CARIBE RUM

THE ORIGINAL GUIDE TO

CARIBBEAN RUM AND DRINKS

BarMedia ©2001

BY ROBERT PLOTKIN

Dedication

This book is dedicated to my friend,
Col. Ronald Gibson,
You meant the world to my family and me.
Now go and get some rest.

RP

OTHER BOOKS BY ROBERT PLOTKIN

Successful Beverage Management: Proven Strategies for the On-Premise Operator (2000)

¡Toma! Margaritas! The Original Guide to Margaritas and Tequila (1999)

Preventing Internal Theft: A Bar Owner's Guide — 2nd Edition (1998)

Increasing Bar Sales: Creative Twists to Bigger Profits (1997)

The Bartender's Companion: A Complete Drink Recipe Guide — 3rd Edition (1997)

The Commercial Bartender's Training Manual — 2nd Edition (1994)

Reducing Bar Costs: A Survival Guide for the '90s (1993)

501 Questions Every Bartender Should Know How to Answer: A Unique Look at the Bar Business (1993)

The Professional Guide to Bartending: The Encyclopedia of American Mixology (1991)

The Intervention Handbook: The Legal Aspects of Serving Alcohol — 2nd Edition (1990)

Publishers:	Robert Plotkin, Carol Plotkin
Editors:	Karen Schmidt, Sheila Berry, Elisa Carrizoza
Managing Editor:	Robert Plotkin
Production Manager:	Carol Plotkin
Cover Design:	Miguel Castillo, Carol Plotkin
Book Design:	Miguel Castillo
Photography:	Eric Hinote
Additional Photography:	Artwork comes from archival sources and may not be reproduced without the written consent of the respective companies.

Published by: **BarMedia**
P.O. Box 14486
Tucson, AZ 85732
520.747.8131
www.barmedia.com

Library of Congress Card Catalog Number: 2001-130543
ISBN: 0-945562-28-4

Printed in the U.S.A.

Caribe Rum
THE ORIGINAL GUIDE TO CARIBBEAN RUM AND DRINKS

Table of Contents

THE CARIBBEAN

Carnes/Lafferty 97

ACKNOWLEDGEMENTS

Mine may be the only name on the cover, but I assure you that this book was entirely a collaborative effort. It required the participation and the creative talents of numerous individuals, all of whom I want to recognize at this time.

We received a great deal of support, information and archival photography from our featured rum producers, without whom this book would have suffered greatly. All of us at BarMedia would like to thank: Bacardi USA Inc. and The Baddish Group; John Mutterperl and Claire Jordon of Remy Amerique and Robyn Gollop-Knight of Mount Gay Rum; Larry Watson and Tania Myers-Marley of Appleton Estate; Winston Stonea of Busha-Browne, Jamaica; Martin Crowley of St. Maarten Spirits and Anguilla Rums; Thomas Valdes, Tony Moreno, and Michelle Cuomo of Todhunter Imports and Cruzan Rum; Tyler Phillips, Mark Tramont and Marilyn Biercuk of Angostura International; Stanislas Ronteix of Cointreau S.A. and Saint James Rhum and J. Bally Rhum; Peter Schwartz of International Beverage Company; James Tirrell and Silvio Leal of Ron Matusalem; Charles Tobias of Pusser's Limited; Susan Wall and Susan Overton of Rhum Dillon and Heaven Hill Distilleries; E. Malcolm Gosling, Jr. of Gosling Brothers; Tonia Pizzuti and Charlotte Conner of Cockspur Rum and the Sazerac Company; Ewan Gunn of Wm. Cadenhead and Henry Preiss of Preiss Imports.

I also want to thank Karen Schmidt, Sheila Berry and Elisa Carrizoza for their endless encouragement while editing and proofing every page of the book. Thanks also to Eric Hinote for his outstanding photography.

I want to thank Miguel Castillo for the countless improvements he made to this book, from designing its cover and interior layout, to his good humor, good judgement and dedication to excellence.

My gratitude and humble admiration to my wife and partner, Carol Plotkin, for overseeing the project, running the company, managing our personal life and being the role model for our daughters.

A special thank you to my daughters, Sarah and Hannah, for their love, understanding and affording me guilt-free time to write this book.

And finally, to Hugo Lewis, my guide and new friend in Trinidad. Thank you for your time, insights and friendship. See, I told you I would get you into the book.

INTRODUCTION

It was my first trip to the island of Trinidad. I had already had a long day traveling from Arizona to Miami, and then the long trip across the Caribbean to a tiny point of light on the horizon.

It was after 11:00 PM by the time I walked onto the tarmac of the Port of Spain airport, just about the same time that passengers from a Dutch airline were disembarking. I picked up my luggage and headed for customs, when I found myself at the end of a long line in a large room filled with long lines. The room was filled with tired, sweaty bodies and a cacophony of shuffling feet and foreign sounding chatter.

Overburdened with my briefcase, camera case and garment bag, I shuffled one linoleum tile at a time until I reached a red line painted on the floor, meaning I was next. I was also the last person in the room, with the exception of several well-armed soldiers off to the side and a burly, immigration officer waving me forward.

The man looked as tired as I felt. I handed him my passport and entry card, expecting it would get the usual glance, stamp and nod treatment. I was wrong.

He must have read every word and considered every bit of information on the documents. Concern washed over me. What a lousy spy I'd make. He finally looked up at me, slowly and deliberately. He had a large imposing face and immense eyes, which were trained on mine.

A few, painfully long moments later he asked, "What brings you to Trinidad?"

"Business," I said. The word seemed to reverberate off the walls. My breathing quickened when I heard my voice. I sounded like I was lying.

Again time stopped. Completely deadpan he asked, "What kind of business?"

"I'm a writer…working on a book about rum. I'm here to visit the Angostura distillery." I forced a thin smile across my face and hoped for the best. Maybe writers aren't welcome on Trinidad, what then I worried.

He leaned back in the chair, rubbed his chin, and then actually smiled. It wasn't an official, I'm-about-to arrest-you smile, it was a genuine, bemused smile. "A book about rum? That's it?"

All of a sudden it sounded like a bad idea. Slightly shaken I said, "It's about Caribbean rums, but yah, the book is just about rum and rum drinks."

"Who would want to have such a book?" he asked. At least he was still smiling.

"Well…people who sell it and people who drink it. Rum has a lot of fans."

The immigration officer leaned forward, stamped my passport and handed it back to me. "You want to know which Caribbean rum is the best? Whichever one is in my glass." He chuckled and motioned me through; his day was over.

I owe that man a debt of gratitude, because he was exactly right. The best Caribbean rum is the one in your glass. Shortly thereafter I realized that there'd be no comparative ratings in this book; no "this rum is better than that rum" business.

I've reviewed over 125 Caribbean rums in this book. There are many different styles and types of rum from more than a dozen different nations represented herein. For each individual rum, I looked to provide a combination of practical information and an assessment of its inherent characteristics. I wrote about where each rum is made, what it is and how it's made, as well as what it looks, smells and tastes like.

As you're about to find out, the book is set-up like a guided tour of the Caribbean. Each chapter focuses on the history, culture and rums of a particular island. Because of space constraints, each chapter highlights one of that island's major distillers. Making the decision of which distiller to feature was a simple process of gravitating to the one that shined brightest. Without exception, it turned out to be the most interesting and historically relevant. Invariably the rums the featured distiller produce also served as ideal representations of the island's individual style.

The selection process behind assembling the book's rum drink recipes was a labor of love for all of us who worked on this book. There are over 400 recipes included in the collection, and we have a close relationship with nearly all of them. Rest assured, each of the recipes warrant inclusion in the collection, fulfilling some mission within the body of work.

Why write a book about rum? As someone who writes about beverage trends, I can tell you that rum is a popular phenomenon in the making. And why not? These highly mixable spirits come from the beautiful, exotic islands in the most romantic of seas. Rum tastes and smells great; there's no learning curve necessary to enjoy it. It's a spirit that takes well to barrel-aging, which adds a whole other dimension to the subject.

The Caribbean region produces an intriguing array of styles and types of rum. There are overproof, vintage-dated, flavored, agricole, naval and single barrel rums. One evening you could be sipping a 1929-vintage J. Bally agricole rhum, the next quaffing a grog made with British naval rum. It's just really easy to stay interested in rums.

Another advantage rum enjoys over other spirits, such as brandy or single malt scotch, is that it is relatively inexpensive. Appleton Estate Extra, which is aged in wood for a minimum of 12-years, wholesales for about $20 per 750ml. Compared to most 12-year old spirits, that's a considerable bargain.

Perhaps the best explanation for rum's enormous popularity is that it's fun. You remember fun, don't you? So take a moment, stick your feet in some sand and enjoy a sunset.

Robert Plotkin
BarMedia
Tucson, Arizona

Chapter 1

The Lore of the Caribbean

The Caribbean Sea encompasses 1,000,000 square miles. Among the one hundred plus volcanic islands within its waters are 29 sovereign nations. In the southeast corner of the Caribbean is a chain of islands called the Lesser Antilles. Principal among its Windward Islands are Trinidad and Tobago, Barbados, Grenada, and Martinique. Included in the Leeward Islands of the Lesser Antilles are Guadeloupe, Antigua, Anguilla and the Virgin Islands.

Near the Caribbean's northern edge are the Greater Antilles, which is primarily comprised of the islands of Puerto Rico, Jamaica, Cuba, the Caymans and Hispaniola, the home of Haiti and the Dominican Republic. On the Atlantic side of the Greater Antilles is the Bahamas group, a chain of more than 700 coral islands including the Turk and Bahama Islands.

Perhaps no place on Earth enjoys a greater diversity of climates and exotic landscapes than the Caribbean. The region includes active, dormant and extinct volcanoes, imposing mountain ranges, vast rain forests, and closer to sea level, unexpectedly hot and arid climes. The constant temperature of the ocean and the steady, temperate trade winds blowing in from Africa make the weather in the Caribbean, by any definition, nearly perfect. Temperatures rarely vary 25° from a high of around 90°F at sea level, to nighttime lows of 65°F in the higher elevations.

In addition to being extraordinarily lush and teeming with life, the islands of the Caribbean are endowed with a fabulous wealth of natural resources, including gold, silver and other precious metals. Few things attract the attention of man more than exploitable riches. Herein lies much of the history of the Caribbean.

By the time Columbus set foot on the shore of Guadeloupe, many of the principal Caribbean islands had been inhabited by two dynamic, thriving civilizations. These indigenous peoples originated from the delta forests of the Rio Orinoco in what is now northeastern Venezuela.

The first of the native civilizations to migrate north up the rim of the mountainous Lesser Antilles islands were the Arawaks. While predating written historical records, the Arawaks were by all accounts a peaceful people, who by living off the sea, met their needs easily. They spent much of their time as artisans making pottery, baskets, woven clothing, stone tools and sculpting stone statues. The Arawaks also sculpted with gold, crafting intricate, ornate jewelry. Ironically, this would contribute to their eventual downfall.

In sharp contrast, the Caribs were a fierce, hostile people. In fact they excelled at making weaponry, war and piracy. The Caribs fashioned huge dugout vessels from hollowed-out trees, some as long as 80-feet. These vessels were so large that they could carry 100 warriors, gear and provisions distances of up to 1000 miles.

Following the path taken by the Arawaks before them, the seafaring Caribs set off and proceeded to raid and sack the islands in the Lesser Antilles. The Arawaks were supremely outmatched and one by one the islands fell victim. The Carib invaders would drink hallucinogenic casava beer and revel in the ensuing carnage. Women were raped and killed or taken as slaves. Like the Vikings, the Carib warriors had no use for material goods. Other than slaves, all the warriors took with them was gold.

The march up the Lesser Antilles continued until the seafaring marauders reached the wide, hazardous expanse of open water between what is today Puerto Rico and Hispaniola, a perilous stretch now called the Anegada Passage.

Perhaps what is most remembered about the Caribs is that they were cannibals. Cannibalism held religious significance to them. It was thought that eating the bodies of their enemy would transfer the virtues of the slain. The braver the warrior the more savagely the victim was eaten. The Caribs also placed a high value on pain, thinking that in pain and torture one would transcend the corporal world and enter the spiritual realm.

In October 1492, when Columbus first set foot on the shore of San Salvador, what is now known as Watling's Island, his men soon stumbled upon a hastily vacated Carib encampment. There they found a simmering cauldron. Inevitably curiosity got the better of them and one of the sailors lifted the lid. The human remains stewing inside so revolted the Spaniards that the Caribs were branded as inhuman, savage animals.

SPAIN STAKES ITS CLAIM

Upon discovering Hispaniola, Columbus set out to offer the timid and peaceful Arawaks protection from the Caribs. In his journal Columbus noted of the Arawaks, "They should be good servants and intelligent for I observed that they quickly took in what was said to them. So that they are good to be ordered about, to work, to sow and do all that may be necessary."

Columbus' promise of protection turned out to be a horrible perversion of the truth. In 1498 he shipped 600 Arawak natives to Spain, effectively beginning over 250 years of slavery in the region. Within 20 years of the arrival of Columbus the West Indies Arawaks and Caribs were all but exterminated.

The economic windfall of Columbus' discovery sent shock waves through the treasury of Spain. An unprecedented flow of gold, silver and other precious metals poured into Spain's coffers, an unbelievable amount of wealth that greatly bolstered Spain's global imperialism. By the turn of the 16th century, Spain—and to a lesser degree Portugal—had staked their claim to the entire Lesser Antilles and Greater Antilles chains of islands.

As a finishing touch, Pope Alexander VI, a Spaniard, issued the now infamous "Inter Caetera Proclamation" of 1493. In essence the papal edict confirmed Spain and Portugal's annexations and was long used as the pretext for colonialism. It authorized Christian countries to occupy and convert any non-Christian nation, asserting the supremacy of Christianity over paganism and making non-Christian indigenous people subject to the domination and enslavement of the Spanish crown. In the proclamation the Pope declared that should any man violate his edict, "he would incur the indignation of Almighty God and the blessed apostles Peter and Paul."

The plundering of the Caribbean and the West Indies islands quickly caught the attention of Spain's enemies, principally England and France. The extraordinary magnitude of Spain's windfall staggered her rivals. The Crowns of England and France feared a major shift in world power. The flash point of global conflict would slowly, yet inexorably, shift to the Caribbean Sea.

By the middle of the 16th century, England's Queen Victoria and King Francis I of France were publicly repudiating the Papal proclamation. Spain had grown enormously powerful, possessing the largest and most feared navy in the world, the Armada.

England and France resorted to several strategies to counteract Spain's strangle hold on the Caribbean, the most effective of which was piracy. In 1522 Florentine buccaneer Giovanni da Verrazanno, acting under the auspices of the King of France, captured three Spanish galleons, two filled with treasure from Mexico, and the third loaded with sugar, pearls and hides from Hispaniola. When presented with the treasure from these ships, the King of France exclaimed in amazement, "The Emperor (of Spain) can carry on war against me by means of the riches from the West Indies alone."

Piracy proved to be such a viable method of disrupting Spain's flow of riches, as well as a lucrative source of capital, that both England and France adopted it as a matter of national policy and self-interest. In 1559 France and Spain entered into the Treaty of Cateau-Cambresis, in which the parties tacitly acknowledges the undeclared war in the Caribbean. In the treaty France and Spain agreed that, "west of the Prime Meridian and south of the Tropic of Cancer…violence by either party to the other shall not be regarded as in contravention of the treaty."

England's foray into piracy yielded enormous profits. By far the most successful and feared English pirate of the time was Sir Francis Drake. Funded by Queen Elizabeth, Drake attacked the Spanish shipping lanes at will throughout the Caribbean. So successful were Drake's forays that his expeditions yielded dividends of £47 Sterling for every one invested. Spain's response was to shoot first and ask questions later, targeting all ships sailing under foreign flags as potential enemies.

Nevertheless, Spain was slowly losing its steel grip on the region. In 1588 the British Royal Navy destroyed the mighty Spanish Armada, further crippling the ability of King Philip to monopolize the Caribbean. In the decades to follow, state sanctioned piracy slowly gave way to a new, more frenzied form of chaos. Pirates with loyalties to a sovereign eventually were replaced by buccaneers, the majority of whom were fugitives from the law, savage, ruthless and driven solely by greed and lawlessness.

The shipping lanes of the Caribbean were soon plunged into terror as the ranks of pirates and buccaneers swelled. By the 1660s, thousands of pirates and buccaneers were operating out of Port Royal (Jamaica), Tortuga, St. Croix and Curaçao. While the British, French and Dutch were considered fair prey, Spanish ships were still the choice targets of opportunity.

Being terrors of the sea was apparently not enough, for in 1666 the pirate community turned their collective attention to raiding coastal towns. The most famous buccaneer raid was lead by Briton Henry "Captain" Morgan. With ten ships and a force of 700 men, Morgan sacked the city of Puerto Principe in Cuba. He then stormed the well-fortified and heavily armed garrison of Porto Bello, Panama. For 31 days, Morgan and his men held the city captive repelling numerous Spanish counter-attacks. When the governor of Panama saw the futility of further military action, he authorized the payment of a £10,000 ransom for the return of the city.

For the governments that connived the strategy that let loose these dogs of war, piracy was becoming a considerable problem. Britain and France were also suffering terrible losses on the seas. In 1668 France and Spain signed the Treaty of Aix-la-Chapelle bringing an end to the war between them. The buccaneers refused to participate in the negotiations or abide by its conditions. Two years later, Britain and Spain agreed to terms, one of which was to punish all acts of piracy.

Unfortunately for the world's superpowers, these treaties and accords did little to stem the growing scourge of piracy. In January 1669, Morgan and his pirates sacked the Cuban towns of Gibraltar and Maracaibo, seizing a considerable amount of booty as well as extracting a sizeable ransom from the Spanish for the return of the city.

A veritable army of buccaneers plundered Trinidad in 1673 yielding a booty of 100,000 "pieces of eight." Then they seized what was at the time the wealthiest city in the "New World," Vera Cruz, Mexico, carrying off what in today's dollars amounted to $6,000,000.

It wasn't until 1720 and the demise of Edward Teach, alias Blackbeard, that the combined efforts of the world's greatest military powers were able to eradicate pirates from the Caribbean, but not before every ploy, scheme and enticement were used to lure buccaneers into another profession. In St. Dominique, buccaneers were offered huge tracts of land upon which to cultivate tobacco. The British offered pirates amnesty to surrender. Others were offered a bounty to capture buccaneers still at-large. Still others were given huge sums of money, land and title to retire. Such was the fate of Henry Morgan, or one of the several people who posed as Captain Morgan. The once feared pirate was knighted, given the title of Sir Henry Morgan and made the Deputy Governor of Jamaica.

By the end of the 17th century, after two hundred years of systematic plundering and autocratic dominion over the entire region, Spain's territorial holdings in the Caribbean had been reduced to Cuba, Puerto Rico, the eastern two-thirds of Hispaniola, and the island of Trinidad.

THE "NEW WORLD" SETTLES IN

By the time Columbus arrived in the region, the Arawaks and the Caribs had discovered and inhabited virtually every island in the Caribbean Sea. Between his three voyages, however, Columbus visited and laid claim to nearly every significant landmass. Sticking a flag into the sand and claiming an island in the name of Spain, however, is hardly sufficient to convince the inhabitants that they now were under the dominion of the King and Queen of Spain.

While the superpowers fought for control of the seas, the 16th and 17th centuries were dominated by European settlers, outcasts and indentured servants from Britain, Spain, Holland and France vying for control of the roughly 30 principal islands. In nearly every case, control meant battling the indigenous peoples living there, which in the case of the Caribs, was no easy feat.

By the middle of the 17th century, however, the majority of the islands were settled and politically aligned with a European power. Settlers initially attempted to scratch out an existence growing various agricultural products. None flourished as well as tobacco, but the superiority of Virginia tobacco out competed the Caribbean commodity in the world market. Slowly, yet inexorably settlers on one island after another became involved with either the cultivation of sugar cane, the slave trade, or both.

Of the many things that can be said about Christopher Columbus, arguably the most important contribution he made to the "New World" was the introduction of sugar cane. On his second voyage he brought with him what became known as the Creole variety of sugar cane, which remained the dominant type in the Caribbean until around 1750 when the Otaheite variety of sugar cane became the preferred strain.

Conditions for cultivating sugar cane were ideal in the Caribbean. When Ponce de Leon arrived in Puerto Rico in 1508 he found large tracts of land flourishing with sugar cane. In his travels he discovered that sugar cane was bountiful throughout the West Indies. The famed explorer even took to cultivating sugar cane at his home near present day San Juan. Shortly thereafter, the Spaniards on Hispaniola began experimenting with the distillation of the fermented sap of the sugar cane. The often fiery spirit, which they called *brebaje*, quickly became a local favorite.

By the end of the 17th century, Europe had developed a nearly insatiable appetite for sugar, which sent demand soaring. On many islands sugar became a form of currency.

To some degree all of the Caribbean islands became integrated into the sugar plantation system. On the British islands of Jamaica, Antigua, Barbados, and Tortola, sugar became the only crop resulting in the development of a monoculture. On the French islands of St. Lucia, Guadeloupe, Martinique, Grenada and St. Barts, there were more diversified economies, however, sugar remained a dominant commodity. The plantation system significantly affected even the islands on which sugar didn't grow. So dominant was sugar to the Caribbean economies that the Bahamas remained unsettled because of its unsuitability for growing sugar cane.

Cultivating sugar cane required agricultural knowledge and a great deal of labor. The insatiable demand for inexpensive labor directly resulted in the slavery trade flourishing. Sufficient labor could only be acquired by opening up the African slave trade. The labor of African slaves was the economic underpinning of the sugar islands from the 17th century.

About two-thirds of all Africans captured and shipped across the Atlantic ended up on sugar plantations. By 1680, the average sugar plantation on Barbados had 60 slaves. One hundred and fifty years later, Jamaican plantation owners had an average of 150 slaves.

Slaves were used exclusively in the cane fields, using hoes to dig five-foot round, six-inch deep holes. The tops of mature plants were lopped off and several pieces of cane would be placed into the hole and covered with several inches of soil. As the cane grew slaves would tend to it by supplementing the soil with mold and dung until the hole was ground level. This method of planting is extremely arduous work. Only the most stalwart of slaves could endure it for any length of time.

The harvesting process was equally laborious. Using machetes or a sharp, hooked instrument called a bill, slaves would chop down the cane close to the ground. They would then strip the cane of its leaves and cut it into 3 to 4 foot length pieces. Scores of these pieces were then bundled together and carried either by slaves or pack animals to the mill.

Processing sugar cane into crystallized sugar required industry, capital and technology. By controlling the cultivation of the sugar cane and the total reliance on slave labor, Caribbean sugar plantations became the largest and most profitable enterprises in the contemporary 18th century world.

The first sugar mill was established in Hispaniola in 1516. Horses, oxen or windmills were used to turn a huge wheel to crush and extract the juice from the sugar cane. In areas with close proximity to an abundant water supply, water wheels were used to supply the power necessary to mill the cane. The extracted cane juice was boiled and then crystallized into sugar.

In addition to sugar, many of the plantations sold the liquid by-products of the milling process. The cane juice skimmed from the surface of the boiling syrup could be fermented. It was a raw, inexpensive and highly potent liquor that became a favorite of laborers and slaves.

As a final step in the milling process, many of the plantations began distilling the molasses—the residue remaining from the clarification process—in liquor at the still house. On the French islands this distillate was known as *Tafia*, on the British islands it eventually became known as rum. While sugar cane became destined to change the collective economies of the Caribbean, it was the distilling of cane juice that would make the islands renowned around the world.

Chapter 2

The History of Caribbean Rum

The soil conditions, temperature and humidity of the Caribbean make it the definitive place on the planet to cultivate sugar cane and produce and age rum.

In the simplest possible terms, rum is a spirit distilled from fresh sugar cane juice, cane syrup or molasses. When the harvested sugar cane stalks are crushed and ground the process expresses a sweet, green-colored sap rich in sucrose. This sap is referred to as fresh sugar cane juice. Most of the rums produced on the French islands are distilled from fresh sugar cane juice and called *Rhum Agricole*.

There are also rums distilled from sugar cane syrup, which is derived from boiling and clarifying the cane juice. The majority of rums are distilled, however, from molasses, which is the final by-product in the production of crystallized sugar. Molasses is a thick, sticky, slightly bitter black liquid obtained after the third boiling of the cane juice. Even after being boiled three times, it still contains a significant amount of uncrystallized sugar, along with other organic compounds that greatly contribute to the bouquet and flavor of the finished distilled spirit.

While theories abound, the origin of the word "rum" is uncertain. One theory suggests that it is an abbreviation of the Latin words for sugar, *saccharrum officinarum*. Another theory suggests that the name "rum" originated on the island of Barbados as a derivation of the words "*rumbullion* or *rumbustion*," which were common terms for fighting or causing trouble.

On Barbados, rum was also called *Kill Devil*, likely because as a strong spirit it was used to cure a wide range of afflictions. Among the other island references for rum were *Devil's death*, *red eye*, and *guildive*. On the French islands, rum was referred to as *rhum* and *tafia*.

The Spanish Conquistadors brought the science of distillation to the Caribbean. Shortly after the English, Dutch and French began establishing colonies on the islands, many of them began experimenting with distilling sugar cane. By the 17th century, sugar cane spirits were being distilled throughout the Caribbean.

PRODUCING THE "NEW WORLD" SPIRIT

It takes new cane plants approximately 1-1½ years under optimum conditions to reach maturity. The sugar cane is harvested by cutting it close to the ground, either by hand or with a cane-cutting machine. The mature, spongy cane is rich with sweet sap, which may become diluted if left in the rain. Once harvested, the cane must be taken to the mill promptly, typically within 24-hours. Like any other fresh produce, sugar cane begins to deteriorate quickly, and its juice will be diminished in both quantity and quality.

The sectioned cane is then milled and put through a series of grinders and rollers to extract the juice from the fibrous stalks. On the French islands this fresh cane juice is then fermented and distilled to make the famed *Rhum Agricole*.

To produce molasses, the cane juice is boiled, clarified, and in some instances, sent into an evaporator to remove any excess water from the juice. Once cooled, the dark liquid is referred to as cane syrup or light molasses. The third boiling renders the syrup into black molasses.

The distillation process requires that the molasses be allowed to ferment, or in other words, to create an alcoholic liquid. This warm, sweet liquid—called "wash"—is comprised of molasses, water and yeast. The active yeast converts the sugar in the molasses into alcohol and carbon dioxide. The quality and taste of the water has a significant impact on the character of the finished rum. The same is true for the specific strain of yeast used to start fermentation. Many firms have maintained the exact same strain of yeast as a proprietary trade secret and have done so for generations.

To create a dark, full-flavored rum, a portion of a previous distillation is added to the fermenting wash. This residue contributes greatly to the finished rum's bouquet and flavor. Other distillers add "limings" to the fermenting wash to develop a fuller bodied and more flavorful rum. Limings are obtained by skimming the surface of the sugar boilers during the process of rendering the molasses.

The duration of fermentation is a crucial factor in the taste and body of the rum. For a light rum, fermentation takes roughly 12-48 hours. Heavier-bodied rums require slower fermentation, a process that requires up to 4 days. Once fermentation has ceased, the liquid is referred to as a "dead wash."

Distilling rum is essentially the simple process of boiling the dead wash such that the alcohol in the liquid evaporates and is collected as condensate. Alcohol has a lower boiling point than water (78.5°C versus 100°C), so it will be the first liquid in the wash to evaporate. Distillation also removes from the unrefined alcohol the vast majority of impurities and toxins, elements such as esters, aldehydes, acids and light alcohols. Some of these congeners, also known as fusel oils, are distilled off first, the others are obtained after the ethyl alcohol has evaporated. Only the heart of the distillation is collected and redistilled. The fusel oils derived in the "heads" and "tails" of the distillation are frequently discarded.

There are three primary types of stills used to distill rum. The traditional type is the alembic still, or pot still. While their size and volume vary, all alembic stills function in the same manner. It is comprised of a kettle-shaped vessel in which the wash is heated. As the alcohol vapor rises it is funneled into the neck and collected in the condenser coils. This coil is often surrounded by a unit containing cold water that accelerates the vapor condensing into alcohol. The condensate is then pumped into a second alembic still to be redistilled, concentrating the flavors and further purifying the spirit.

After the first distillation the rum is roughly 70% alcohol by volume. The second distillation often yields a spirit containing approximately 80% alcohol by volume. Alembic stills, the same type used to make the world's finest whiskies and brandies, are typically used to produce full-flavored, full-bodied rums.

The other two primary types of stills both utilize columns instead of pots or kettles. The column still allows the alcohol to be distilled continuously. In this case, the dead wash is pumped into the top of the column still, which is constructed with numerous levels of plates and holes. As the wash slowly filters through the top of the maze, steam is pumped into the bottom of the column. The steam rises through the various levels, heating the wash and causing the alcohol to evaporate. The steam becomes saturated with alcohol, which is collected near the top of the column. By the time the wash reaches the bottom of the still it no longer contains any alcohol.

The modern column still is widely used in the Caribbean and presents distillers with certain advantages. One advantage is that the process is continuous, rather than the alembic still's batch by batch process. Column stills are economical, efficient and yield lighter-bodied spirits, an attractive feature to many master rum distillers.

The final distillation technique is the Coffey still, which essentially is a device that utilizes column stills hooked in a series. As the ethyl alcohol is condensed it is pumped into the second column still to be redistilled.

MASTERING RUM SPEAK

Regardless of the type of still used, distilled spirits exit the still absolutely crystal clear. So if all rums are distilled from sugar cane in some form, what distinguishes one rum from another? There are a number of factors that affect on the quality and character of a finished rum.

• **MICRO-CLIMATE AND RAW MATERIAL**—Sugar cane is a grass, and as is the case of all plants, it is highly affected by the micro-climate in which it is cultivated. Conditions such as elevation, temperature, humidity and soil composition all impact the quality of the sugar cane, and the quantity and quality of the juice.

• **PRODUCTION VARIABLES**—Among the first of the production variables is whether the rum is distilled from fresh cane juice, cane syrup or molasses. Each yields a different tasting rum. Another of the variables is the length of fermentation. The longer the fermentation process, the fuller-bodied, and fuller-flavored the resulting rum will be.

The unique qualities of the particular strain of yeast will play a significant role in determining the characteristics of the finished rum. Most distillers use carefully cultured strains of yeast to start the fermentation, while others rely on wild yeasts present in the air to jump start fermentation. Some yeasts rapidly precipitate fermentation, others take longer.

The quality of the water used throughout the production process will affect the taste of the finished rum. The water used to irrigate the cane fields will affect the flavor of the cane juice. Water is also used during fermentation and distillation.

The addition of "dunder" or "limings" to the fermenting wash plays a large role in creating the final character of the rum. Both dunder and limings help achieve consistent conditions for fermentation. They also both contribute to the finished rum's bouquet and flavor.

It is certainly ill advised to disregard the alcohol content of the rum. In addition to the commonly noted affects of rum, alcohol content can be perceived on the palate.

• **DISTILLATION**—There are three types of stills used to distill rum. Heavier, fuller-flavored rums are typically distilled in alembic (pot) stills. Lighter rums are most often distilled in a column still or continuous still.

• **AGING**—Take a fiery spirit straight from the still and age it in wood for a decade and magical things happen. Over time, the rum will begin to soften and become mellow. Rum gathers its color from aging in wood. Barrel aging affects every dimension of the finished rum. Rums produced in pot stills are invariably aged in wood. This allows its constituent elements to marry, while the wood works to smooth out any rough edges.

While length of aging is a principle point of distinction, the type of wood in which a rum is aged is significant. Rum is often aged in used bourbon barrels, however, a wide variety of different wood type casks are used to age Caribbean rum. Both the type of wood, as well as what was in the cask previously, play a role in creating the finished rum.

The last of the aging variables are the specific conditions under which the rum is aged. Temperature and humidity are the two primary factors. Certainly resting in an open-air warehouse in Barbados is very different than being aged in the Scottish Highlands or along the Irish coast.

• **FILTERING AND BLENDING**—There are rums that are bottled unfiltered and undiluted. The rum is essentially drawn directly from the cask and bottled. Others are fastidiously filtered to remove any particulate from the rum, then diluted down to alcoholic proof with purified water.

The majority of all rums are created by marrying numerous rums together of various distillations and ages. The practice of blending spirits requires a heightened olfactory sense and a highly developed palate. The objective is to combine a number of different rums to create a spirit that best showcase the outstanding qualities of the constituent elements. It's a classic case of something becoming more than the sum of its parts.

A GUIDED TOUR OF CARIBBEAN RUMS

Nearly all rums fall into one of two major categories—heavy and light. Heavy rums are typically distilled in alembic or column stills. Continuous stills are also capable of producing heavy rums, although the spirit is likely removed from the first column. Heavy is an unfortunate label for these highly flavorful spirits, one that casts the impression that these rums are dense and chewy. While more substantial than their lighter counterparts, heavy rums are labeled as such because they are loaded with flavoring agents (congeners). They are aromatic, full-bodied, full-flavored spirits with long lasting finishes. Heavy rums are invariably aged in wood.

Light rums are usually distilled in column or continuous stills. They have light bodies and crisp, clean palates. Light rums are distilled to high proof rendering them extremely pure. They are occasionally aged for brief periods to round out their character. Light rums are unsurpassed for their mixability.

While there are scores of different brands of Caribbean rums, the good news is that there are only a few types of rum to distinguish between. Take heart, here's a brief guide to get you started.

• **WHITE RUM (A.K.A. LIGHT, SILVER RUM)**—These are dry, clear and light-bodied rums. The majority of rum distillers have at least one of these spirits in their repertoire. White rums are typically blended and left unaged.

• **GOLD RUM (A.K.A. ORO, AMBRÉ RUM)**—These rums are typically medium-bodied and slightly more flavorful than the white version as a result of being barrel aged. Most derive their golden color during aging, however, many contain a touch of caramel coloring to enhance their presentation.

- **DARK RUM (A.K.A. BLACK RUM)**—These aromatic rums are most often distilled in alembic stills and barrel aged for extended periods of time. Dark rums are invariably full-bodied, full-flavored with long, lingering finishes.

- **AGED RUM (A.K.A. AÑEJO, RHUM VIEUX)**—Rums age extremely well in wood. The peak age being somewhere between 15 to 20 years, after which the rum begins to decline. *Rhum Vieux* are aged a minimum of three years in barrels of no less than 650 liters in capacity. *Rhum Trés Vieux* are barrel aged a minimum of ten years.

- **OVERPROOF RUM**—These spirits are most frequently white rums bottled at an extremely high alcohol content. Technically overproof spirits are those bottled at more than 50% alcohol by volume (abv), however, most overproof rums are bottled in the range of 150-151 proof (75-75.5% abv).

- **FLAVORED AND SPICED RUM**—As the names would imply, these rums are altered by the addition of natural fruit flavorings or a small bevy of spices. White rums are most often married with fruit flavoring, while gold or aged rums are more often used as the base for spiced rums.

- **VINTAGE & SINGLE BARREL (A.K.A. SINGLE CASK, SINGLE MARK RUMS)**—There are a number of vintage rums on the market. A vintage on the label of a rum signifies the year that the sugar cane was harvested and the rum distilled. Single barrel rums—also known as single mark rums—are spirits drawn from a single cask. These rums are singular in as much as each barrel of rum is slightly different, making these rums unique, never to be repeated products.

Chapter 3

Puerto Rico and the Rums of Bacardi

L ocated between the U.S. Virgin Islands and Hispaniola, home of Haiti and the Dominican Republic, Puerto Rico is the smallest and most easterly island of the Greater Antilles. Slightly smaller than Jamaica, the island is rectangular in shape and is about 100 miles long by 35 miles wide. Extinct volcanic mountain ranges, a matrix of fresh water rivers and wide, rich valleys dominate the interior of the island. Sloping down towards the sea are the coastal plains, which are fertile, highly productive agriculture areas.

Speculation abounds as to when the Arawaks first settled on the island of Puerto Rico, the best estimates being somewhere around 800 A.D. They established a cultured, agrarian society and named the island *Boriquén*, meaning "land of the great lord." Peace lasted only until various Carib tribes invaded the island. Ill prepared to defend themselves against the fierce Caribs, the Arawaks were exterminated.

On November 19, 1493, during his second voyage to the "New World," Columbus landed on the island, which he named San Juan. Columbus was accompanied on the voyage by a young nobleman, Juan Ponce de León. Drawn by tales of fabulous reserves of gold, León brought a royal writ granting him permission to colonize the land. Colonization actually began in 1508 when Ponce de León established a settlement called Caparra in the island's northeast. A year later the Spanish Crown appointed León the first governor of Puerto Rico.

The Spanish quickly discovered that the island held little or no gold. They soon divided the island into vast plantations and enslaved the natives to work the cane fields. Conditions were horrendous and the mortality rate was staggering. The Caribs mounted widespread rebellions on several occasions, the first launched in 1511. Large numbers of settlers and even larger numbers of natives were killed, but superior firepower and tactics quashed each successive uprising. In less than a century the Carib population was wiped out.

Caparra proved to be disease-ridden, so in 1521 Ponce de León moved the capital to the natural port of present day Old San Juan. The Spanish fortified San Juan with a large fortress and the port served as a central staging area for defending the Spanish Empire's interests in the region. The Port of San Juan also became an integral hub in Spanish commercial trade routes and the port of entry for the growing trade in African slaves. Those Africans not purchased for use on the sugar plantations were exported to other Spanish colonies.

While the Spanish maintained autonomy over Puerto Rico for more than 400 years, it was not without a heavy cost. They were forced to withstand numerous attempts to take the island. The first was an attack by the English pirate, Sir Francis Drake in 1595. The conflict was fought at a fevered pitch and Drake ultimately withdrew. Three years later, English troops under the command of the Earl of Cumberland invaded the island and established a temporary foothold on the island. The Spanish eventually repelled the British. Then in 1625 the Dutch attacked and sacked the Port of San Juan.

By the beginning of the 18th century, Spain's empire in the Caribbean had been reduced to Puerto Rico, Cuba, Trinidad, and two-thirds of Hispaniola. The liberation movement was growing throughout the region. Anti-colonial sentiment and the inherent instability created by slavery were creating a political ground swell. Spain highly valued its possessions in the Caribbean. The government openly referring to Puerto Rico and Cuba as "the limbs of Spain."

In February 1797, Britain went to war against France, which again threw the Caribbean into turmoil. During the conflict, Britain captured Trinidad from the Spanish, seized Guyana from Holland, and unsuccessfully invaded Puerto Rico.

Political unrest continued to build on the island. In 1815, Spain was forced to grant Puerto Rico political concessions. A year later the colony was rocked by a massive slave revolt that wrought tremendous damage and loss of life. Slavery was eventually abolished in Puerto Rico in 1873.

Spanish rule on the island of Puerto Rico ended in 1898 with the conclusion of the Spanish-American War. The United States invaded the island and overwhelmed the Spanish defensive forces. In the ensuing peace treaty of 1899, the United States was ceded possession of the island, which immediately abolished the existing government. The United States established a governing executive council and appointed an American governor.

The people of Puerto Rico took no better to the autocratic rule of the United States than they did to being subjects of Spain. In 1917, the American government passed legislation that granted U.S. citizenship to all Puerto Ricans and supplemented the Executive Council with a popularly elected Senate and House of Delegates. In 1948, Puerto Rico enjoyed its initial taste of self-rule with the election of the first Puerto Rican governor, who had the authority to appoint his cabinet and justices of the Supreme Court. Four years later, Puerto Rico became a Commonwealth, voluntarily associated with the United States. Statehood remains a highly controversial political issue on the island.

Puerto Rico today is a popular tourist destination with posh resorts throughout the island. The country has one of the strongest economies in the region, a thriving middle class, and a dynamic culture rich in the arts.

RUM AND THE ISLAND OF PUERTO RICO

Puerto Rico is the world's leading producer of rum, or ron as it is referred to in Spanish. In fact, roughly 80% of all the rum consumed in the United States is distilled and blended on the island. Columbus brought sugar cane to Puerto Rico on his second voyage in 1493. By the time Ponce de León established the settlement in Caparra fifteen years later, sugar cane was flourishing on the island. Puerto Rico's rum industry, however, took much longer to reach its potential.

Like other islands in the region, Puerto Rico is an ideal environment for cultivating sugar cane. The volcanic soil of the coastal plains is rich and fertile. Fresh water is plentiful and the climate is temperate and not overly humid. Sugar has been the cornerstone of Puerto Rico's economy for 400 years, with tobacco running a distant second.

It is conjectured that the sugar industry spread from Hispaniola to Jamaica, Cuba and Puerto Rico. By 1528 there were 10 *ingenios*—water-powered mills used to process sugar cane— on the island, compared to the thirty *ingenios* operating on Jamaica. Founded in 1510, the city of Ponce on the southern coast became a hub of the island's sugar industry.

The majority of Puerto Rico's coastal plains were divided into vast sugar plantations. As was the case with other Caribbean

islands, plantation owners found the distillation of rum a profitable venture. Molasses was essentially little more than a by-product, the remnant of processing sugar. Therefore nearly every plantation had facilities for the production of rum. There the molasses would be mixed with fresh water and yeast to precipitate fermentation. The fermented wash would then be distilled in small copper pot (alembic) stills.

The single largest impediment to the growth of rum on the island was the halting, unsteady development of Puerto Rico's economy. The Spanish put little effort into developing a broad-based economic infrastructure. While the cities of Old San Juan and Ponce thrived as centers of trade and industry, Puerto Rico's third city wouldn't be founded until 1646, a span of 136 years.

Unlike the growth experienced on other Caribbean islands, Puerto Rico's sugar industry floundered. In 1860 the island was producing 70,000 tons of sugar. Thirty years later the output had dropped to 48,500 tons. The changing fortunes of the major sugar plantations caused the early development of rum on the island to be lackluster.

This slow growth, however, would ultimately prove fortuitous. In 1863, Aeneas Coffey patented the two-column still, an ingenious, revolutionary piece of equipment that allowed distillers to produce a light bodied spirit in large quantities and at great economy. While the few serious distillers on the island at the time were using pot stills, no real distilling tradition had been established. Conditions were right for accepting this innovative distilling technique. As a result, Puerto Rico became world renowned for producing light, dry rums.

Sales of Puerto Rican rum surged during World War II. Stocks of whisky had all but dried up, which caused a thirsty world to turn for relief to rum. Sales dipped dramatically shortly after the war, prompting the American government to intervene with the passage of the Mature Spirits Act of 1948. The legislation established stricter production standards for the island's rum and improved its quality and market acceptance. As a result,

Puerto Rican rum must be aged a minimum of one year in oak barrels prior to bottling, dark rums must be aged for a minimum of three years, and no neutral spirits can be added to the blend.

Undoubtedly, the single most important event to happen to the island's rum industry was the arrival of Bacardi in 1936. From that date forward, Puerto Rico permanently secured its position as a world class rum producer.

In 1829, Don Facundo Bacardi y Massó emigrated from Catalonia, Spain to the colonial city of Santiago de Cuba. He was an avid aficionado of rum who experimented with distillation at home. Bacardi considered the local rums to be fiery, harsh and unrefined, so he became dedicated to creating rums that would transcend contemporary standards.

Don Facundo Bacardi began scrutinizing every step of production, such as improving the quality of raw ingredients, trying different strains of yeasts, length of fermentation and various aging and blending techniques. Bacardi then added a step to the production process never attempted before. He filtered his

rum through charcoal to remove congeners, particulate and impurities. The result of his efforts was a light rum, smoother and more refined than any other contemporary rum. Bacardi also produced dark, richly flavorful aged rums that exceeded anything produced in the world.

In February 1862, Don Facundo Bacardi purchased a small, tin-roofed distillery in Santiago de Cuba, complete with a copper and cast iron alembic still. That same month he established a rum company called Bacardi y Compañía. Bacardi became the first producer to release a white rum, *Bacardi Carta Blanca*, which in short order became the most popular and successful brand in Cuba.

The modest distillery also came with a colony of fruit bats living in the rafters. According to local lore, bats were harbingers of good health, fortune and family unity. Don Facundo's wife, Doña Amalia, suggested that the image of the bat be used as the rum's trademark. The image of the bat has graced every bottle of Bacardi rum since the company's inception.

The family-owned Bacardi y Compañía has been a continuing legacy of innovation, insight and achievement. Bacardi was the first distillery to utilize the Coffey continuous still. In its first forty years, Bacardi rums earned 10 gold medals in international competition. Overseas production commenced with the 1910 opening of a distillery in Spain and another in Mexico in 1930. The company also built a distillery in San Juan, Puerto Rico in 1936. Bacardi began production in Puerto Rico after the appeal of Prohibition.

In 1960, the Castro government nationalized the Bacardi production facilities in Santiago and confiscated the company's assets. The family had years before taken the precaution of transferring all of its trademarks out of Cuba.

THE RUMS OF BACARDI

The rums of Bacardi are distilled from fermented molasses. As an organic substance, the storage and shipment of the molasses is of critical concern. Bacardi has developed sophisticated facilities at each of their production sites worldwide to provide a controlled, dry and surgically clean environment for the molasses.

The particular strain of yeast used to precipitate fermentation is the same native Cuban strain discovered and cultivated by Don Facundo Bacardi in the early 1860s. This yeast is singular to Bacardi and gives the rums their distinctive flavor and character.

Along with the yeast, purified water and nutrients are added to the molasses to create the fermentable mash. Fermentation lasts roughly 30-35 hours under strictly controlled conditions.

Bacardi relies on both four-column continuous stills and alembic stills for distilling its rums. The continuous stills are used predominantly to produce Bacardi's famous rums. Copper alembic stills are used to produce the fuller-bodied rums. Bacardi charcoal filters its rums after distillation. The charcoal is obtained from different types of carefully selected wood, such that when they are carbonized they produce a dynamic filter. Filtration eliminates impurities harmful to the finished product.

All of Bacardi's rums are aged in select American white oak barrels. The barrels are charred on the inside to create a charcoal-dominated environment in which the rums can mature and mellow. Bacardi stores its barrels of rum in completely closed, dark warehouses, far away from the noise and unwanted influence of civilization.

Bacardi's master bender is responsible for creating the finished rum. Several of the brand's rums are a carefully balanced blend of continuous- and pot-distilled spirits. Bacardi's añejos are sophisticated blends of well-aged rums.

Although originally from Cuba, Bacardi rums are now synonymous with the island and people of Puerto Rico. Sold in 175 countries, the Bacardi line of rums is the largest selling spirit brand in the world.

BACARDI SUPERIOR CARTA BLANCA (LIGHT-DRY)®

This legendary white rum is the best selling distilled spirit in the world. Its origins can be traced back to 1862 in Santiago de Cuba. Don Facundo Bacardi was intent on creating a smooth, light-bodied rum, a stark contrast to the rums of the day. After experimenting with every variable in the production process, Bacardi hit on the notion of charcoal filtering the rum before and after it had been aged in wood, something that had never been attempted with rum.

The charcoal filtration had several remarkable effects. The process filters the rum by removing impurities and particulate. The charcoal also softened the rum, mellowing its naturally robust character. Perhaps most striking was that the charcoal removed all traces of color from the rum leaving it crystal clear.

The world's most popular spirit is a blend of light, continuous-distilled rums and hardy, pot-distilled rums. BACARDI CARTA BLANCA is aged for a minimum of one year in American white oak barrels. The insides of the barrels are charred to enhance the maturation process. When the rum is emptied from the cask it has a rich, golden color. It is then filtered through charcoal for further mellowing and to strip away any trace of color.

Bacardi Carta Blanca is a brilliantly clear rum with a delicate bouquet comprised of almonds and tropical fruits. It has an extremely light, smooth body that glides onto the palate without a trace of heat. The rum expands in the mouth revealing slightly sweet flavors with a finish that is clean and balanced.

In addition to Puerto Rico, Bacardi Carta Blanca is also distilled in Brazil, Spain and Mexico. Regardless of where it is produced, every batch is checked and certified for quality assurance at Bacardi's state of the art laboratory. In addition, the rum must pass a series of blind taste tests before it is bottled and offered for sale. Bacardi Carta Blanca is marketed in the United States at 40% abv (80 proof), however, it is also produced at 37.5% abv.

Perhaps it's stating the obvious, but Bacardi's dry, light-bodied Carta Blanca is ideally suited for drink making. It marries with just about anything that can be put into a glass. To experience just how smooth a spirit can be, try sampling the rum neat. Then you'll get an opportunity to appreciate how remarkable Bacardi's revolutionary white rum is.

BACARDI SUPERIOR CARTA DE ORO (GOLD)®

This rum tells its own story. Swirling it in a glass you get a good sense of what Don Facundo Bacardi was looking to achieve when he first stepped into his distillery. BACARDI CARTA DE ORO was created to be something entirely different from the other rums of the day.

Armed with Cuba's first Coffey continuous still, Don Facundo Bacardi began distilling light-bodied rums. After aging in wood, these spirits were blended together with the distillery's growing reserves of hardy, fuller-bodied, pot-distilled rums. The result was something never before seen on the island, a light-bodied, golden rum.

Bacardi Carta de Oro is the same blend of continuous-distilled and pot-distilled rums as Carta Blanca. There are, however, two notable differences between these rums. Carta de Oro is aged in charred, American white oak barrels for up to two years, as opposed to the one year Carta Blanca spends in wood. Secondly, Carta de Oro has less filtering.

The rum has excellent clarity, a silky smooth texture, and an alluring golden hue. Carta de Oro is lightly aromatic with aromas of walnuts, spices and tropical fruits. The rum has a light to medium body and a spicy, vanilla-laced palate. The Carta de Oro has a soft, flavorful and lingering finish. It is marketed in the United States at 40% abv (80 proof), however, it is also produced at 37.5% abv.

When mixed in cocktails, the differences between the two rums are most noticeable. While the Carta Blanca is content to meld effortlessly with the other ingredients, Carta de Oro actually becomes one of the players. Its color, bouquet, body and taste are invaluable additions to nearly any cocktail.

BACARDI SELECT®

BACARDI SELECT is a lively, full-flavored spirit. Unlike some dark rums that deliver their full-bodied flavor with a mouthful of heat, Bacardi's entry is a surprisingly smooth, dark rum with a heady aroma and a rich full body.

Bacardi Select is crafted from a blend of continuous-distilled and pot-distilled rums. The constituent rums are aged between one and four years in charred, American white oak barrels.

This is a rum you'll want to initially taste neat before you add it to your favorite cocktail. While it enjoys scores of drink-making applications, it is a solid performer in its own right.

Bacardi Select has a brilliant amber color with auburn hues. The semi-sweet bouquet reveals notes of molasses, toasted oak and vanilla. The rum's appearance would suggest that its body would have plenty of heft and weight to it, but that's not the case. It has a trim, slender body that lilts over the palate. The rum presents a pleasant array of slightly smoky, slightly sweet flavors that build in intensity during the lingering finish.

The rum is 40% abv (80 proof), however, it is also produced at 37.5% abv.

BACARDI 151°®

Overproof rums are a traditional style of Caribbean rum. These spirits are often white rums bottled at an extremely high alcohol content. Technically, overproof spirits are those bottled at more than 50% alcohol by volume (abv). BACARDI 151° is an overproof rum made from a blend of light, continuous-distilled rums, charcoal filtered and aged in charred oak barrels for up to two years. The extended aging is pivotal in curbing some of the rum's aggressive character.

Bacardi 151° has a subtle bouquet, a featherweight body and a surprisingly smooth texture. The rum immediately fills the mouth with sizzling, effervescent flavors. The finish is quite warm and protracted.

This highly potent rum is 75.5% abv, which is an important consideration when serving. It is not intended to be consumed neat. On the contrary, Bacardi 151° is designed for use in drink making, and is often featured in exotic drinks such as the Mai Tai.

BACARDI 8®

Since its initial release in October 1998, BACARDI 8 has been the company's super-premium brand. A quick swirl, sniff and sip and you'll know why this is a classic añejo rum, once reserved solely for the Bacardi family's private consumption.

Crafted using the original recipe and aging process created by Don Facundo Bacardi in 1862, Bacardi 8 is a blend of continuous-distilled and pot-distilled rums. The rums are filtered through charcoal and aged a minimum of eight years in hand-selected, charred American white oak barrels. The rum is bottled at 40% abv (80 proof).

Bacardi 8 has a golden amber hue, excellent clarity and is highly aromatic. Its complex bouquet is imbued with the aromas of apricots, cocoa, molasses, caramel and vanilla. Remarkably soft and well rounded, the rum gracefully glides over the palate without a hint of harshness or biting edge. Within moments it opens up revealing a generous and long lasting array of toasty flavors. The rum finishes warm and relaxed. Bacardi 8 is a luxurious, añejo rum, one to be savored neat in an unhurried moment.

BACARDI® LIMÓN™

Clearly Bacardi is a company that places a premium on innovation. In 1995, Bacardi launched a revolutionary new style of rum, BACARDI LIMÓN. Two years in development, Limón is an imaginative infusion of Bacardi Carta Blanca rum and a proprietary, all-natural blend of lemon, lime and grape-fruit essence. It was an immediate success, shattering the company's previous sales records by selling more than 350,000 cases in the first nine months.

The undercarriage of Bacardi Limón is a blend of continuous-distilled and pot-distilled rums that are twice filtered through charcoal and aged a year in charred oak barrels. Fresh citrus extracts are added to the rum during blending. Even the packaging is a departure from the expected.

Bacardi Limón has a light body and silky smooth texture. Its character is loaded with fresh, sun-ripened aromas and tangy, citrus flavors. The rum finishes long and flavorful. Frankly, everything about Bacardi Limón is refreshing.

Its singular flavor makes it exceptionally refreshing and mixable. Bacardi Limón is a natural with lemonade, fresh juice or blended in a piña colada or daiquiri. It's also excellent when featured in a Cosmopolitan, Martini, Bossa Nova, or Gauguin. The rum is marketed in the United States at 35% abv (70 proof).

TROPICO®

One of the first things someone learns about rum is that it marries beautifully with fruit juice. There's just something about the way the flavors complement each other that makes it a timeless taste combination. This was clearly the working premise behind the 1999 release of TROPICO, a unique blend of Bacardi añejo rum and seven exotic fruit juices.

Tropico is almost identical to the color of a ripe papaya with a lush bouquet of fresh tropical fruit. Its substantial body is more reminiscent of a well crafted cocktail. The palate is well balanced with a slightly tangy flavor and a hint of rum in the semi-sweet finish.

Tropico earned "Best of Show" and "Award of Excellence" honors at the 2000 San Francisco World Spirit Competition. In addition, it also took double honors in the Awards of the Americas competition judged by the prestigious panel of Chefs from the American Tasting Institute Advisory Panel. The refreshing drink, Tropico Tango won top honors at the Most Sensual Drink Competition hosted by *Penthouse Magazine* in July of the same year. While it enjoys numerous creative applications, it's a marvelous cocktail straight from the bottle over ice. Tropico should be refrigerated after opening and is 16% abv (32 proof).

OTHER PUERTO RICAN RUMS

Compared to the experiences of other Caribbean islands, the rum industry in Puerto Rico got off the ground relatively late. Since the mid-19th century, several other distilleries have succeeded in creating rums of merit and distinction.

The origins of the RON DEL BARRILITO brand can be traced to the Fernández estate, a sugar plantation named Haciendo Santa Ana in Bayamón, Puerto Rico. Pedro Fernández established a distillery and in 1888 he began selling a rum he dubbed "Ron del Barril" meaning "rum of the barrel."

Renamed Ron del Barrilito, the brand remains a favorite among locals. It is made by the Edmund Fernández company. The blend is aged in large 132 gallon European oak wine barrels. The TWO STAR RON DEL BARRILITO is a blend of three year old rums, and the THREE STAR RON DEL BARRILITO is a blend comprised of rums aged a minimum of six years. Both are 43% abv (86 proof).

The Serrallès Distillery was founded in 1865. Sebastian Serrallès equipped the facility with a five-tray continuous column still imported from France. The distillery closed during Prohibition in the United States. It reopened at its present site in 1935 and was equipped with six continuous column stills. Today the distillery can output 55,000 proof gallons per day and has approximately 500,000 barrels of rum maturing in their warehouses.

The Serrallès Distillery produces several different brands of blended rums. There are four labels of DON Q, including a white and gold version (40% abv), a 151° OVERPROOF (75.5% abv), and GRAN AÑEJO, a blend of rums aged between three and twelve years. The distillery also produces RONRICO, a 130-year old brand produced in three styles, a white, gold (40% abv), and 151-proof; and EL DORADO, a blend of light rums aged five years, (40% abv).

Perhaps the distillery's most famous brand is CAPTAIN MORGAN RUM. Named after the famous buccaneer, the brand is produced in four styles. CAPTAIN MORGAN BLACK LABEL is a dark, medium-bodied blend of pot-distilled and continuous-distilled rums, aged up to seven years (37.5% abv and 40% abv). CAPTAIN MORGAN ORIGINAL SPICED RUM is the best selling brand in its category (35% abv). It was reprised by the release of CAPTAIN MORGAN PRIVATE STOCK, a premium spiced rum made from a blend of older, more mature rums (40% abv). Released in 1998, CAPTAIN MORGAN PARROT BAY is a clear rum with tropical flavors and natural coconut (25% abv).

LEEWARD ISLANDS
PUERTO RICO
San Juan
Ponce
St John
St Thomas
B.V.I.
VIRGIN Is
St Croix
Anguilla
St Martin
St Barts
BARBUDA
ST. KITTS
ST. NEVIS
St. John
ANTIGUA
MONTSERRAT
LESSER ANTILLES
WINDWARD ISLANDS
GUADELOUPE
Pointe-a-Pitre
Portsmouth
Marigot
DOMINICA
Fort de France
MARTINIQUE
Castries
ST. LUCIA
BARBADOS
ST. VINCENT
Bridgetown
The Grenadas
GRENADA
St George
THE CARIBBEAN
CARIBBEAN SEA
Rogues Is
Orchita
Blanquilla Is
Los Testigos
TOBAGO
Margarita Is
Tortuga
Porlamar
Port of Spain
TRINIDAD
Arima
San Fernando
Carapano
Caracas
Puerto Cabello
Los Teques
Cumaná
Maracay
Valencia
Barcelona
Caripito
San Juan
Maturia
Valle
VENEZUELA
Ciudad Bolivar
San Pernando

Chapter 4

The Island of Barbados and Mount Gay Rum

Barbados lies 90 miles east of the islands known as the Lesser Antilles. On a map, the island looks comparatively large, green and difficult to overlook. Approaching Barbados from the sea, however, tells a different story and offers a plausible explanation for the island's relative calm history.

Barbados is essentially flat. In fact the highest point on the 166 square mile island is Mount Hillaby at a mere 1,116 feet above sea level. It barely makes an impression on the horizon until you're several miles out. What's the relevance? Barbados' minimal elevation and gently rolling countryside made the island challenging to be seen from the sea and difficult for ship's navigators to find.

Barbados was essentially uninhabited when the Portuguese first set foot on the island in the early part of the 16th century. However, it is widely contended that the Arawaks actually discovered the island centuries before. The Portuguese were apparently unimpressed because the island remained mostly uninhabited for more than a century until the English established a settlement at what is now Bridgetown in 1627.

The English found the lush island quite hospitable. The level terrain and the porous, fertile soil, composed primarily of limestone, sandstone and volcanic ash, was well suited for agriculture and the eventual cultivation of sugar cane. Fresh water was pumped from subterranean aquifers for irrigation.

In 1637, a Dutchman named Pieter Blower purportedly was the first to bring sugar cane to the island. He established a small, simple plant to process sugar cane into crystallized sugar. The skimmings from the boiling molasses were distilled into what the locals called "kill devil," thereby beginning the rum industry on Barbados.

The island's economy soon revolved around the cultivation of sugar cane, production of processed sugar and the distillation of rum. Sugar plantations dotted the countryside.

By 1650, the settlement at Bridgetown was flourishing and included among its population were 120 taverns. At that time nearly a million liters a year were being distilled in pot stills on the island. Near the end of the 17th century there were 460 windmill-driven sugar mills and estate distilleries.

While it appears that Barbados wasn't necessarily the birthplace of rum, the British colony was likely the first to make the export of rum a significant aspect of their economy. A burgeoning rum industry in the American colonies sought to prohibit the import of superior Bajan rum. To protect the scores of local distilleries, in 1654 the General Court of Connecticut ordered the confiscation of "whatsoever Barbados liquors, commonly called rum, kill-devil or the like."

The judicial degree had little impact. Soon Bajan rum was the alcoholic potable of choice in colonial America. George Washington freely distributed 75 gallons of rum from Barbados during his election to the Virginia House of Burgesses in 1758. When Washington was inaugurated as president he purchased a barrel of the best Bajan rum for the celebration.

Until the beginning of the 20th century, Bajan rum was distilled on sugar plantations. Few governments, however, can leave well enough alone. Laws were soon introduced, prohibiting those who cultivated sugar, from distilling it into rum. In addition, distillers were prohibited from bottling or distributing their own product. These legal provisions are still in effect today.

It is conjectured that because Barbados has ideal natural defenses and lies upwind of the Antilles chain of islands, it was hard to attack from the sea. As a result, the island never changed allegiances during the colonial wars of the 17th and 18th century. In fact, Barbados has only been colonized by the British. In 1966, Barbados achieved independence from Britain and became a sovereign nation in the British Commonwealth of Nations.

Today, Barbados has a population of approximately 265,000, making it the third most densely populated Caribbean island. It is the highest ranked Caribbean nation on the United Nation's Human Development Index, which ranks countries based on life expectancy, per capita income and the amount of GNP devoted to education.

RUM AND THE ISLAND OF BARBADOS

The history of rum and the island of Barbados are intertwined. It has been produced in Barbados continuously since the early 1600's. Rum is not only an essential element of the island's economy, it is an integral aspect of the social fabric. The island of Barbados sports some 1200 rum shops, local "watering holes" where the locals congregate, socialize and enjoy the finest Barbadian spirits. Bajans are rum connoisseurs, most of who have well-articulated opinions on the various attributes of any brand. Suffice to say that the island's rum shop culture has created a sophisticated rum market.

The people of Barbados are justifiably proud of their indigenous spirits. The truth is that the island—measuring all of 14 miles wide by 21 miles long—is an ideal place to cultivate sugar cane and distill rum. The all-important water source is underground aquifers fed with filtered spring water. The gentling rolling terrain and porous, fertile soil are tailor-made for agriculture. The climate is temperate and the air is invariably laden with humidity.

Of the various brands of Barbadian rum, the oldest and most recognized around the world is Mount Gay. There are reasons to believe that rum was being distilled on the Mount Gay Estate as early as 1663. The earliest historical evidence of rum production, however, is a property deed dated February 20, 1703. The legal document states that on the property there existed "two stone windmills...one boiling house with seven coppers, one curing house and one still house." All these items are essential to the distillation of rum.

The spacious Mount Gay Rum Estate is located in the northernmost parish of St. Lucy. It is situated on a prominent ridge overlooking the expanse of countryside. In the early 1700s, William Sandiford consolidated a number of smaller sugar plantations into one, 280-acre estate. The newly created estate was given the name of Mount Gilboa and from the onset the plantation flourished. The estate stayed in the Sandiford family until 1747 when it was sold to fellow Englishman John Sober.

Sober lived in England so he chose family friend Sir John Gay Alleyne to personally oversee the sprawling Mount Gilboa sugar cane plantation and rum still house. Alleyne excelled at business and the plantation prospered. Upon Sir John Gay's death in 1801, John Sober's son, Cumberbatch, honored the man by renaming the plantation, Mount Gay Rum Estate (the place name Mount Alleyne was already taken).

Businessman Aubrey Ward purchased the Mount Gay Rum Plantation at the turn of the 20th century. Faced with increasing worldwide demand for Mount Gay Rum, Ward looked to expand production while strictly maintaining the rum's unsurpassed quality and traditional character. The Ward family continued to expand the production capacity of the distillery throughout the century. Ward's partner, John F. Hutson, succeeded in greatly expanding Mount Gay's worldwide distribution, eventually making the brand among the most recognized labels of Caribbean rum.

In 1989 the Remy Cointreau Group acquired a majority interest in the Mount Gay Distillery. The acquisition further solidified the presence of Mount Gay Rum in international markets.

The rums of Mount Gay are the best selling in Barbados, with nearly 25% of the distillery's output being consumed on the island, and 40% exported to the United States. There are several primary reasons for the market preeminence of Mount Gay Rum.

The sugar cane grown on the island is especially high quality. The cane takes 12-18 months to reach maturity. Harvesting takes place between February and June, and commences when the cane has reached its peak sugar content. Once harvested the sugar cane is taken immediately to the sugar refinery.

The cane is crushed and heated to produce sugar crystals. The residue is boiled repeatedly to create a thick, black molasses. This rich, flavorful molasses is mixed with spring water in large oak vats. Yeast is added to the mixture to precipitate fermentation, a process that takes three days.

Mount Gay rums are produced using one of two different distillation methods. Some versions of the rum, those distilled once, are produced in a particular type of two-column still called a Coffey still. This process yields an extremely pure spirit, one with a light, delicate character and high in alcohol.

The second method employed at Mount Gay is alembic distillation in traditional copper pot stills, which have been in use on the estate for approximately 300 years. These stills are used when crafting small batch, double-distilled rums. The resulting distillate has a more robust, distinctive character. Because they are produced at a lower alcohol content by volume, the rums are intensely aromatic and far more flavorful. Pot still rums also take well to aging in wood.

The rums obtained from the two different methods of distillation are rested in select American white oak casks. These charred barrels were previously used to age Kentucky bourbon. The char on the inside of the barrel imbues the rum with the flavors of vanilla, caramel, toffee and toasty oak. The rum also gets its rich, dark color from aging in wood.

Mount Gay ages its rums in open-air warehouses. Seemingly endless rows of barrels stacked on their sides are exposed to the climatic changes of the seasons. The master distiller carefully monitors the maturation process of each cask, some of which are over 20-years in maturity.

Once matured, the single and double distilled rums are blended together to create the various rums in the Mount Gay Rum portfolio. The single distilled spirits add a light body and aromatic qualities. The double distilled rums contribute greatly to the finished spirit's alluring bouquet, supple body and full-flavored palate. The pot still rums are also primarily responsible for creating the spirit's finish, the persistence of taste after the rum has been swallowed.

The Mount Gay Rum master blender is responsible for deciding the exact composition of the finished rum. It is a complex process of combining differing types and ages of spirits together to achieve the desired aroma, texture, body, taste and finish of the particular end product. Each of Mount Gay's rums is as individual as a signature. They are in essence the spirits of Barbados.

THE RUMS OF MOUNT GAY

MOUNT GAY ECLIPSE®

One of the most recognized labels of rum in the world is MOUNT GAY ECLIPSE. Flagship of the Mount Gay portfolio of rums, the brand was created in 1910 and its name commemorates the total solar eclipse that occurred that year. It is crafted from a blend of pot still and continuous still rums that are two-years in maturity. It is marketed in the United States at 40% abv (80 proof), however, it is also produced at 37.5%, 43% and 77% abv.

The enticement begins with the first glance. Eclipse has a luminous, golden amber hue that is a marvelous entrée for the sensations to follow. The rum has a compact bouquet featuring the aromas of flora, spice, nuts and fresh fruit with a touch of vanilla and oak thrown into the mix.

The rum has a well-textured, light- to medium-body. Its complex array of flavors settles lightly on the palate and slowly each individual flavor can be discerned. Most prominent among its smooth tastes are tropical fruit, vanilla and a hint of toasty oak, caramel and apricot. Eclipse has a marvelous, semi-sweet, lightly smoked finish that is both complex and long lasting.

Little wonder Mount Gay Eclipse has gained worldwide renown. It's a soft, well-balanced rum that can be enjoyed both neat or mixed with a bevy of mixers or juice. It also has a starring role in scores of cocktails and classic mixed drinks.

MOUNT GAY
SPECIAL RESERVE®

One of the earliest offerings in the estate's repertoire, MOUNT GAY SPECIAL RESERVE is a crisp, unassuming spirit. Also marketed as Mount Gay Premium White Rum, it is made from a blend of pot and continuous still rums that are two-years in maturity. Special Reserve is carefully filtered to attain purity and remove the coloring congeners in the pot still rum.

The rum has brilliant clarity and an interesting appearance. In the bottle it has a pale tint, similar in hue to that of a light whisky. In the glass, however, the rum has only a touch of color; add a splash of water and the color disappears. Rendering the rum absolutely clear would be possible, yet it could be argued, undesirable. Letting a trace of its natural color shine through is appreciated and a pleasant point of difference.

Special Reserve is also surprisingly aromatic. Many brands of white rum are devoid of any discernable bouquet, made with nary a suggestion of aroma. Frankly it's disappointing to nose a rum and come away without a hint of what it will taste like. Mount Gay must agree because they imbued Special Reserve with a delicate yet satisfying bouquet.

This is a lively, light-bodied spirit. It immediately fills the mouth with subtle, fruit flavors best perceived on the finish. After the rum drifts over the palate it drifts away warm and relaxed.

Mount Gay Special Reserve is marketed in the United States at 40% abv (80 proof), however, it is also produced at 43% abv. Before committing this splendid, unassuming rum to a chilled daiquiri, take a moment to enjoy it neat or with a cube or two of ice.

MOUNT GAY SUGAR CANE®

Most of the world knows this rum as Mount Gay Sugar Cane Brandy. Legal restrictions in the United States and US Virgin Islands caused the distillery to make a slight alteration on the label and call it MOUNT GAY SUGAR CANE RUM. Regardless of the name on the paper, the rum is exceptional, a celebration of the sugar cane and rum making tradition.

The likely reason why the distillery dubbed this gem a brandy is that it drinks like a brandy. Mount Gay  Sugar Cane Rum is a blend containing a high proportion of pot still rums, some of which are a minimum of seven-years in maturity. It is marketed in the United States at 40% abv (80 proof). The rest of the world though gets to appreciate the version labeled as Sugar Cane Brandy at 43% abv, which, while subject to personal taste, is a more appropriate strength for such an exuberant rum.

Mount Gay Sugar Cane Rum is bred with all the character of an alembic spirit. It's a big, full-bodied rum brimming with aroma and taste. It has marvelous clarity and is a deep, golden amber color, perhaps a shade lighter than Eclipse. It's when you nose this spirit that you first become aware of its special qualities. The expansive bouquet is layered with the aromas of sugar cane, spice and toasted oak.

The Sugar Cane Rum is remarkably elegant upon entering the palate. Slowly, almost patiently it starts to fill the mouth with a broad range of warm, toasty flavors, such as spice, vanilla and molasses. The highlight of the experience, however, is saved for the finish. Not only is the rum long lasting, it's loaded with flavor and warmth.

This is a highly versatile performer. Mount Gay Sugar Cane Rum is so complex and well balanced it warrants sipping it in a snifter. On the other hand, the rum is so full-flavored that the temptation of showcasing it in a cocktail is hard to resist. Ultimately the choice is yours.

MOUNT GAY EXTRA OLD®

This rum is testimony to why you need a master blender like Jerry Edwards. Marrying together numerous spirits of different maturities and differing compositions such that they become something much more than the sum of their parts is a daunting task. When done really well it yields something noteworthy, such as MOUNT GAY EXTRA OLD RUM.

Edwards and his staff spent three years developing this rum. It is a blend comprised of some of the oldest, most prized rums in the Mount Gay reserves. The mature pot still and continuous still rums selected for the blend range between 12 and 17 years in age. The rum is bottled at a lip tingling 43% abv (80 proof). The overall result is a spirit worthy of a fine brandy snifter.

Mount Gay Extra Old has a rich, amber brown color and brilliant luminescence. The pronounced greenish tint around the edges of the rum confirms its extensive wood aging. It possesses a generous, well-balanced bouquet offering up the sweet aromas of oak, honey, vanilla, and fruit. The more the rum aerates, the more expansive and pleasant the bouquet becomes.

Extra Old is remarkably light and delicate, not unlike the body of an aged alembic brandy. The rum immediately fills the mouth and splashes the palate with waves of flavor; tastes of banana, vanilla, caramel and toasted oak. The finish, while not overly protracted, is seamlessly smooth and loaded with flavor. Extra Old is in every sense a luxurious rum.

Not surprisingly the brand has garnered numerous awards at international competitions. In 1999 it earned a fourth Grand Gold medal at the *Monde Selection Quality Institute* in Brussels. That same year Mount Gay Extra Old Rum was judged "Best in its Class" at the prestigious *International Wine & Spirits Competition* in London.

Suffice to say that the best way to enjoy this rum is to pour some in a brandy snifter or inhaler glass and experience it neat and unadulterated. Its character will change every minute. Prepare to be fascinated. But we're reasonable, there are other ways to enjoy the rum. If you want to drop in an ice cube or a milliliter or two of water, go ahead. Just don't let us know.

OTHER BARBADIAN RUMS

For over 300 years rum has played a historically significant role in the nation's economy. While the best known expression of Barbadian rum is Mount Gay, there are other capable craftsmen on the island of Barbados.

Just north of Bridgetown is the West Indies Rum Refinery. Since 1893 the firm has made all of the alcohol distilled on the island of Barbados, with the notable exception of those distilled by the Mount Gay Distillers. The West Indies Rum Refinery provides scores of rums of different ages and compositions to numerous bottlers on the island and around the world.

One such famous brand of Barbadian rum is COCKSPUR. The rums that comprise these full-bodied blends are distilled at the West Indies Rum Refinery, but blended by the capable craftsmen of brand owner Hanschell Inniss Limited. The rums of Cockspur are described in detail in chapter thirteen, "Caribbean Rums Off The Beaten Path."

The third largest blender and bottler of Bajan rum is R. L. Seale & Company Limited. The 17th century Hopefield Sugar Plantation is located in the southern parish of Christ Church. The company is wholly Bajan owned and operated and is presently building its own distillery.

R. L. Seale & Company produces several distinctive brands of rum, each of which are extremely popular in the region. The firm produces the best selling white rum in Barbados, STADE'S WHITE RUM (43% abv). Popularly referred to as "see through," Stade's is a filtered, aged rum and not yet available in the States.

The company blends and bottles rums under the Doorly's name. DOORLY'S FINE OLD BARBADOS RUM (40% and 43% abv) is an amber, 5-year old blend; DOORLY'S MACAW (40%, 43% and 75.5% abv) is an unaged blend available in both a white and dark version; and DOORLY'S HARBOUR POLICEMAN (40% abv) is a local favorite marketed in a figural bottle.

Under the label of Alleyne Arthur & Hunte, the firm blends and bottles OLD BRIGAND BLACK AND WHITE (40% abv), a filtered, nearly black rum made from a blend of rums aged less than five years. There is also OLD BRIGAND BLACK LABEL SUPERIOR (37%, 40% & 43% abv), a blend of rums aged up to 13-years.

R. L. Seale & Company also produces an award winning, super-premium spiced rum named FOURSQUARE SPICED RUM. Seales' Foursquare Spiced Rum is made from a blend of barrel-aged Barbados rum and ground nutmeg, cinnamon and vanilla. Foursquare Spiced Rum was rated as the number one spiced rum at the Rum Expo 2000, the largest annual gathering of rums in the world.

Chapter 5

Jamaica and the Rums of Appleton Estate

Archaeological evidence suggests that the Arawaks settled on the island of Jamaica somewhere around the year 1000 A.D. They developed an agrarian society and lived in relative peace for nearly 500 years, free even from the onslaughts of the Caribs. The Arawaks even gave the island its name; Jamaica is derived from the Arawak word *Xaymaca* meaning, "Land of wood and water."

Jamaica is 90 miles south of Cuba and some 100 miles west of Haiti. Measuring 146 miles by 51 miles, it is the 3rd largest island in the Greater Antilles. The landmass is actually an outcrop of an oceanic mountain range. The center of the island is mostly mountainous with peaks exceeding 7,000 feet. Jamaica has an abundance of flora, fresh springs and spacious forests. There are fine coral beaches and broad, expansive plains where coconuts, citrus fruits and sugar cane grow. When Columbus landed on its shores on May 4, 1494 it is said he declared, "This is the fairest island eyes have ever beheld."

Fifteen years later the Spanish colonized the island. They established two settlements, one near St. Ann's Bay on the northern coast named Seville Nueva, and Villa de la Vega located across the island at present day Spanish Town. The fulcrum of the Spaniards economy was cultivating sugar cane, and to drive the burgeoning industry, they introduced the indigenous population to the realities of slavery. When the Spanish arrived in 1509, there were an estimated 100,000 Arawaks living in Jamaica. Within two generations, disease and slavery wiped out the entire population. To replace the labor force the Spanish brought in African slaves.

In 1654, England's government, led by Oliver Cromwell, looked to wrest control of the Caribbean from the Spanish and made their first target the large island of Hispaniola, a campaign that failed miserably. Looking to garner a small margin of gain, the English invaded Jamaica. They knew the island's small Spanish garrison militarily stood little chance. On May 10, 1655, the English landed 6,000 men off 38 warships, easily capturing Kingston and all of the Spanish strongholds.

The British allowed the Spanish settlers to leave the island and thereby abandon their land and possessions. Instead, many of the slaves escaped into the mountains. From there they mounted a guerilla war, harassing and marauding the English settlements. The slaves became known as the Maroons, (from the Spanish word *"cimmarones,"* meaning runaways).

For five years the Maroons fought a battle of attrition waiting for reinforcements from Mexico and Cuba, relief that never came. Direct Spanish involvement on Jamaica ended in June 1658 when an invading Spanish force was defeated after fierce fighting near St. Ann's Bay.

After a short period of military rule, the colony adopted an English-type constitution and legislative body. Once firmly in control of the island, the British made overtures to Europe's pirates and buccaneers to make Port Royal on the Kingston peninsula their port-of-call. It soon drew a large population of pirates from around the Caribbean, including Henry Morgan. For decades they plundered the Spanish fleet, laid siege to Spanish cities and came back to the city of Port Royal. It eventually earned the notorious reputation as the "richest, wickedest city in Christendom." In 1692 things came to a screeching halt when a horrific earthquake dropped most of the city into the sea.

Unless you owned one of the few sugar cane plantations, life on Jamaica during the last half of the 17th century was harsh. Of the roughly 12,000 British settlers, only 3,470 lasted the first six years. Disease, disaster and an invasion by France kept mortality high during the century. Those that survived gained a foothold on the island and prospered greatly.

This concentration of wealth spawned the growth of the sugar cane industry. It required large amounts of capital to develop and operate an economically viable plantation. At the close of the 17th century much of the best land on the island was centralized between a number of large estates. Vast acreage of cane fields dominated the plains.

In addition, the plantations required a large, cheap labor force to cultivate the sugar cane, an arduous, demanding task. The course the owners took was slavery. Under British rule the slave trade flourished. By 1700, there were an estimated 45,000 African slaves in Jamaica, outnumbering the free population seven to one. Over the century, nearly a million Africans were sent to Jamaica as slaves.

The growing work force allowed the estates to extend their holdings as the plantation owners ordered vast tracts of thick tropical forests be cleared into fertile, cultivatable fields. The gulf between the large and small plantation owners continued to grow, and prominent owners dominated local governments. Production of sugar cane skyrocketed in the 1720s, cementing the wealth and importance of the plantation owners for the next century.

Things were about to change greatly for the nation of Jamaica. In 1832, about 150 slaves worked the average sugar plantation on the island. The following year slavery was abolished throughout the British Empire. The decline of the sugar plantations after the emancipation of the slaves had a devastating impact on the economy. Soon waves of Chinese and East Indians were imported into the country as indentured servants to rejuvenate the sugar cane and rum production.

The newly freed slaves deserted the plantations and established themselves as free settlers in the hills. They formed independent peasant communities and through hard work most of these cooperative efforts thrived. In 1865 an insurrection by former slaves was repelled with such ferocity that the government was forced to conduct an investigation. The following year the Representative Constitution was abolished, and in 1866 a new form of government was established. The foundations for Jamaica's modern political system were laid in the 1930s. The two current political parties were formed by the mid-1940s. In 1960 the Jamaican government nationalized the sugar industry.

Jamaica was among the first of the British West Indies nations to gain independence. On August 6, 1962 Jamaica became an independent member of the British Commonwealth, with the Queen of England as a titular head of state. The island has its own constitution based principally on British legal, religious, educational and political traditions.

Today, Jamaica has a population of approximately 2.5 million, over 90% are of West African descent. With a population of 700,000, Kingston is the largest English speaking city south of Miami. The sugar industry is the oldest continuing industry in the country and the third largest source of foreign exchange. The industry is the largest employer of labor. Jamaica is a thriving tourist destination and continuing among the island's economic mainstays are the production and exportation of rum.

RUM AND THE ISLAND OF JAMAICA

The Spanish introduced the science of cultivating sugar cane and the art of distillation to the island of Jamaica, both of which found a conducive environment in which to flourish. The plains along the north coast, with its fertile volcanic and limestone soil, proved ideal for growing sugar cane. So too were the climate, precipitation, humidity and terrain. The water sources for irrigation and the production of rum were pristine mountain fed springs and underground aquifers of limestone filtered spring water.

Distilling rum became a serious endeavor for the plantation owners. The distillation and sale of what was essentially a by-product of processing sugar provided an attractive source of revenue. Nearly every Jamaican sugar cane plantation of the day had the facilities necessary to distill rum. In many cases it proved more profitable to sell rum than sugar.

After harvesting, the sugar cane is taken to the plantation's mill where the cane juice is extracted from the plant. The juice is boiled repeatedly and eventually rendered into molasses. Jamaican rums are produced by fermenting a wash of molasses, spring water and yeasts, and then distilling it in copper pot (alembic) stills.

Jamaicans have made many contributions to the evolution of rum, among these was the practice of adding a portion of the previous distillation to the fermenting wash. This was done in an effort to create a more flavorful and aromatic spirit.

By the turn of the 20th century there were nearly 32,000 acres of sugar cane under cultivation. Nearly

90% of the island's plantations had a distillery on the property. Because of the shortage of whiskey during World War II, Jamaican rum jumped in popularity as people began trying it for the first time. Otherwise, the century was difficult for the Jamaican sugar and rum industries, partially as a result of the growing reliance on sugar beets for processing sugar. Most of the rum distilleries have ceased operation. Those that remain have developed a worldwide reputation for greatness.

There is no better representation of everything that Jamaican rum has become than Appleton Estate. The oldest sugar estate and distillery in Jamaica, Appleton Estate has been continuously producing rum for over 250 years. While the earliest documentation of rum production was dated 1749, the origins of the estate can be traced back to 1655 when the British wrested control of the island from the Spanish.

It is believed that the sprawling estate was part of a land grant given to Francis Dickinson in recognition of his military service for the Crown. Located in Jamaica's picturesque Nassau Valley in the parish of St. Elizabeth, Appleton Estate encompasses a total of 11,400 acres and includes cane fields, a sugar processing plant, distillery, its own natural spring and aging warehouses. The distillery is  equipped with large, copper pot (alembic) stills—three of which are over 100 years old—and state of the art column stills.

Appleton Estate stayed in the Dickinson family until 1845. At the time, there were roughly 17 acres of sugar cane under cultivation. In 1907 control of the estate was given over to J. M. Farquharson, who in 1916 sold the property to J. Wray and Nephew Ltd., a company with a well-established tradition for producing world caliber rums and spirits.

J. Wray and Nephew Ltd. is the largest distiller, blender and bottler of Jamaican rum. In fact, it is the oldest company in Jamaica and has grown to be among the largest exporters in the Caribbean. John Wray opened the Shakespeare Tavern on the north side of Kingston in 1825. He began blending his own rums and selling them in the tavern. The next year Wray won three gold medals for aged rum at the London International Exposition.

The acquisition of Appleton Estate in 1916 allowed J. Wray and Nephew Ltd. to greatly expand its production and aging capabilities. It gave the growing company access to unsurpassed, estate-grown sugar cane and a source of limestone-filtered spring water. Appleton Estate currently provides J. Wray and Nephew Ltd. with two-thirds of the firm's sugar cane needs. In addition to the Appleton Estate rums, the company also blends and bottles Coruba and J. Wray and Nephew White Overproof Rum.

Exported to over 60 countries, Appleton Estate has become the best known Jamaican rum in the world. It has been continuously producing rum since 1749. The estate's sugar plant can process in excess of 150 tons of sugar a day. The distillery production capacity is nearly 28,000 liters of rum per day.

Some of the finest sugar cane in the region is grown on the Appleton Estate. After the cane has reached its peak sugar content, it is harvested and brought directly to the mill. There the sugar cane juice is boiled repeatedly and produced into black, high-grade molasses. Still heavily laden with sugar, the molasses is transferred into a large, vat where it is blended with spring water and a special, proprietary strain of yeast to precipitate fermentation. The fermentation process is completed in approximately 30-hours. The wash is then distilled using either the traditional copper pot (alembic) method or the more modern column still.

The rums distilled in the three-column still are typically lightly flavored, and have delicate bodies with subtle taste profiles. Those that are distilled in the copper pot still are made in small batches and double distilled. These rums retain high concentrations of congeners and flavoring agents. These full-bodied pot still rums are highly aromatic and loaded with flavor and character. They are also best suited for extended aging in wood.

Appleton Estate ages all of its rums in select American white oak casks, that were previously used to age Kentucky bourbon. Over the years the char on the inside of the barrel greatly affects every facet of the finished rum's character, imbuing it with rich color, toasty aromas, warm, caramel-like flavors and a long, luxuriant finish.

The estate maintains several huge, open-air warehouses. Inside ,countless rows of barrels are stored on their sides in racks that tower to the warehouse's high ceiling. In hotter climates,

such as Jamaica, rum matures more quickly than in cooler climates. This phenomenon is known as "Tropical Aging." A rum aged in Jamaica for a year will have the characteristics of a rum that has been aged for two or three years in a cooler climate. The barrels are monitored closely by Joy Spence, and occasionally are rotated, but mostly the barrels are left alone, allowing the rum inside to mature at its own pace. Appleton Estate has an extremely large stock of well-aged rums, some in excess of 50-years old.

The master blender combines numerous types of column-distilled and pot-distilled spirits to create the fine line of Appleton Estate Jamaica rums. The rums distilled in the three-column still feature light bodies and delicate bouquets. The hearty, pot-distilled rums are more exuberant in character and are primarily responsible for creating the finished rums expansive bouquet, full-flavored palate and long, luxurious finish.

Appleton Estate's master blender has the responsibility of determining the exact composition of each brand of rum. The process of blending differing types and ages of spirits together to achieve the desired aroma, texture, body, taste and finish, is a challenging task. The end results are a work of art and rate among the most vivacious and flavorful rums in the region.

After blending, the rum is left to rest in large oak vats. This process allows the elements in the blend to "marry" into one cohesive spirit. It's an extra step in production that pays large dividends.

A sniff, sip and swallow leaves little doubt why Appleton Estate Jamaica rums epitomize the spirit of Jamaica.

THE RUMS OF APPLETON ESTATE

APPLETON SPECIAL JAMAICA®

This singular spirit is made from a blend of pot-distilled and continuous-distilled rums that have been aged in American oak barrels. APPLETON SPECIAL JAMAICA RUM originated at the height of World War II. The worldwide supply of whisky was nearly exhausted, so Appleton Estate set about creating a rum with a whisky-like character. The result of their efforts was labeled as Appleton Estate Special. Its name proved accurate as the brand became an immediate success.

Now labeled simply as Appleton Special, the rum has an amber-gold hue and a medium, well-rounded body. It is richly aromatic. On the nose the expansive bouquet presents the aromas of caramel, spice and honey, with a tantalizing chaser of smoke. The bouquet gives the first glimpse into this marvelous rum's dual personality.

Appleton Special enters the mouth quietly, never revealing that it is 43% abv (86 proof). The rum is impressively smooth and mild. It has a medium-body and a palate that features the flavors of spice, caramel and apples. The lingering finish is more reminiscent of whisky—dry, spicy and laced with a bit of smoke.

Appleton Special is an intriguing marriage of styles. Sampling it neat is an interesting experience because it very much drinks like a rum with a whisky personality. Appleton Special is ideally suited for cocktails. Its aroma, body and taste shine through when mixed.

APPLETON ESTATE V/X JAMAICA®

The hugely successful APPLETON ESTATE V/X JAMAICA RUM is the brand's flagship and ranks among the most recognizable Jamaican exports. It is a skillful blend of pot still and continuous still rums, which have an average age of five to ten years. After blending, the rum is rested in large oak vats to allow the blend to "marry." The V/X on the label is not an age designation, rather a reference that the rum is "very exceptional." It is available in the United States at 40% abv (80 proof), however, it is also produced at 43% abv.

Appleton Estate V/X has a deep golden-amber color similar to that of an old Highland single malt whisky. The bouquet is marvelously generous and complex. It is endowed with the aromas of oranges, molasses, nuts and spice. The rum's silky smooth, medium body lilts over the palate, filling the mouth with firm, moderately sweet flavors, the most prominent of which is caramel, vanilla and spice. Possibly the best part of the experience is the creamy, long lasting, flavor-filled finish.

Appleton Estate V/X is a refined pleasure from start to finish. It is tempting to simply present this rum in a snifter neat, or with a few cubes of ice, and leave it at that. While the rum is certainly elegant enough to warrant the high brow treatment, you'd be missing out on much of its versatility. Appleton Estate V/X is a spirit bred for featuring in a cocktail, such as a daiquiri, or mixed with your choice of fresh fruit juice.

APPLETON ESTATE
EXTRA JAMAICA®

If you're looking to impress someone special with your savior-faire and not drain your pocketbook in the process, giving them some APPLETON ESTATE EXTRA JAMAICA RUM would certainly fit the bill. This is a lot of rum for the money. It is crafted using pot still and continuous still rums. The spirits selected for the blend are aged in American white oak barrels up to 18 years. After blending, Appleton Estate Extra is rested in large oak vats to allow the blend to "marry" into one, well-defined expression. The rum is bottled at 43% abv (80 proof).

The seduction begins even while the rum is in the bottle. Appleton Extra is luminescent with a fabulously dark color, a deep amber with crimson tints, perhaps closest in hue to well-aged cognac. The rum has a huge, assertive bouquet. It's delightfully complex, showcasing the aromas of allspice and citrus.

Appleton Estate Extra has a well-rounded, medium body and a bold, powerful palate comprised of the tightly compacted, semi-sweet flavors of brown sugar, spice and oak. The finish is warm, relaxed and of moderate duration.

This rum is one of the best buys in the entire category. It retails for less than half of other comparable aged spirits. Appleton Estate Extra should definitely be sampled neat and allowed a few minutes to "breathe." The rum also holds up well with an ounce or two of spring water or a few ice cubes.

APPLETON ESTATE
21-YEAR OLD JAMAICA®

Turning 21-years old is a special, once in a lifetime event. It is the age of majority and therefore worthy of celebrating. That's precisely what APPLETON ESTATE 21-YEAR OLD JAMAICA RUM is, a celebration of the coming of age. It is made from a blend of pot distilled rums aged in American white oak barrels a minimum of 21-years. The blend is then placed in an oak vat for an additional year to allow the constituent rums to fully marry. The rum is bottled at 43% abv (80 proof).

Appleton Estate 21-Year Old Jamaica Rum has the same captivating, luminescent deep amber color as the Appleton Estate Extra with the same brilliant red highlights. Tilt the glass and the rum develops a greenish tint around the edges that confirms the long aging in wood. While it possesses a lavish bouquet, the fragrance of the Appleton Estate 21-year old is several degrees less intense than that found in the Extra. The bouquet is a sultry mix of oranges, musk, cocoa and vanilla.

The rum sports a satiny, medium-body that slowly blossoms on the palate, filling the mouth with warm, extremely spicy flavors. The finish is huge, long lasting and marvelously flavorful.

There should be no confusion as to how to best present this elegant and sophisticated spirit. It is similar in character to an old alembic brandy and as such should be savored neat. Let it breathe and get its bearings for a few minutes. This 21-year old gem opens up with time and still presents the palate with an exuberant treat.

APPLETON ESTATE 250TH ANNIVERSARY EDITION®

If turning 21 years old is a big deal, imagine the fuss there'll be for your 250th birthday, presuming you make it that far. Founded in 1749, Appleton Estate celebrated its 250th anniversary in 1999 and commemorated the milestone with the release of a limited edition rum worthy of the event. In fact, for the past 50 years, Appleton Estate blenders have been setting aside reserve rums to blend together for just this purpose.

The APPLETON ESTATE 250TH ANNIVERSARY EDITION is a blend of pot distilled rums, several of which exceed 50 years in age. Presented in an etched crystal decanter, the rum has a deep, walnut brown color with golden reflections. The pronounced greenish tint around the edges of the rum confirms its extensive wood aging. The rum has a tightly compacted bouquet, one that requires several minutes of breathing time to fully open up. Even then the bouquet is light and delicate with the semi-sweet aromas of vanilla and nuts.

This rare edition of Appleton Estate Jamaica rum is full-bodied and sensationally smooth. On the palate there are the sumptuous flavors of brown sugar, vanilla, caramel, fruit and oaky notes. The finish is warm, enduring and remarkably spicy.

The rum has remarkable finesse, much like well-aged cognac. The company produced only 6,000 bottles of the 250th Anniversary Edition. Appleton Estate's chief blender Joy Spence, the first woman to acheive this position in the industry, has every reason to be proud. This rum is a fitting tribute to Jamaica's oldest and most successful estate and distillery.

OTHER JAMAICAN RUMS

The microclimate on the island makes Jamaica an ideal place to cultivate sugar cane and distill rum. Taking advantage of these optimum conditions has led a number of Jamaican distillers to produce their own rums.

In addition to facilitating rum production at the Appleton Estate, J. Wray and Nephew Ltd. also craft several other rums, two of which carry the J. Wray and Nephew name. The first is the award-winning J. WRAY AND NEPHEW WHITE OVERPROOF RUM, the world's best selling high-strength white rum. It is an unaged spirit blended from light and full-bodied rums from the J. Wray and Nephew estates. White Overproof is bottled at 63% abv (126 proof). The rum has crystalline clarity, a sweet and fruity bouquet and a molasses-like palate. The brand won a gold medal at the Wine and Spirits International Competition in London.

The firm also produces C. J. WRAY, a brand promoted as the world's first dry rum and named after the founder of the business. It is made from a blend of aged white rums and bottled at 40% abv (80 proof). The rum is bone dry with a light herbal flavor with woody undertones.

J. Wray and Nephew Ltd. also owns the rum company, Jamaica Ltd., producers of the highly popular CORUBA DELUXE DARK RUM, a traditional small batch, pot distilled rum. Coruba Deluxe is a robust, full-bodied rum with the aromas and flavors of brown sugar, cocoa and caramel. The rum is bottled at 37.2% abv (74.4 proof) and 40% abv (80 proof).

LANG'S FINEST OLD BANANA RUM is a gold, pot distilled rum produced in Jamaica and bottled in the United Kingdom by Lang Brothers Ltd. in Glasgow. The rum is aromatic, full-bodied and full-flavored. It is bottled at 40% abv (80 proof).

Fred L. Myers & Son was founded in 1879 in Kingston. They are best known for the bronze colored, molasses-based MYERS'S PLANTER'S PUNCH RUM, a blend of up to nine different pot distilled rums aged up to four years in white oak. The rum's assertive bouquet features tobacco, pepper, anise, and the semi-sweet palate presents flavors of molasses and chocolate. The rum is bottled at 40% abv (80 proof).

Myers's also produces PLATINUM WHITE, a full-flavored white rum, and MYERS'S LEGEND, a blend of rums aged a minimum of 10-years. Both are bottled at 40% abv (80 proof).

Archival photographs and registered trademarks in this chapter may not be reproduced without the written consent of J. Wray and Nephew, Ltd.

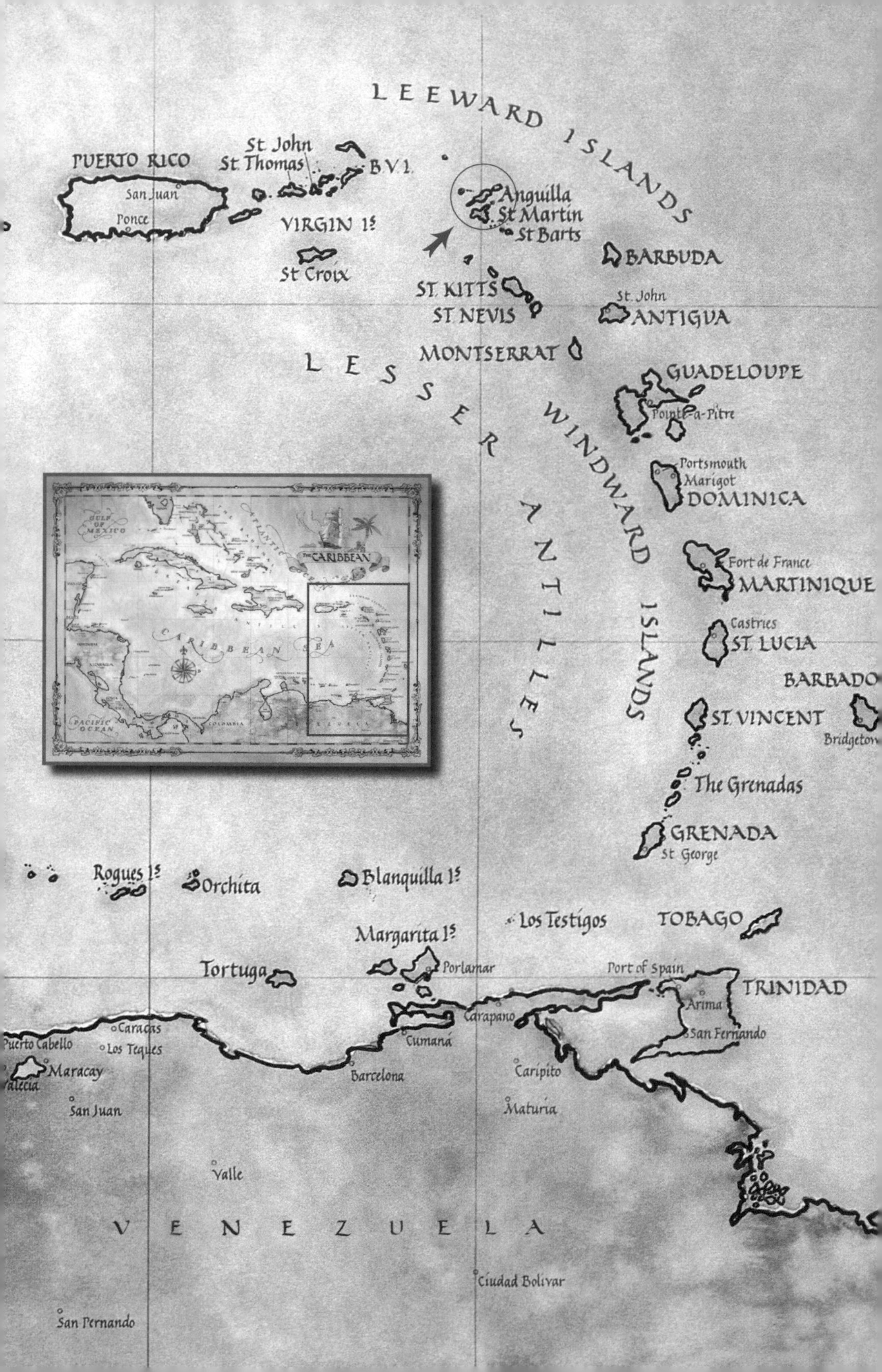

Chapter 6

The Island of Anguilla and Pyrat Rums

L ocated in a remote corner of the Leeward Islands five miles north of St. Maarten, Anguilla is a scant 35 square miles in area and its highest point—Crocus Hill—measures a mere 214 feet. From a historical standpoint, the coral island of Anguilla is one of the small players, an extra in the struggles of the Caribbean. But the island's charm lies in its quality, not quantity. Well, the word's out. The world has "discovered" Anguilla, with one popular guidebook dubbing it the "best kept secret in the Caribbean."

Anguilla (pronounced ang-gwil'uh) closely matches the definition of paradise. The tiny island features coastlines of pristine beaches with gently rolling dunes and a climate that rarely gives one reason for complaint. The island is lightly populated and quite enchanting.

From a geo-political perspective, though, Anguilla barely registered on the screen. The island was first inhabited by a tribe of Ciboney Indians more than a century before the birth of Christ, and around 200 A.D. by the Arawaks. They lived on the island undisturbed until the Caribs invaded around the time of the Crusades. The Caribs named it *Anguilla*, meaning "eel" in Spanish, an apparent reference to the long, narrow contour of the island. Anguilla was among the few Leeward Islands not "discovered" by Columbus.

In 1650, British settlers from nearby St. Kitts were the first Europeans to establish a colony on Anguilla. The Crown maintained continuous sovereignty over the island for more than 300 years, one of only a handful of islands to never be a pawn in an international conflict. While the British were forced to repel invasion attempts by the French in 1745 and 1796 and several raids by the Caribs, they never lost control of the tiny island.

The country's 15 minutes in the spotlight began in 1967 when Anguilla became part of the West Indies Associated States, a federation that included the island nations of St. Kitts and Nevis. Claiming political and economic discrimination, Anguilla seceded from the federation that same year. In February 1969 the people of Anguilla voted to sever all ties with Great Britain and become an autonomous republic.

The British took exception to the move and in March landed troops on the island. It turned out to be a public relations disaster as worldwide opinion ran heavily against the British use of force. Anguillans took to the streets in protest. The British responded by bringing in brigades of policemen to restore the peace. By the end of the month, the two sides signed a truce, ending the bloodless insurrection and making Anguilla a self-governing British dependency. In 1982, Anguilla drafted a new constitution and created a government with elected representatives.

RUM AND THE ISLAND OF ANGUILLA

For centuries Anguilla served as a convenient staging area for rum smugglers. Brigands looking to avoid an expensive and dangerous confrontation with the royal navies of Spain, Britain and France, sought the remote sandy dunes of Anguilla for storage and transfer of smuggled rum. Large pots were sometimes used for blending what became known as "bush rum."

The most famous rum concern associated with the island is the Planter's Rum Company. Founded by a sailor named C. J. Planter at the turn of the 20th century, the company produced blended rum that was said to be among the finest in the West Indies and beyond. The worldwide economic depression and Prohibition in America forced the Anguilla Rums company to cease production in the 1920s. Little documentation exists about the firm or its rums, and it would have slipped from the historical record if it weren't for the efforts of an American named Martin Crowley.

Crowley is an avid rum enthusiast and past owner of a hotel on the nearby island of Antigua. Long an admirer of traditional rums, he decided to recreate the alembic spirits made famous by the

Anguilla Rums company. Crowley had previous experience successfully developing spirit brands. Considered something of a marketing genius, he created the mega-popular line of Patrón 100% Blue Agave Tequilas, now the best selling super-premium tequila in the world.

In the early 1990s, Crowley sought out Caribbean producers who he knew distilled the highest

quality rums in small copper alembic stills. He eventually chose seven different producers and began investing in stocks of aged alembic rums. He built facilities located at Road Bay on the island's northeast shore for the blending and aging of the rums. Crowley named the venture Anguilla Rums, Ltd. in honor of the previous incarnation.

At his plant Crowley set about creating a line of artisan, handcrafted rums. The products were to be comprised solely of aged alembic rums. Crowley christened the line Pyrat Rum, using the Old World spelling of the word, "pirate." After the various rums were blended, Crowley decided to further mature his rums using the Solera aging system, the same system originated by the Spanish to produce sherry.

The Solera aging system is used to assure consistency in the blends. The system involves the use of a series of oak casks arranged in tiers. The barrels on the top tier contain the youngest rums. The middle tier casks contain older rums and the barrels on the bottom tier are filled with the oldest rums.

When deemed appropriate, the master blender, who in this case happens to be Martin Crowley himself, will order that half the contents of each barrel from the lowest tier are emptied for bottling. The emptied barrels are then filled to capacity with rum from the middle tier. Young rums from the barrels on the highest tier are used to fill the casks on the middle tier. In this way the spirits marry in the barrel, the older rum "educating" the younger rum and enhancing their taste and character.

Instead of aging his rum in 55-gallon barrels constructed from one type of oak, Crowley opted to have his casks custom built in France from two different types of oak, Limousin and Gascon. Famous for use in aging brandies and fine wines, each type of oak imbues the spirit with different characteristics. The Limousin oak is

an extremely fast-growing tree, resulting in the widest grain pattern of the species. Its loose pores allow the spirit to extract more flavorants from the wood, which for Limousin means a slightly higher level of vanillin (vanilla). The Gascon oak yields higher levels of tannins.

The rums are put into the wood at high proof. After blending, the rum is diluted to proof using spring water from an underground aquifer. Crowley now maintains aging reserves amounting to approximately 200,000 cases.

The Pyrat Rum labels bear the image of the Zen patron saint Hoti, the protector of little children, fortune tellers and bartenders. These are special rums from a singular corner of the British West Indies.

ANGUILLA'S PYRAT RUMS

PYRAT XO RESERVE RUM— PLANTER'S GOLD®

Introduced in 1998, PYRAT XO RESERVE RUM—PLANTER'S GOLD is made from a blend of nine, well aged alembic rums. These barrel-aged spirits were obtained from seven distillers throughout the Caribbean, then further matured in 55-gallon French oak barrels according to the Solera aging system. The nine rums in the blend have a range in age from 8-40 years. After the extended aging, the rum is reduced in proof using coral-filtered spring water. The rum is bottled at 40% abv (80 proof).

Pyrat XO Reserve Rum—Planter's Gold is a marvelous treat from start to finish. The rum has a lustrous amber color and a soft, medium-weight body. The broad, expansive bouquet is enticing, offering the comforting aromas of vanilla, allspice and molasses. The XO Reserve is exceptionally smooth upon entering the palate, then builds in intensity, quickly filling the mouth with warmth and flavor. The palate features a wide array of savory flavors, including cinnamon, vanilla, caramel and a hint of honey. The finish is long, warm and exceptionally flavorful.

As a finishing touch, Crowley markets the Pyrat XO Reserve Rum—Planter's Gold in a hand-blown, cork-finished decanter reminiscent of the rum bottles from the 1880s. The look is convincing. The bottle is numbered, which will appeal to collectors.

Before you mix this rum with your favorite mixer, take a moment to sample the rum neat. It's guaranteed you won't be disappointed.

PYRAT PISTOL®

Also introduced in 1998, PYRAT PISTOL RUM is made from the same nine, barrel-aged alembic rums used to make XO Reserve, however, the proportion of each rum is different. Pyrat Pistol is purposely blended to be lighter than either the XO Reserve or Cask 23.

The rum has an amber/honey hue and a noticeably lighter body. While subtle in comparison to its counterparts, the bouquet of cinnamon and vanilla is pleasant and beckons good things. The rum expands quickly in the mouth and brings some heat with it. The warm, toasty flavors of this blend surge forth quickly and then linger off.

Pyrat Pistol is an exuberant blend, one that's appropriately named. It is ideally suited for drink making. Its aroma, body and taste shine through when mixed. Crowley celebrates its distinctive character by marketing it in tall, narrow 375ml bottles, the size and shape often used on old sailing ships.

PYRAT CASK 23®

As an aficionado of classically structured, pot-still blends, Martin Crowley set out to create an assertive rum, brimming with high-ester character and taste. In PYRAT CASK 23 RUM he achieved his objective. This is a luxurious, thoroughly engaging rum.

Introduced in 1999, Pyrat Cask 23 is crafted from the same blend of nine, barrel-aged alembic rums as the XO Reserve, although the rums are used in different proportions. The rums are Solera aged and range in age from 8 to 40 years. The blend is diluted to 40% abv (80 proof) with spring water.

Pyrat Cask 23 Rum is an extremely impressive spirit, not dissimilar to a well-aged cognac. The rum has a luminescent, deep amber hue and a lush, smooth body. The bouquet is soft and alluring with the aromas of vanilla, chocolate and oranges. Tilt the glass and the rum will develop a prominent greenish tint around the edges confirming its extended aging in wood.

The Pyrat Cask 23 tracks over the palate without a trace of excess heat or harshness. It slowly builds in intensity revealing layers of spicy flavors. It's a refined and well-orchestrated experience. The body and flavor of the rum swells for a moment or two, then gradually ebbs away. This rum has depth and a splendid finish.

As remarkable a global success as Patrón Tequila has become, Pyrat Cask 23 may be Martin Crowley's crowning achievement. Only three thousand hand-blown, cork-finished bottles (750ml) are produced each year. The price tag is $250 (US). Demand for the rum is high, the production run is usually allocated before it even hits the bottle.

Archival photographs and registered trademarks in this chapter may not be reproduced without the written consent of St. Maarten Spirits Limited.

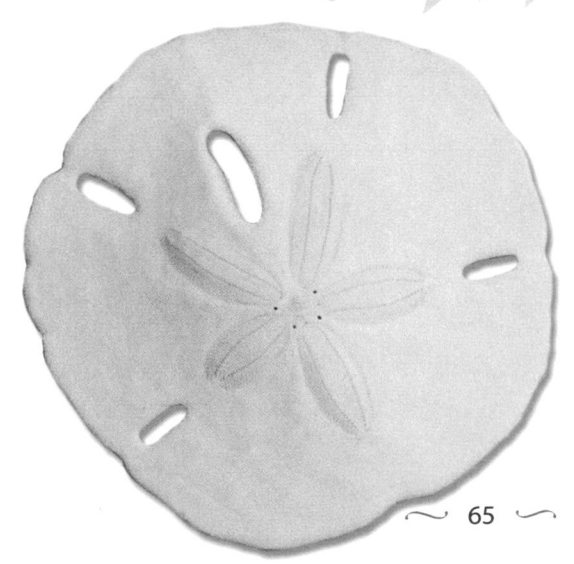

Chapter 7

The Virgin Islands and Cruzan Rum

The Virgin Islands are a group of about 100 small Leeward Islands located east of Puerto Rico between the Atlantic Ocean and the Caribbean Sea. The islands were first inhabited by the Arawaks in 700 A.D. Several centuries later the Caribs invaded the islands and vied for control. The balance of power shifted considerably when in 1493 Christopher Columbus "discovered" the islands. On his second voyage, Columbus sailed a fleet of 17 ships and 1,500 men into Salt River Bay on the north side of St. Croix and claimed the island, and all the islands within the group, in the name of the Spanish crown.

The islands had no gold reserves and were therefore of little interest to the Spanish, who concentrated their efforts on colonizing Puerto Rico, Hispaniola, Mexico and beyond. The island was left undefended, so in the mid-1600s the French invaded St. Croix and forcibly seized control.

Despite the French domain over the island of St. Croix, the expansive group of islands was essentially an open territory. The islands provided sanctuary for pirates and buccaneers. Scores of islands served as makeshift bases and the burying sites of untold riches. Edward Teach, the infamous Captain Blackbeard, took residence on the nearby Dutch island of St. Thomas.

The French brought with them the science of sugar cane cultivation. Vast tracts of land on St. Croix were eventually devoted to the growing of cane. The French governor of the island connived to gain title to nearly the entire island of St. Croix, then in 1664 transferred the holdings to the Knights of Malta for what is presumed to be a tidy sum. When learning of the situation, France sent forces to seize control of the island.

In 1733, the Danish West Indies & Guinea Company negotiated the purchase of St. Croix from the French government. Established on St. Thomas since 1671 and St. John in 1718, the company successfully fostered the development of St. Thomas. The firm's improved techniques for growing and harvesting of sugar cane greatly increased the island's output of molasses. The company began the widespread use of windmills to power sugar production.

On the eastside of the island, the Danish West Indies & Guinea Company founded the defended harbor city of Christiansted in 1735. Sixteen years later the harbor of Fredriksted was built on the westside of St. Croix. Aware of the growing prosperity of the islands, King Frederick V of Denmark purchased the entire holdings of the Danish West Indies & Guinea Company in 1755.

Looking to create a conducive environment for commerce, the Danish government declared the harbors on the three principal Virgin Islands to be "free and open." This allowed the sugar and cotton plantations under their domain to compete favorably with the English colonies without the burden of excise taxes and tariffs. The pro-American sentiment of the islands caused the British to attack and occupy St. Thomas in 1800 and again in 1807 through 1815.

The economies of the Virgin Islands slumped during the 18th century. Sagging sugar prices stymied the industry and caused most plantations to cease operations. The abolition of slavery through the Danish colonies in 1848, changing trade routes and the growth of the sugar beet cultivation in America virtually halted the production of sugar on the islands. Most of the plantations went fallow.

Commerce throughout the islands increased with the beginning of the American Civil War. International trade flourished in the free ports of the Virgin Islands during the war, with much of the goods eventually shipped to the United States, principally to the Confederacy.

In 1917, the United States purchased the islands of St. Croix, St. Thomas and St. John, including roughly 50 smaller islands from Denmark for $25 million in gold. The transaction concluded negotiations between the two countries that had begun fifty years prior.

Thus were born the U.S. Virgin Islands, supervision of which transferred to the U.S. Department of the Interior in 1931. The following year the Virgin Islands Company was formed to revive the slumping sugar and rum industries. The biggest boon to the economy, however, would take place in 1934 with the repeal of the Volstead Act and the end of Prohibition in America.

RUM AND THE VIRGIN ISLANDS

Molasses production in the Virgin Islands dates back to the middle of the 17th century. The majority of it, however, was shipped to New England for distillation. When the Danish government declared the ports of the Virgin Islands to "be free and open," it gave the small, rum producers on the islands an immediate boost. Without the burden of excise taxes and outrageous trade tariffs, it became far more profitable to export rum than molasses.

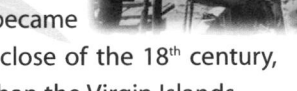

By 1750, St. Croix was home to 241 sugar and cotton plantations. Scores of windmills dotted the landscape and soon the island's ports became international rum trade centers. With the close of the 18th century, only Barbados was exporting more sugar than the Virgin Islands.

In 1760, the distillery on the Estate Diamond Plantation began producing rum. The estate was a sprawling, richly fertile plantation, with a huge sugar cane mill. The Estate Diamond Plantation was located on the west side of the island, and its rum became highly sought after in the island's pubs. The busy ports were crowded with thirsty sailors and ship captains, who soon developed a taste for the Cruzan rum, making it the best-known, best-selling rum on St. Croix.

In the late 1700s the plantation and distillery were purchased by the Nelthropps, a family that had emigrated from England. The Nelthropp family began raising cattle and cultivating cotton on the plantation, as well as maintaining the sugar cane crops and the distillation of rum. The distillery at Estate Diamond flourished under the expertise of the Nelthropp family. By 1856, the distillery's output of Cruzan Rum had greatly increased. The year's sales alone amounted to 10,054 barrels of rum, most of which was exported.

The Cruzan Rum Distillery Company ceased operations in 1920, due largely to the beginning of Prohibition in the United States. The facility remained closed for nearly 14 years, until January 6, 1933, when upon hearing news of the repeal of Prohibition, the Nelthropps re-opened the distillery. In 1995, Todhunter Imports, Ltd. of West Palm Beach, Florida, purchased 100% of the Cruzan Distillery on St. Croix. The Nelthropp family continues to oversee the distillation and aging of Cruzan Rum to this day.

The ruins of the original Estate Diamond Plantation serve as the site for the present day distillery, one of the largest facilities in the Caribbean. There are no longer any sugar cane mills on St. Croix, so the company must import all of its molasses from other Caribbean producers. The advantage is that they can be more discriminating in their quality standards, purchasing only the highest quality molasses available. It takes 100 gallons of molasses to produce one barrel of rum.

The molasses is diluted with spring water and repeatedly boiled prior to the introduction of the distillery's proprietary strain of yeast. After fermentation, the wash is pumped into the first column of Cruzan's five-column still. The multiple distillations remove the fusels, aldehydes, esters, ethyl alcohol and any remaining trace elements from the rum. When the vapor is condensed from the final distillation, the alcohol is 94.5% alcohol by volume and extremely pure.

Cruzan ages all of its rum in oak barrels prior to bottling. There are approximately 25,000 charred oak barrels of rum aging in the distillery's warehouse at any point in time. Barrel aging ranges from

a minimum of two years up to twelve. To enhance the aging process of the older rums, oak chips are added to the barrels, increasing the amount of oak in contact with the rum.

With one notable exception, all of the Cruzan Rums are blended. The master blender, Hardy Nelthropp, expertly integrates various aged rums to create a blend with a consistent flavor profile for each Cruzan Rum. He also leads a panel of tasters on a daily basis to assess 30 different production samples of rum to assure that quality standards are diligently being maintained.

The Virgin Islands are a tremendous tourist destination, and the rum of choice is Cruzan. Its fame has spread and it is now available worldwide. By any standards, Cruzan is the rum of the Virgin Islands; in fact, Cruzan (pronounced with a soft "z") is what the inhabitants of St. Croix call themselves.

THE RUMS OF CRUZAN

CRUZAN ESTATE LIGHT®

In the evolutionary scale, CRUZAN ESTATE LIGHT RUM followed the dark version in development. It can be found on every back bar in the Virgin Islands, and in nearly every tourist's glass. It's a silky smooth rum, undoubtedly one of the best values in the entire category.

Originally labeled as St. Croix Premium Light, Cruzan Estate Light is a blend of triple-distilled rums produced in Cruzan's five-column continuous still. The blend is aged in charred American oak bourbon barrels between two and three years. United States regulations require that age statements on labels reflect the youngest spirit used in the blend, thus the two-years on the label of Cruzan Estate Light Rum.

After aging, the rum has a golden hue. It is then filtered through activated charcoal to remove impurities and much of the color it obtained maturing in the barrel. Some of the color remains, giving the rum a hue reminiscent of a pale white wine.

The Cruzan Estate Light Rum is an unexpected treat; rarely are light spirits so easy to drink neat. The rum is crystal clear, medium-bodied and has a delicate, floral bouquet. It has a dry, light palate, one marked with creamy flavors of vanilla bean and spice. The finish is crisp and of medium duration.

Blindfolded it would be easy to mistake the Cruzan Estate Light for a gold rum. Its body, bouquet and palate reflect its barrel aging. The rum makes an excellent base for nearly any type of cocktail. It is marketed at 40% abv (80 proof).

CRUZAN ESTATE DARK®

Upon further consideration, CRUZAN ESTATE DARK RUM is likely the best value in the category. It has everything one could hope for in a gold rum, all at a suggested retail price of $12 (US).

After many decades of being labeled as St. Croix Premium Dark, the famous rum was recently renamed Cruzan Estate Dark. There was, however, absolutely no reason to change anything else about the product. It is a blend of triple-distilled rums produced in a five-column continuous still. The blend is aged in charred American oak bourbon barrels between two to four years. The rum is then lightly filtered through activated charcoal to remove impurities and particulate, but not so much so that it compromises its inherently rich flavor or alters its naturally golden-yellow color.

After only a minute or two in the glass, the bouquet Cruzan Estate Dark offers up is a sampling of things to come, with warm aromas of vanilla and spice. Gone are the floral notes present in the light rum. Almost immediately upon entry the rum goes to work, filling the mouth with energy and flavor. The vanilla and spice build in intensity, then exactly at the right moment slowly tapers off in a warm, flavorful finish.

By anybody's measure, this is a lot of rum for the money. Cruzan Estate Dark drinks like an older rum. Here again, federal regulations are the reason the label states that it is a 2-year old rum rather than 4-year old. Like the white version, the rum tastes great in any cocktail or circumstance. It is marketed at 40% abv (80 proof).

CRUZAN ESTATE DIAMOND®

Known on the island simply as "Diamond Rum," CRUZAN ESTATE DIAMOND is the distillery's flagship blended rum and the most recognized label of Cruzan Rum. It was once an indulgence only available on the islands, but tourists brought home word of its existence and it is now becoming widely available. For those looking for a savory añejo at an amazingly low price (SRP $17 US), this rum is just the ticket.

Cruzan Estate Diamond is a blend of triple-distilled rums produced in a five-column continuous still. The constituent rums are aged in charred American oak bourbon barrels between five to ten years. After aging, the rums are hand-blended in small batches to assure consistency and maintain the highest quality control. The blend is then lightly filtered through activated charcoal to remove impurities and particulate.

Cruzan Estate Diamond Rum has an alluring orange-amber hue, the result of its extended aging and a medium-weight body. The expansive bouquet immediately fills the glass with the toasty aromas of vanilla, chocolate, spice and oak. The rum enters the mouth softly, without a trace of heat, and bathes the palate with rich, delectable flavor, including the tastes of coffee, cocoa, caramel, and vanilla. The finish is dry, warming and of moderate duration.

This is a rum that should be appreciated neat, or on-the-rocks before playing with it in a cocktail, although it is highly versatile and excellent when mixed. Cruzan Estate Diamond Rum is skillfully crafted and a pleasure to drink. It is marketed at 40% abv (80 proof).

CRUZAN SINGLE BARREL ESTATE®

Introduced in 1997, CRUZAN SINGLE BARREL ESTATE RUM is a limited production, handcrafted rum made from a blend of triple-distilled rums produced in Cruzan's five-column continuous still. The constituent rums are aged between five and twelve years in 55-gallon, charred American oak bourbon barrels.

After blending, the rum is placed in a new American white oak cask for secondary aging, the inside of which has been toasted to their specifications. Secondary aging allows the elements of the blend to "marry" together and further mature. The barrel is then moved to a specially designed, climate-controlled aging warehouse. Each bottle bears the hand-written number of the cask in which the rum was aged. No batch is bottled until a panel of tasters, headed by master blender Hardy Nelthropp, deems the rum ready for release.

"Doubling Casking" spirits is a technique most frequently employed with whiskies. The result of the secondary aging can be perceived in every aspect of the rum's character. It has a lustrous, tawny red color and a medium to full body. The prominent, greenish tint around the edges of the rum confirms its extensive wood aging. The sumptuous bouquet is loaded with the aromas of butterscotch, spice, vanilla, and a hint of smoke. The palate is brimming with flavor and tannin from the oak, all of which taper off to a smooth, medium finish.

Cruzan Single Barrel Estate Rum is impressively similar in character to an aged alembic brandy with rum notes on the palate and finish. In 2000 it was named the "Best Rum in the World" at the San Francisco World Spirits Competition. This is a rum that should be doted over, sipped neat or on-the-rocks. The rum is marketed at 40% abv (80 proof).

CRUZAN JUNKANU CITRUS®

Also introduced in 1997, CRUZAN JUNKANU CITRUS RUM is a dry and tangy citrus-infused rum. Everything about this product screams of fun. With its playfully designed label and brightly colored, gecko logo, Cruzan Junkanu Citrus Rum is a contemporary, lighthearted product, not one intended for a pompous, uptight consumer.

The rum is made from a blend of triple-distilled rums produced in Cruzan's five-column continuous still. The blend is aged in charred American oak bourbon barrels between two and three years. After aging, the rum has a golden hue. It is then filtered through activated charcoal to remove impurities and particulate, and much of the color it obtained maturing in the barrel. Natural orange and lemon flavorings are added to create the finished product.

Cruzan Junkanu Citrus Rum is clear, although there is a hint of coloring similar in hue to the Estate Light. It has a satiny, featherweight body and a prominent bouquet balanced between orange and lemon zest. The flavors open up quickly in the mouth with just enough heat to remind you that this citrus blast is 35% abv (70 proof). The rum finishes long, warm and flavorful.

The orange/lemon taste profile of Cruzan Junkanu Citrus Rum is superb in many different styles of drinks. It works well in rum classic cocktails, and also as a creative substitute for vodka in such popular favorites as the cosmopolitan and kamikaze. Have fun…that's why they make it.

CRUZAN FRUIT-FLAVORED®

There are numerous popular flavored-vodkas on the market. They're popular because they deliver what people inherently are looking for when they order a mixed drink—flavor. The vodka portion of the equation, however, does nothing for the drink except add alcohol.

Cruzan took this popular equation to the next level when in 1996 they introduced CRUZAN PINEAPPLE® RUM, CRUZAN CO-CONUT® RUM and CRUZAN BANANA® RUM, and then a year later, CRUZAN ORANGE® RUM. Marketed at a suggested retail price of $12 (US - 750ml), these rums are made from a blend of triple-distilled rums aged in oak bourbon barrels between two and three years. After aging it is filtered through activated charcoal to remove impurities and the color it obtained maturing in the barrel. Natural flavorings are added to create the finished product.

These rums are delicious. They have light/medium bodies and bouquets that lead with the aroma of their namesake flavor. Because they are relatively low in alcohol at 27.5% abv (55 proof), the dry, silky smooth flavors stay on the palate for a considerably long time.

The taste of the Cruzan premium light rum can easily be perceived, a taste that complements the featured fruit or coconut flavor.

These four rums are ideally suited for drink making. In fact, be prepared to get rid of the flavored schnapps and cordials collecting dust on your back bar. These rums are lighter, drier and far more flavorful. They make much better cocktails than products we relied on in years past. Clearly it's why they were created.

CRUZAN RUM CREAM®

CRUZAN RUM CREAM is actually produced in Ireland, but since Cruzan premium light rum provides the principal flavoring, it is fitting to mention the product here. It is made with Irish cream, caramel, vanilla and Cruzan light rum. The rum is a blend of triple-distilled rums, aged two to three years in oak bourbon barrels and filtered through activated charcoal.

This light, coffee-colored product has a compact, creamy bouquet of vanilla, cream and toffee. It has a medium body that immediately coats the palate with the prominent flavors of caramel, vanilla and dairy fresh cream. The rum shines through in the lingering finish. It is marketed 17% abv (34 proof).

To get the most out of the experience, sample Cruzan Rum Cream neat with a slight chill, or with the addition of ice. It is easy to drink and is devoid of the sweet cloying finish that plague so many of the other cream liqueurs. It is also delectable when added to coffee, or mixed with Tia Maria, amaretto, or a score of other complementary flavors.

OTHER U.S. VIRGIN ISLAND RUMS

While the Cruzan Rum Distillery produces the best-selling and most recognized spirits from the U.S. Virgin Islands, other producers have attained a fair measure of acclaim.

The A. H. Riise Company was founded on the island of St. Thomas in 1837. The firm's founder, Albert Riise, perfected the process of double distilling bay rum, a spirit flavored primarily with bay leaf. In rapid succession Riise and his bay rums won medals at the international competitions between 1884 to 1893. The Riise family continues to operate the firm to this day.

A. H. RIISE CUSTOM RUMS are made from a blend of rums distilled by Cruzan at their facilities in St. Croix. The Riise Company then blends their rums on the island of St. Thomas. A. H. Riise Custom Rums are marketed at two ages: a blend of golden rums aged 3-6 years, and a savory blend aged 6-12 years.

Also on St. Thomas is the firm of Calypso, Limited. The company purchases rums, then blends them with local flavorings. CALYPSO ISLAND PINEAPPLE RUM (24% abv) and SAINT THOMAS COCONUT CHOCOLATE LIQUEUR (27.5% abv) are two popular brands. The company also markets SALT RIVER PLANTATION SPICED RUM made in St. Croix and a key lime liqueur named BUBBA TOUEE (20% abv).

The RON CARIOCA COMPANY on St. Croix produces three versions of 40% abv (80 proof) rum: a dry blanco, a light-bodied gold and a dark añejo.

Now popular in the United States is REDRUM, a shooter category liqueur made from a blend of Virgin Island rum and natural fruit flavorings. It is produced and imported by the Three-D Company of San Francisco.

Archival photographs and registered trademarks in this chapter may not be reproduced without the written consent of Todhunter Imports Limited.

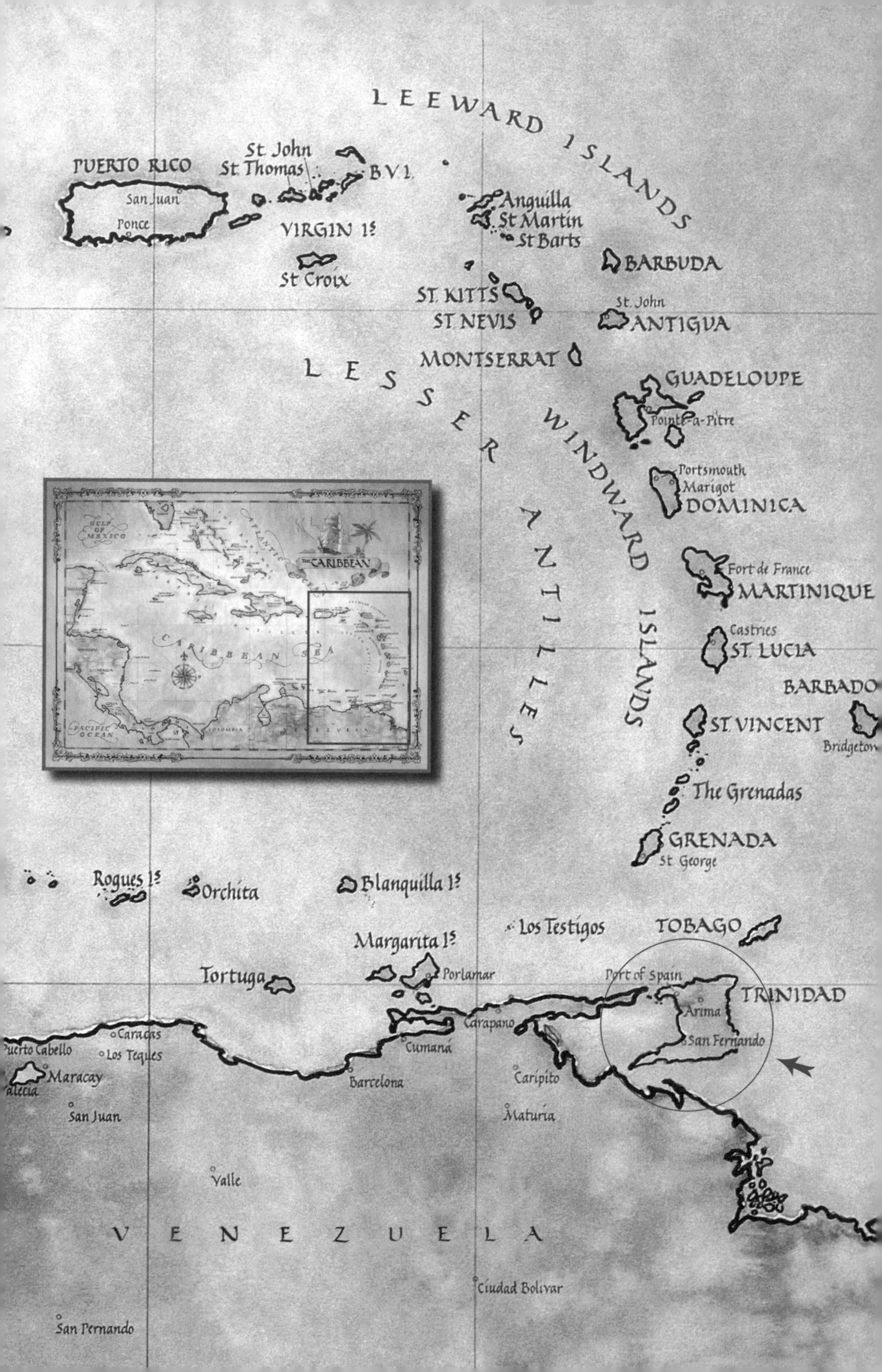

Chapter 8

Trinidad and the Rums of Angostura

Trinidad is the southernmost island in the British West Indies chain, and at 2000 square miles is second only to Jamaica in size. The island lies 8 miles off the coast of Venezuela, and was once geologically a part of South America. Lying 21-miles northeast of Trinidad is the significantly smaller island of Tobago. Over the centuries, possession of the two islands has been contested by the region's superpowers—Spain, Holland, France, and Britain—until the early 1960s when both gained their independence from England and became one island republic.

The original inhabitants of Trinidad and Tobago were tribes of Amerindians. A thousand years before Columbus arrived in 1498, the Arawaks, Caribs and several other tribes lived on Trinidad, with the warlike Caribs inhabiting the more, mountainous north. The Caribs held the island of Tobago. When Columbus caught sight of Tobago, one of the first things he observed was the Caribs tending to their crop of tobacco, which led him to give the island its name. By the mid-1800s, disease and slavery would wipe out the native population.

Columbus claimed the islands in the name of the Spanish Crown, but after learning that the islands held no reserves of gold, Spain showed little interest in colonizing the islands. Successive attempts at establishing settlements on Trinidad failed, until 1592 when Spain founded the town of San Jose just east of the present-day capital of Port of Spain.

Over the next two centuries the Spanish settlers found life on Trinidad a difficult challenge. Raids by the Caribs, repeated failures to establish cacao and tobacco plantations, and a total lack of support by the Spanish government left the settlers barely scratching out an existence.

The Dutch seized control of Tobago in 1658. They cultivated numerous cash crops, including tobacco, cotton, cacao and sugar cane. The Dutch withstood numerous attacks from the Caribs and

Spanish, but finally lost Tobago to the French in 1662. The French quickly learned that possession did not necessarily translate to control.

In response to an increasingly unstable situation on Tobago, France in 1704 declared the island a neutral territory. The proclamation only added fuel to the turmoil as pirates quickly overran the island and established it as a base from which to launch raids throughout the Eastern Caribbean. After more than 50 years of chaotic rule, France was forced to concede possession of Tobago to the British in the Treaty of Paris in 1763.

England quickly established colonial rule over the island. Within 20 years the British brought over 10,000 African slaves to Tobago to work the various plantations. While France made several attempts to retake the island by force, England eventually was able to establish firm control over the island by the beginning of the 1800s.

In 1783, concern over the British intentions led Spain to issue a decree known as the Royal Cedula, which offered generous land grants to Roman Catholics as incentive to settle on Trinidad. As a result, a large influx of mostly French-speaking settlers immigrated to the island. People relocated from neighboring islands and the population on Trinidad began to swell. The new settlers brought slave labor to work the sugar and cotton fields.

The Spanish strategy of developing the island to improve its defenses failed miserably, when in 1797, a British military force landed on Trinidad, overran the Spanish garrisons and quickly seized control of the entire island. Five years later, Britain gained permanent possession of Trinidad when it was ceded by Spain in the Treaty of Amiens.

Large numbers of African slaves were brought in to work the sugar and cotton plantations abandoned by the French. When the British banned the slave trade in its colonies (in 1807) and then abolished slavery altogether (in 1834), the economies of Trinidad and Tobago went spiraling downward. Without slaves, the crops failed and fields went fallow. Eventually many of the owners were forced to sell or abandon their plantations. By the mid-1880s sugar and rum production on the islands were in serious decline.

Between 1840 and the beginning of the 20th century, there was a tremendous wave of immigration to Trinidad and Tobago. Indentured workers came from neighboring islands, Europe, America and Africa to work the fields and try to grab a plot of land for themselves. In

1845, the British government began importing indentured laborers from East India by the thousands. The date of their arrival—May 30th—is now commemorated by a national holiday.

In 1888, the islands of Trinidad and Tobago were politically united as a Crown Colony of Britain. Political organizations began surfacing in the 1930s, amidst the riots, strikes and social unrest of the economic depression. The British government finally granted the people of Trinidad and Tobago suffrage in 1946. The first popularly elected cabinet was formed in 1956, headed by Dr. Eric Williams.

Trinidad and Tobago became an independent republic in 1976. The oil boom in the late 1970s brought prosperity to the islands, especially Trinidad. It continues to have one of the most thriving economies in the Eastern Caribbean.

RUM AND THE ISLAND OF TRINIDAD

Trinidad is the birthplace of Carnival, and the celebration is the largest in the Caribbean, third biggest in the world behind New Orleans and Rio de Janeiro. It takes place several days before Ash Wednesday, which marks the beginning of the Christian holiday Lent. Carnival is held in the streets of beautiful Port of Spain. It is a celebration of life with calypso music, steel drum (pan) bands, dancing in the streets, and rum.

Sugar cane cultivation has been an economic mainstay on Trinidad since the latter part of the 1700s. The massive influx of indentured laborers between the 1840s and 1900 prevented a total collapse of the sugar industry. By 1882, Trinidad ranked just behind Barbados as the largest exporter of sugar in the Caribbean. The island had the second largest acreage devoted to sugar cane cultivation—again just behind Barbados. By 1895, export of sugar from Trinidad exceeded 54,000 tons, by far the most of any Caribbean nation.

It is conjectured that the difficulty navigating under the typically light winds around Trinidad contributed to the slow

development of the rum trade on the island. While molasses-based rums were being distilled at numerous plantations on Trinidad, no major brands were created, or if they were, there is scant evidence of their existence.

The rum industry on Trinidad legitimately began in 1875 with the arrival of the House of Angostura to the island. The story of this famous rum distillery began in Venezuela in 1820. A 24-year old, Prussian army surgeon named Dr. J. G. B. Siegert came to South America to enlist in the cause of independence under General Simón Bolívar. The highly decorated Siegert was made Surgeon General of the military hospital in Guyana.

In 1824, Dr. Siegert formulated a compound using tropical herbs, spices and a base of alcohol as a medicinal tonic to cure the numerous disorders prevalent in the jungles of South America. The aromatic bitters proved a highly effective remedy and its reputation as a curative rapidly spread. Demand grew for what became known as Dr. Siegert's Aromatic Bitters.

Siegert eventually left the military and turned his complete attention to the production of his bitters. He changed the name of the secret blend to Angostura Aromatic Bitters, this after the small town of Angostura on the Orinoco River where Bolívar had been headquartered. The business—The House of Angostura—was soon a thriving success. The bitters had become an established international export. When Dr. Siegert died in 1870, he was succeeded in business by his sons.

In 1875, the political climate in Venezuela was rapidly deteriorating. Riots and civil unrest caused the Siegert family to move their business to neighboring Trinidad. With the island being a major producer of sugar cane, Angostura began purchasing locally distilled rums for aging, blending and bottling under the Angostura label. While the formula of the bitters is a closely guarded secret, it is widely conjectured that rum is the alcohol base used in the production of the bitters.

In 1936, Robert W. Siegert, great-grandson of the company's founder, initiated the construction of a modern distillery for the production of molasses-based, column-distilled rum. Equally important, Siegert built a research laboratory at the distillery to

scientifically ensure the utmost quality control standards were maintained. All of the raw materials used in the production of the rum were tested for purity. In addition, the entire distillation process was closely monitored and the distillate was tested for quality throughout the process.

The Angostura distillery—named Trinidad Distillers Limited—now is one of the most advanced and technologically sophisticated facilities in the region. The company operates an extremely large, five-column still at its Port of Spain complex. After the molasses has been inspected for quality and sugar content (brix), it is transferred to the fermentation vat, where it is mixed with purified, demineralized water and Angostura's proprietary strain of yeast. Fermentation lasts for 24-hours.

After distillation, only spirits obtained from the first and last columns are used and sent on to be barrel aged. The master distiller has the ability to create light and heavy spirits, which is ideal for blending purposes. A significant percentage of the rum Angostura produces is shipped in bulk to other producers around the Caribbean.

In 1973, Angostura purchased the assets and brands of Trinidad's second most popular rum producer, Fernandes Distillers Ltd. The Fernandes line of blended rums continues to be produced by Angostura. Recently the House of Angostura was awarded the prestigious and difficult to obtain ISO 9002 and 14001 certification for its strict adherence to quality control and environmental standards throughout its production facilities.

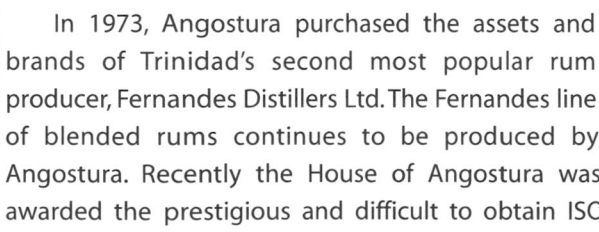

THE RUMS OF ANGOSTURA

ANGOSTURA OLD OAK WHITE®

The ANGOSTURA OLD OAK WHITE RUM, along with the gold version, are the best selling rums on Trinidad and Tobago. The brand is stocked at every restaurant, resort and roadside bar on the islands, and with good reason. Its simple label design and small price tag belies that it is a quality, exceptionally easy to drink spirit.

The Old Oak White is made from a blend of light and heavy rums distilled in Angostura's five-column continuous still. The blend is aged in charred American oak bourbon barrels between 3 and 5 years. After aging, the rum is twice filtered through activated charcoal to remove impurities and the golden color it obtained during barrel aging.

The rum is clear, light-bodied and bred with an impressively big bouquet. The nose is loaded with the crisp, fresh aromas of herbs, maple and a hint of vanilla. The rum has an exceptionally dry palate with a delicate array of spicy flavors. It builds gradually in intensity, bearing no harshness or excessive heat, then tapers off in a relaxed finish of medium duration. Depending on the market, the rum is marketed at 40% abv (80 proof).

The Angostura Old Oak White is among the best values in its class. Understandably the natural tendency is to use it exclusively in drink-making, a role at which it is more than capable of excelling. But before you rush off and add it to your next daiquiri, sneak a sip first. You may be surprised at how pleasantly smooth a white rum can be.

ANGOSTURA OLD OAK GOLD®

The ANGOSTURA OLD OAK GOLD RUM is a familiar sight in watering holes around Trinidad and Tobago. On an island where the people take pride in their rum, Old Oak Gold and White outsell all other brands of rum.

The Angostura Old Oak Gold is made from a blend of light and heavy rums distilled in the company's five-column continuous still. The blend is aged between 3 and 5 years in charred American oak bourbon barrels. After aging, the rum is filtered through activated charcoal to remove impurities, but not so much so that it compromises its inherently rich flavor or alters the wood-induced, pale amber color.

The rum is light-bodied and has a compact bouquet laced with the aromas of toffee, vanilla and a hint of smoke. Like the Old Oak White, the gold version has an extremely dry palate. It enters the mouth softly, then builds in intensity revealing flavors of caramel, nutmeg and toasted oak. The rum has a warm, medium finish. The rum is marketed at 40% and 43% abv (80 and 86 proof).

Angostura Old Oak Gold is an energetic, flavorful rum that is ideally suited for use behind the bar. It is an excellent candidate for use in a wide array of cocktails, contributing color, taste and aroma to the drink.

ANGOSTURA ROYAL OAK EXTRA OLD TRINIDAD®

Trinidad has the perfect climate for sitting on a veranda after dinner and sipping an añejo rum. It's almost as if the master blender at Angostura created the ROYAL OAK EXTRA OLD RUM premium blends especially for an occasion such as this.

Angostura Royal Oak Extra Old is made from a blend of light and heavy rums distilled in the Angostura five-column continuous still. All of the añejo rums used in the blend are aged up to 8 years in charred American oak bourbon barrels in Angostura's warehouses. After aging, the rum is twice filtered through activated charcoal to remove impurities and particulate.

Royal Oak Extra Old has a golden amber hue and a satiny, light/medium body. The bouquet fully comes into its own after a minute or two in the glass, releasing the aromas of chocolate, caramel, mint, and a hint of smoke. The rum prickles the palate with energy and quickly engulfs the mouth with warmth and spicy flavors. The sensations continue to build, move slowly toward the back of the throat and then almost reluctantly taper off.

Do not mix this rum in the libation of your choice until you sample it neat first. It is a well-bred añejo rum that still retains some vestiges of youthful vim and vigor. Each bottle is stamped with the master blender's registration number. Depending on the country in which it is being marketed, the rum is bottled at 40% or 43% abv (80 and 86 proof).

ANGOSTURA 1824 LIMITED RESERVE®

Introduced in 1999 to commemorate the company's 175th anniversary, ANGOSTURA 1824 LIMITED RESERVE RUM is a luxurious, super-premium spirit. This classy, top-shelf añejo is a rare pleasure from start to finish.

Angostura 1824 Limited Reserve is blended from select casks of mature, continuous distilled rums. The rums used in the blend are aged for a minimum of 12 years in charred American oak bourbon barrels in Angostura's warehouses. The rums are skillfully hand-blended in small batches and then recasked. The master blender regularly monitors the progress of the aging barrels. When the rum has reached its optimum maturity, it is then hand-drawn, filtered and hand-bottled.

Angostura 1824 Limited Reserve Rum has an amber/bronze color, a seamlessly smooth texture, and a well-rounded, medium to full body. The bouquet is seductive and it quickly fills the glass with the aromas of sweet molasses, vanilla, honey, spice and brandy-like notes. As delightful as the bouquet is, the rum's palate is even better, presenting the mouth-watering flavors of honey, fruit, chocolate, spices and herbs. The rum has a remarkably long and flavor-packed finish.

This outstanding rum deserves its day in a snifter. It is a straightforward proposition of pour and enjoy; no ice or water please. Each bottle is individually numbered, finished with a cork closure, and dipped in red wax with the imprint of the master distiller's seal. It is marketed at 40% abv (80 proof).

FERNANDES "19"®

The Fernandes Distillery was founded in 1919 at the Forres Park sugar plantation and distillery in Trinidad. The Fernandes brand grew in popularity on the island, eventually becoming one of the best selling, most recognized labels on Trinidad. In 1973, Trinidad Distillers Limited purchased the company's assets and trademarked names. The Fernandes brand continues to prosper and the rums are produced in the same still used to make the Angostura rums.

FERNANDES "19" RUM is made from a blend of light and heavy rums distilled in the Angostura five-column continuous still. The blend is aged between 3 and 5 years in charred American oak bourbon barrels. There are two versions of Fernandes "19" Rum. After aging, the Fernandes "19" White Rum is twice filtered through activated charcoal to remove impurities and the golden color it obtained during barrel aging. The Fernandes "19" Gold Rum is filtered to remove impurities, but does not alter its wood-induced, pale amber color.

It's easy to see why the Fernandes "19" rums are a popular success. Both versions are light-bodied and have subtle, yet pleasant bouquets. Give these spirited rums a few moments to open up and you won't regret it. They have crisp, dry palates packed with energy

and delicate, tightly knit flavors. Both of the Fernandes "19" rums finish long and feisty. They are marketed at 40% and 43% abv (80 and 86 proof).

FERNANDES FORRES PARK PUNCHEON®

Fernandes Forres Park Puncheon ranks among the region's most famous overproof rums. It is clear and amazingly drinkable for something comprised of 75% alcohol by volume (150 proof). The name refers to the site of the company's original distillery, and a puncheon is a large cask with a capacity of 378 liters (formerly 262 liters) used in the West Indies for aging rum.

Overproof rums by their very nature are created for use in mixed drinks. Before you commit Forres Park Puncheon to your next Zombie or Mai Tai, consider pouring a dram or two in a glass, letting it aerate for 5-10 minutes, and allowing your taste buds to take it out for a spin. The rum is light-bodied, with a fetching bouquet and a mouthful of sizzling, fruit flavors.

Fernandes Forres Park Puncheon has a great deal of finesse for such a strong, athletic spirit. It certainly warrants a spot on every rum enthusiast's shelf.

ANGOSTURA CARIBBEAN RUM CREAM®

The Angostura Caribbean Rum Cream Liqueur is a savory blend of fresh cream, proprietary flavorings, and aged, continuous distilled rum. There is no substitute for using fresh cream in a liqueur of this type. Shipping and preserving the dairy-based product proved unfeasible, so the finished product is formulated and bottled in Maine.

Angostura Caribbean Rum Cream is extremely well balanced with a medium body and smooth texture. The bouquet is a delicate offering of dairy fresh cream, chocolate and a hint of rum. The flavor of the chocolate is prominent, with rum playing a supporting role.

The liqueur has a rich, dessert-like appeal. Try it on the rocks or served chilled. It is a highly mixable product, marrying well with brandy, and other liqueurs such as Tia Maria (coffee), Chambord (raspberry), Frangelico (hazelnut) or Di Saronno Amaretto (nutty almond). It presents a creative option to using the cream liqueurs on the market.

OTHER TRINIDADIAN RUMS

Caroni is the other established label of Trinidadian rum after Angostura and Fernandes. The Caroni Sugar Factory was founded in 1918, making rum as a natural offshoot of processing sugar. The company originally distilled their molasses-based wash in a cast iron alembic still. During World War II the company installed a wooden, two-column still, allowing the company to improve the character of their lighter styles of rum. Wood was used for the making of the still presumably because of material shortages due to the war.

In 1980 the company upgraded its operations including the construction of a stainless steel, four-column continuous still. The four-column still allowed Caroni to further refine their existing brands and introduce several new brands. A large percentage of the rum Caroni produces is shipped in bulk to foreign markets. The remainder is casked and aged in the Caroni warehouse.

Caroni produces six labels of rum, and although not widely distributed, they have found a niche in the local market. Two labels have achieved distinction in their own right. CARONI STALLION PUNCHEON RUM is appropriately named. This muscular beast is bottled at 78% abv (156 proof), making it the strongest rum on the island and among the most potent spirits in the region. CARONI FÉLICITÉ GOLD RUM is possibly the oldest label of rum on Trinidad. It was originally introduced in 1820 as a blend of rums distilled on the Félicité Estate.

Produced in both a white and gold version, CARONI AUTHENTIC RUM is a premium blend made exclusively for export (43% abv). Caroni also markets a charcoal-filtered, three-year old white rum named WHITE MAGIC LIGHT RUM (40% and 43% abv), and SPECIAL OLD CASK RUM, a reddish colored blend of rums aged up to ten years (40% and 43% abv).

Chapter 9

The Nation of Haiti and Rhum Barbancourt

The republic of Haiti occupies the western third of the island of Hispaniola. Its neighbor to the east is the Dominican Republic, and to the west, 50 miles across the Windward Passage is the nation of Cuba. Haiti is largely mountainous with isolated fertile valleys and plateaus. The country's major cities are located principally on the coasts, the two largest being the capital, Port-au-Prince in the south and Cap Haitien in the north.

This former French colony was first inhabited by the Ciboneys who migrated from North America around 400 A.D. They were followed some 500 years later by the Tainos, a peaceful, agrarian people related to the Arawaks, who emigrated from the Amazon valley. They named the island Ayiti, which meant "land of mountains." The beginning of the end of a millennium of peace came when Caribs from neighboring islands began a series of murderous raids on the Tainos.

During his second voyage of discovery, Columbus landed on the northern coast of the island in December 1492. Claiming Haiti for Spain, Columbus was enthralled with the island and the native inhabitants. The Tainos warmly greeted Columbus, thinking that the Europeans were sent from heaven to protect them from the Caribs. When Columbus' flagship—the Santa Maria—ran aground near the coast of Haiti, the Tainos helped in the rescue and subsequent salvage of the ship. Timber from the ship was used to build the first Spanish settlement in the New World, La Navidad.

Before leaving the island for Cuba, Columbus traded with the Tainos for their gold, which they had fashioned into bracelets and other ornaments. Columbus eventually presented these to the King and Queen of Spain. Fueled by desire to capture the island's gold, Columbus was sent back to the island with a significantly larger force of 12 ships and over 1200 men.

Upon his return to Haiti, Columbus found that the Caribs had overrun the settlement of La Navidad, killed all of the European and Taino inhabitants and completely razed its structures. He abandoned the site and moved his fleet west along the north shore, landing at what is today the Dominican Republic. Columbus established another settlement and departed leaving his brother Bartolomé behind to lead the large contingent of Spanish soldiers.

A regime of terror soon followed. In short order, the Spanish enslaved or killed the native population. They looted their villages, taking gold and supplies then razing the encampments. Between 1492 and 1508, the estimated Taino population dropped from 400,000 to roughly 60,000. By 1525, the entire native population on the island was all but eliminated. With the gold reserves exhausted and the native population either dead or already in slavery, the Spanish moved on, leaving the island of Hispaniola largely unpopulated.

In 1644, French and British buccaneers established a base near Port-de-Paix on the northern coast of Haiti. From there, the pirates launched attacks against the Spanish treasure fleets. The attacks proved enormously costly to the Spanish, so much so that Spain ceded the western third of Hispaniola to France in the Treaty of Ryswick in 1697. The territory was renamed Saint-Domingue.

By the 18th century, France had developed Haiti into the most economically prosperous Caribbean colony. The sugar, cotton, cacao and coffee industries on Haiti flourished, with exports exceeding those from the American colonies. The island had become the largest sugar producer in the West Indies, and by 1790, there were over 3000 working coffee plantations.

The island's plantation economy relied exclusively on African slaves for labor. In 1789, the French Revolution and the subsequent Déclaration des droits de l'homme (Human Rights Declaration) had a tremendous impact on Haiti. Slavery came under attack in France, but the French colonists on Haiti refused to grant freedom to the slaves. Tensions mounted and isolated slave uprisings occurred.

Then in 1791, a slave revolt in the north led by former slave Toussaint L'Ouverture sparked widespread violence and destruction. Thousands of white inhabitants were killed and plantations were set aflame. L'Ouverture had formed an army that at times reached 500,000 African slaves. On August 29, 1793, the French Commissioner on Haiti abolished slavery.

The following 11 years on Haiti were filled with bloodshed, strife and hardship. Both the British and Spanish invaded the island, and each was forced to withdraw after fierce and prolonged fighting. The French eventually lost control of the island, leaving L'Ouverture in political control. In 1801, L'Ouverture conquered the eastern portion of Hispaniola, abolished slavery and declared himself governor of the entire island.

Looking to reestablish France's control over Haiti, Napoleon Bonaparte sent 20,000 troops to the island in 1802. During the ensuing conflict, the French captured L'Ouverture and sent him to France where he died in prison. The French overcame the Haitian resistance. But when news reached Haiti that the French were reestablishing slavery on Guadeloupe, a massive insurrection against the French was launched, led by one of L'Ouverture's generals, Jean-Jacques Dessalines. The French troops, decimated by yellow fever, were defeated by Dessalines' armies at the Battle of Vertieres.

Less than two months later, on January 1, 1804, Dessalines proclaimed independence for his country. After 15 years of devastation, the country finally belonged to the black majority. Dessalines replaced the French name Saint-Domingue with the aboriginal name, Haiti. Dessalines became the first leader of a republic born of African descent.

After independence, all of the whites on the island either fled or were killed. The assassination of Dessalines in 1806 marked the beginning of a long series of revolutions and internal power struggles that left the country bankrupt, the economy in shambles and the black population impoverished. Hatred developed between black African Haitians and lighter skinned Haitian mulattoes, who were descendants of white masters and African slaves, further dividing the country.

Between 1843 and 1915, Haiti had 22 heads of state, only one of whom served out his full term of office. Three died in office, one was blown up with his palace, and another was hacked to death by a mob. The other 14 were overthrown by armed insurrections after tenures of 3 months to 12 years. Racial prejudice and factional bitterness between the North and South exacerbated the political turmoil.

In the early 20th century, Haiti borrowed heavily from France and Germany. Continued failure to repay loans brought about the imminent possibility of European occupation of Haiti. In order to restore order and mainly prevent German intervention, President Wilson sent in the U.S. Marines, who remained in Haiti from 1915 to 1934. The presence of the Marines brought stability to the country, and American foreign aid contributed greatly to the rebuilding of Haiti's crumbling infrastructure.

Beginning in December 1956, Haiti was again rocked by a rapid series of governmental collapses, a total of five different governments in less than a year. The free-fall ended when François Duvalier—also known as Papa Doc—seized control over the government. Duvalier declared himself President for Life and maintained control through terror and enforced his will through a Gestapo-like secret police. Thousands of people were murdered, even more fled the country.

Upon Duvalier's death in 1971, his 19-year old son, Jean-Claude assumed control, also assuming the title of President for life. Known as Baby Doc, he relied on the same tactics imposed by his father and committed countless atrocities. In 1986, his reign ended when he was deposed by a military coup and escaped the country to live in exile in a villa on the French Riviera.

Baby Doc's departure only led to further political chaos. There were repeated military coups until pressure from the United States and the world community forced Haiti to hold popular elections in 1990. Father Jean-Betrand Aristide won the election, but a military coup nine months later forced Aristide to flee to the United States.

In September 1991, a military tribunal headed by General Raul Cédras took control of the country through the use of a brutal paramilitary police. Cédras' particular reign of terror lasted until an imminent military invasion by the United States forced him to leave the country.

The world's oldest black republic remains a country in transition. Haiti is the poorest nation in the Western Hemisphere. A large majority of the population lives in unequivocal poverty, the annual per capita income an astonishing $250 (US). While it is unfortunately true that the list of Haiti's social, economic and political problems is long, it is equally true that this amazingly beautiful island is home to a people with a magnificently rich and diverse culture.

RHUM AND THE NATION OF HAITI

Sugarcane was first introduced in the Caribbean in 1493 when Columbus brought the grass from the Canary Islands to the part of Hispaniola that would become Haiti. It was during the French Colonial period in the 1700s that the cultivation of sugar cane flourished on the island. While grown around the island, the most fertile cane-producing region is in northern Haiti.

Despite the country's overthrow of its colonial masters, Haiti has retained its French heritage and employed traditional methods when it comes to rhum-making. While several, extremely small distilleries produce rhum strictly for domestic consumption, there is legitimately only one established brand of Haitian agricole rhum, Rhum Barbancourt. Fortunately for us, it is genuinely world class.

Rhum Barbancourt was founded in 1862 by Frenchman Dupré Barbancourt. His ambition was to apply the techniques that he had learned working in the cognac industry to the rhum-making process. The distillery is located in the small, rural town of Damiens, about 10 miles inland of Port-au-Prince.

The company cultivates and harvests roughly 40% of the sugar it needs for production at its fields in Plaine-du-Cul-de-Sac. The remainder of the sugar cane is purchased from growers in the area. Harvesting occurs between December and May and is done by hand. The stalks are then transported to the mill about 25 kilometers from the fields.

Once at the mill, the stalks are cut into smaller pieces and immediately fed into the crushers. The fresh cane juice—called vesou—is transferred to large stainless steel vats. Purified water and a strain of wild, naturally occurring yeast are added to the fresh cane juice to precipitate fermentation, a process that lasts three days.

After fermentation, the wash is double distilled, first in a single-column continuous still and then in a traditional alembic still. The final distillate leaves the still at 90% abv. It is diluted with purified rain water to 50% abv before being put into large, imported Limousin oak vats for aging.

The three versions of Rhum Barbancourt are highly sought after. Production volumes are low—around 40,000 gallons annually—and demand for these award-winning rhums annually exceeds supply, with the majority of the rhum exported to Europe and North America.

THE RHUMS OF BARBANCOURT

RHUM BARBANCOURT THREE STAR®

The problem with being the youngest in a family is that you're often overshadowed by your older siblings. Such is the case with RHUM BARBANCOURT THREE STAR. With all of the attention heaped onto the distillery's two older rhums, the Three Star is typically relegated to also-ran status. That unfortunate trend stops here.

Rhum Barbancourt Three Star is a delicious, easy to drink spirit. As an agricole rhum, it is distilled from fresh cane juice.

Wild yeast is used to precipitate the three-day fermentation, after which, the fermented wash is double distilled, first in a single-column still and then in a copper alembic still. The final distillate is diluted with purified rain water to 50% abv prior to being aged a minimum of 4 years in large, Limousin oak vats from France. It is available in the United States at 40% abv (80 proof), however, it is also produced at 43% abv.

The Rhum Barbancourt Three Star has a lustrous, amber hue, light/medium body and a dry, compact bouquet featuring the aromas of vanilla, baked apples and oak. The rhum has a soft entry onto the palate, but quickly makes its presence known. At peak intensity, the Three-Star Barbancourt confidently warms the mouth with an array of flavor. The tastes of vanilla extract, pepper, cacao and honey are most prominent. Its finish is long, warm and wonderfully relaxing.

This version of Rhum Barbancourt merits accolades. Perhaps if the Three-Star changed its name and skipped town it would get the attention it deserves.

RHUM BARBANCOURT FIVE STAR RÉSERVE SPÉCIALE®

The RHUM BARBANCOURT FIVE STAR RÉSERVE SPÉCIALE is the most widely distributed of the Barbancourt rhums, which still puts it in the hard to find category. This rhum shoulders half the responsibility for elevating Barbancourt to world class ranking.

Barbancourt's Five Star Réserve Spéciale is an agricole rhum fermented for three days using a strain of wild, naturally occurring yeast to precipitate fermentation. The rhum is double distilled, first in a single-column still and then in a copper alembic still. The final distillate is diluted to 50% abv prior to being aged a minimum of 8 years in large, Limousin oak vats. Depending on the export market, it is bottled at either 40% abv or 43% abv.

The Five Star Réserve Spéciale is an elegant rhum. It has an amber/gold hue with orange highlights, medium body and a seamlessly smooth texture. The rhum's pronounced bouquet offers up a bevy of warm, toasty aromas. It's on the palate that this exceptional spirit shines. The rhum is brimming with the flavors of chocolate, honey, toffee, and almonds. The flavors persist on the palate for an extended amount of time, eventually tapering off into a brandy-like finish.

This rhum was bred for quiet occasions. It comes ready to serve; no ice, water or mixer required.

RHUM BARBANCOURT RÉSERVE DU DOMAINE®

This luxurious rhum was once the private reserve of the Barbancourt distillery, consumed during special functions held at the estate. Fortunately for the world community, someone hit on the magnificent idea of marketing the rhum, and the result is an unbroken string of international awards.

Like the other two releases, RHUM BARBANCOURT RÉSERVE DU DOMAINE is distilled from fresh cane juice and fermented for 3 days. The rhum is double distilled, first in a single-column still and then in a copper alembic still. The final distillate is diluted with purified rain water to 50% abv prior to being aged a minimum of 15 years in large, French oak vats. The greenish tint around the edges of the rum confirms its extensive wood aging. Depending on the export market, it is bottled at either 40% abv or 43% abv.

The extended aging has a profound affect on the rhum. The Réserve du Domaine is slightly darker in color than the 8-year old, pushing it into the single malt whisky range. The rhum has a medium body, a flawless texture and a complex, cognac-like bouquet with oaky, spicy aromas. The palate is a savory offering of brown sugar, nutmeg and honey. The flavors linger before slowly melting away in a graceful finish.

The Rhum Barbancourt Réserve du Domaine is most comparable to a well-aged cognac. It has tremendous complexity and a character full of charm and sophistication. Haiti may be a poor country, but you'd never know it by tasting this rhum.

Archival photographs and registered trademarks in this chapter may not be reproduced without the written consent of Rhum Barbancourt Distillery.

Chapter 10

Martinique and the Rhums of Saint James

Martinique is one of the Windward Islands in the Lesser Antilles. It lies almost equidistant between Dominica 30 miles to the north and St. Lucia 22 miles to the south. By any definition, Martinique is a tropical paradise. Much of the island is dominated by volcanic mountain ranges with dense rain forests that cover the deep gorges and valleys. About a third of the country are elevated plateaus and fertile plains.

On the southern coast there are magnificent stretches of white-sand beaches, while the northern coastline features steep cliffs and miles of black sandy coves. In the south-west, a lateral mountain spur forms a peninsula that forms and protects the Bay of Port-de-France. The island is laced with fresh water rivers, and lush tropical flora and fauna.

Columbus first spotted Martinique in 1493, but didn't come ashore until June 1502. At the time, the island was inhabited by the Caribs, who centuries before had killed or driven off the last remaining Arawaks. While Columbus claimed Martinique for Spain, the Spanish never colonized the island. In fact, the fierce Caribs kept Europeans off Martinique until the French had established the first settlement in 1635 under the leadership of Pierre Belain d'Esnambuc.

The French looked to develop an economy revolving around sugar and tobacco. To facilitate the strategy, King Louis XIII penned a decree in 1636 authorizing slavery throughout the French colonies in the West Indies, thus providing the plantation owners with the labor they badly needed. The settlers began clearing large tracts of rain forest for the crops. This practice encroached on the Caribs' territory, and they retaliated by raiding the plantations.

Tensions mounted and soon the French responded in force. The conflict lasted several years until 1660 when a treaty was signed and the Caribs agreed to remain on the Atlantic side of the island. The conditions of the treaty were not upheld and within several years the Caribs were eradicated.

The wars with the Caribs and Martinique's rugged terrain made the development of the plantation economy slow and challenging. The growth of Fort-de-France as a major port grew steadily. Built on the leeward side of the island, the port of Fort-de-France became the first stop for French ships following the trade winds from Europe. In 1669, the city became the seat of government for the colony and Louis XIV soon made Martinique the capital of France's Caribbean possessions.

The tobacco industry on the island faltered during the 1660s when tobacco grown in the American colony of Virginia became dominant on the world trade market. Sugar plantations, however, continued to thrive. The French government, looking to safeguard the revenue stream from Martinique sugar, treated it as a domestic product, protected it from foreign competition and actively promoted its economic development.

The colonial wars between Britain and France heated up during the 17th and 18th centuries. The English captured and occupied Martinique several times, the first being briefly in 1763, only to cede the island in the Treaty of Paris in exchange for Canada, Senegal, the Grenadines, St. Vincent and Tobago. The French greatly valued Martinique and nearby Guadeloupe for their lucrative sugar cane trade.

The French Revolution in 1789 had a tumultuous impact on Martinique. Impassioned by the civil war over human rights, the African slaves began to openly fight for their emancipation. The abolition movement gained popular support among the island's white artisans, soldiers, small merchants and free people of color. In 1792, a governor loyal to the monarchy wrested temporary control, only to lose control of the island when a rebel force from France overthrew the seated government.

Terrified at the social and economic disorder, and looking to preserve slavery and the status quo, Martinique's plantation owners and ruling class requested that Britain intervene militarily, which they did in January, 1793. The island's economy prospered under the occupation. Instead of selling their sugar in France, the plantation owners marketed their commodity in England. Equally important, the British intervention spared the island from the violence and destruction wrought by the French Revolution. Britain returned Martinique to France in 1815 at the conclusion of the Napoleonic Wars.

France was once again a stable world power and they wasted little time reestablishing a French administration on Martinique. When slavery was abolished throughout the French Republic in 1848, scores of thousands of immigrant workers and indentured servants from India and Indo-China came to Martinique to work in the sugar cane fields. It was roughly this same period of time that sugar prices began to plunge. Introduction of the sugar beet in Europe and a supply glut precipitated the decline.

Through the rest of the 19th century and into the 20th, the French government took steps to protect the sugar industry on Martinique. They levied imposing tariffs on foreign sugar and afforded Caribbean sugar the same status and protection as domestic sugar and French sugar beets. To this day Caribbean sugar is regulated and taxed as a European product by the European Union.

Life on Martinique changed inexorably when on March 8, 1902, the Mont Pelée volcano erupted violently. In less than 3 minutes the then capital of Saint-Pierre was destroyed, killing the city's entire population of 30,000 people. The blast leveled the city of Carbet located 2 miles from the volcano. All told, it was the single most devastating natural disaster in Caribbean history.

The inhabitants of Martinique and Guadeloupe voted for political union with France. The following year, the islands became overseas *Départments*, or administrative districts of France, with all the same rights and political privileges as any metropolitan district. In 1974, Martinique became a region of France, affording it more autonomy and economic advantages and opportunities.

RHUM AND THE ISLAND OF MARTINIQUE

Since the 17th century, the economy of Martinique has revolved around agriculture, with the cultivation of sugar cane eventually becoming the economic cornerstone. The island's rich, volcanic soil and tropical climate create ideal conditions for growing cane.

Rhum production on Martinique dates back to the early 1600s when Dutch and Flemish settlers from South America began relocating throughout the Eastern Caribbean. They brought with them sugar cane cuttings from Brazil, as well as the knowledge of distillation. The Caribs, however, made life on the island for the settlers nearly impossible. They burned the crops, destroyed the settlements and within a few years forced the Europeans off the island.

The arrival of French settlers and the establishment of permanent settlements in 1635 marked the beginning of the sugar industry on Martinique. The French developed vast sugar plantations and Fort-de-France soon became a major port for the exportation of sugar. The French also had a passion for distillation, having long excelled at distilling grape brandy.

The rhums distilled in the French West Indies began strongly competing with France's domestically produced brandies, most notably cognac. This soon prompted King Louis XIV to sign a decree in 1763 prohibiting the importation and sale of rhum in France. Undaunted, the distillers on Martinique began concentrating on the burgeoning markets of the American colonies.

Contrary to the standard practices on English-speaking islands, rhum in the French West Indies is not distilled from molasses, but from fresh sugar cane juice. These spirits are referred to as rhum agricole. After distillation, the majority of the distillate is aged in French Limousin oak barrels. The methodology and techniques used to produce Martinique rhum are similar to those employed to make cognac.

There are over a dozen rhum distilleries in operation on Martinique today, but none are better known, or have a more sterling reputation for quality and taste than those produced by RHUM SAINT JAMES.

In 1765, Father Edmond Lefèbure, a monk of the Charity Hospital Order, founded the original Rhum Saint James distillery in

Saint Pierre on the northwest coast of the island. The monks operated the distillery and the adjacent sugar cane factory, using the net proceeds to fund their work at the Charity Hospital. With the French Prohibition firmly in place, Father Lefèbure decided to concentrate on marketing the rhum to the American colonies.

Father Lefèbure dubbed the spirit Rhum Saint James, a name easily pronounceable to the English speaking colonists. He designed the bottle to be rectangular in shape for efficient packaging and to better withstand the difficulties of shipping from Martinique. Rhum Saint James soon became the most popular brand of West Indies rum in the colonies prior to the American Revolution.

With the departure of the British from Martinique in 1815, the Rhum Saint James company was founded. It included the original distillery, mill and sugar cane plantation. In 1902, the eruption of Mont Pelée leveled the city of Saint Pierre and completely destroyed the Rhum Saint James distillery and adjacent facilities. That same year, the company relocated to Sainte-Marie on the northeast coast of Martinique.

Today, the Saint James distillery is surrounded by company owned sugar cane fields, which supplies roughly 80% of the distillery's needs. The remaining sugar cane is purchased from local farmers. After harvesting, the sugar cane is thoroughly cleaned, ridding it of any micro-organisms contained in the soil that may interfere with fermentation.

The sugar cane is quickly milled to extract the fresh cane juice, a green liquid called *vesou*. The juice is then filtered, cleaned and purified prior to being transferred to the fermentation tanks. Purified water and yeast are added to the juice to precipitate fermentation, a process that takes between 24 to 36 hours.

The fermented wash is distilled in one of the company's six, single-column stills. The distillate leaves the still clear and approximately 65% to 75% abv. It is then put into 68,000 liter, stainless steel vats and allowed to rest for 6 months. This allows the flavor components in the rhum to fully form and for unwanted taste elements to dissipate.

At this point, some of the production is diluted in strength to 50% or 55% abv with distilled water and bottled as Rhum Blanc. Another portion of the production run is aged further in 35,000-liter oak vats called *tuns*. After approximately 18 months it attains a distinctive pale yellow, straw color. It is then diluted to 50% or 55% and marketed as Saint James Rhum Paille (straw rhum). The remainder of the production is aged further in small, 200-liter, French Limousin oak barrels, some in excess of 10 years.

Rhum Saint James also produces a limited release, alembic rhum called Coeur de Chauffe. The rhum is produced using fermented cane juice distilled in a steam-heated pot still. It is an unaged, white rhum marketed at a lip tingling 60% abv (120 proof).

In 1996, the single cane rhums from Rhum Saint James earned the French government's prestigious designation as an Appellation d'Origine Contrôlée (AOC). The designation acknowledges the firm's strict adherence to quality and the preservation of traditional methodology and ingredient use. Each brand of Rhum Saint James bears the Appellation d'Origine Contrôlée designation and states that it is a rhum agricole from Martinique.

THE RHUMS OF SAINT JAMES

SAINT JAMES RHUM BLANC®

The distillery actually bottles two versions of white agricole rhum, something singular to Saint James. After resting in the stainless steel vat for 6 months, some of the rhum is diluted with treated, purified water to 50-55% abv and is marketed as SAINT JAMES IMPERIAL BLANC. Better known is SAINT JAMES RHUM BLANC. While essentially the same rhum, it is diluted with distilled water and bottled at either 50% or 55% abv (100 or 110 proof).

The Saint James Rhum Blanc is a splendid white rhum. It is brilliantly clear and has a remarkably light body and smooth texture for a 100-proof spirit. The rhum is generously aromatic, with the pleasant, herbaceous aroma of fresh cut sugar cane at the lead, followed closely by delicate floral, fruity and spicy notes. Keeping in mind its elevated alcohol content, the rhum is markedly refined on the palate. There's no trace of excess heat or rawness. It initially has a light, grassy taste, then offers subtle fruity flavors. The rhum has a soft, medium-length finish.

Rhum Blanc is tailor-made for cocktails. It has enough body and character to shine even when mixed in a tall, iced libation.

SAINT JAMES ROYAL AMBRE®

The SAINT JAMES ROYAL AMBRE RHUM is the youngest of the distillery's barrel-aged agricole rhums. It represents the ideal marriage between the fresh exuberance of Rhum Blanc and the elegance of the Saint James older rhums. The rhum is aged in 200-liter, Limousin oak barrels for a minimum of 18-months. It is marketed at 45% abv (90 proof).

The Royal Ambre Rhum has a copper/ amber hue with brilliant orange highlights. It has a silky texture and a light to medium body. The rhum has an intriguing bouquet. Initially the grassy aroma of sugar cane dominates, then gradually it is followed by marvelous notes of floral and spice. The rhum energizes and warms the palate, completely filling the mouth with warm, sumptuous flavor. The finish is long and slightly spicy.

There are an unlimited number of ways to enjoy this rhum, the most obvious of which is to sip it neat. Don't overlook this gem when making drinks. It is delicious in a dalquiri or as a float on top of a tall, exotic concoction.

SAINT JAMES
EXTRA OLD®

The name alone suggests you're in for a treat. SAINT JAMES EXTRA OLD (VIEUX) RHUM is one of the best selling rhums on Martinique. It is a savory agricole rhum aged a minimum of 3 years in Limousin oak barrels at the Saint James warehouses. The rhum is marketed at 42% abv (84 proof).

The Saint James Extra Old has a lustrous, bronze color and a supple, medium body. The rhum is quite aromatic; its bouquet immediately fills the glass with a tantalizing mix of spice, vanilla, molasses and oak. It rolls over the palate without a trace of heat. The rhum is remarkably dry at first, but that is soon replaced with a touch of almond and sugar cane sweetness. It has a definite presence in the mouth, similar to an Oloroso sherry or well-aged alembic brandy. The flavors persist throughout the long lasting finish.

Despite the fact that this exemplary rhum performs marvelously when featured in a cocktail, this is a sipping rhum. Savor it first in a snifter before breaking free of convention and adding it to your favorite daiquiri.

SAINT JAMES
(VIEUX) HORS D'AGE®

The first sniff, sip and swallow of SAINT JAMES HORS D'AGE RHUM speak volumes about its breeding and character. The top-of-the-line Hors d'Age is a skillfully crafted blend of barrel-aged agricole rhums aged a minimum of 6 years. The various rhums are aged in 200-liter Limousin oak casks in Saint James expansive warehouses. Considering how rapidly spirits age in the tropical Martinique climate, it is an extremely well aged spirit.

Drinking the Hors D'Age is a first-rate pleasure. It has a rich amber hue with dazzling red and mahogany highlights. The bouquet is brimming with captivating aromas; an array that includes honey, cacao, cinnamon, and fruit. The master blender has endowed this rhum with a luscious palate, one that features all of the above flavors, plus notes of vanilla, nuts, caramel and oak. These sumptuous flavors persist throughout the lingering finish.

The Saint James Hors D'Age is a luxurious rhum, certainly in the upper echelons of the category. It richly deserves the numerous awards and medals it has accrued. All that is required to fully appreciate this rhum is a glass and an unhurried moment.

OTHER MARTINIQUE RHUMS

Martinique should be dubbed the "Rhum Capital of the World." There are more than a dozen active rhum distilleries in operation on the island, the most in the Caribbean. Little wonder then why rhum is Martinique's leading export.

Two of the famed distilleries on Martinique are the J. Bally Distillery and Rhum Dillon. Both produce agricole rhums that are heavily exported and have developed tremendous popular followings. These two notable distilleries and their rhums are described in detail in chapter thirteen, "Caribbean Rums Off the Beaten Path."

One of the premiere brands of agricole rhum on the island is RHUM CLÉMENT, a distillery founded in 1887 at the site of an old sugar refinery by one of the island's most revered politicians, Homère Clément. The Habitation Clément is located south of Le Francois, but distillation now takes place at nearby Distillerie Simon. Clément purchases the unaged, column-distilled agricole rhum from Simon, then ages and bottles the rhum at its estate. Clément is best known for its line of vieux rhums, aged 6, 10 and 15 years. The company also markets three millésimé vieux rhums— vintages 1952, 1970 and 1990.

The Depaz Distillery has been located on the side of Mont Pelée since 1917, only fifteen years after the massive eruption rocked the island. Victor Depaz did so to capitalize on the area's fertile volcanic soil. To this day the plantation enjoys the highest yields of sugar cane. All of the cane is used In the productlon of premium, high quality agricole rhums. In addition to the DEPAZ WHITE RHUMS (50% and 55% abv), the distillery produces RHUM

PAILLE DEPAZ (2-years and 50% abv) and Rhum Vieux Depaz (4-years and 45% abv). Depaz also markets three RHUM VIEUX PLANTATION MILLÉSIMÉ—vintages 1929, 1950 and 1979.

Located on the northern coast of the island is Rhumerie J. M at Fonds-Preville. The distillery was founded in 1790 on the grounds of the Jean-Marie Martin sugar factory. The company originally distilled rhum from molasses, but switched to producing agricole rhum in the 1800s. The distillery cultivates its own sugar cane on the estate and uses two copper, single-column stills for production. Rhum J. M is produced in several different versions: RHUM BLANC J. M (aged 6-months in stainless steel vats and 55% abv); RHUM PAILLE J. M (barrel-aged 1-year and 55% abv), and RHUM VIEUX J. M (aged 10-years and 50% abv).

The Trois Rivières Distillery is located on the southern coast of Martinique near Sainte Luce. It was founded on a sugar plantation in 1660, where to this day the distillery cultivates nearly all of its sugar cane needs. The majority of its production is dedicated to RHUM VIEUX TROIS RIVIÈRES, which is aged in oak barrels 5-years and marketed almost exclusively on Martinique. The Trois Rivières Distillery also produces five millésimé vieux rhums—vintages 1969, 1975, 1979, 1980 and 1982. Its sister label, Duquesne, is primarily produced for export to France. DUQUESNE TRÈS VIEUX RHUM is an agricole rhum aged in American oak barrels for 10-years.

The Le Galion Sugar Factory on the east coast of Martinique is the last remaining sugar factory on the island. It produces two rhums distilled from molasses, the only two labels of Martinique rhum not produced from fresh cane juice.

The La Favorite Distillery dates back to 1842. It produces several labels of column-distilled agricole rhum including LA FAVORITE RHUM BLANC (50% and 55% abv), LA FAVORITE RHUM VIEUX (4-years and 45% abv) and LA FAVORITE CUVÉE SPÉCIALE DE LA FLIBUSTE (33-years and 40% abv), which has the distinction of being the oldest commercial Martinique vieux rhum. La Favorite also distills agricole rhum sold under the Saint-Etienne and Courville labels.

The largest distillery on Martinique is La Mauny. Founded in 1749, the distillery is capable of producing a staggering 35,000 liters of agricole rhum a day, exceeding the annual capabilities of most of the island's distilleries. A local favorite, La Mauny produces several versions of column-distilled rhums: RHUM BLANC LA MAUNY (50%, 55% and 62% abv); Rhum Vieux La Mauny (5-years and 45% abv) and La Mauny Hors d'Age (10-years and 43% abv).

Chapter 11

Cuba and the Rums of Matusalem

uba is the largest island in the Caribbean. At over 66,000 square miles, it has more than twice the area of Hispaniola. In fact, Cuba is almost as large as all of the other Caribbean islands combined. The island lies at the mouth of the Gulf of Mexico, just south of the Tropic of Cancer, a mere 90 miles from Key West. While geo-politically estranged from the United States, Cuba is actually part of the North American continent.

Of all the islands in the Caribbean, Cuba likely had the best initial shot at greatness. From a strategic standpoint, it is ideally positioned between Florida and the Yucatan, thereby defending both passages into the Gulf of Mexico. Likewise, it borders the high-traffic Windward Passage separating it from Hispaniola. Cuba is also one of only a few islands not dominated by mountain ranges, in fact, almost three-quarters of the island is fertile, arable, gently rolling plains. In addition, the island has numerous natural harbors that facilitate commerce and the movement of people.

Columbus first stepped ashore on the island of Cuba on October 27, 1492, landing on the northern coast. He claimed the island for Spain and the indigenous Arawaks greeted the Europeans warmly. Columbus noted in his log that it was "the most beautiful land eyes had ever seen." He returned to Cuba two years later on his way from Hispaniola to Jamaica. When repeated searches revealed that there was no gold, Columbus moved on.

While the Spanish explorer Sebastián de Ocampo was the first to circumnavigate the island in 1508, Spain's occupation of the island really began in 1511 when Diego de Veláquez landed a large force of conquistadors at Baracoa. Veláquez set out on a brutal campaign to conquer the island. The Arawaks desperately resisted the invaders.

Led by a chief named Hatuey, the Arawaks fought a guerrilla war for 3 months before eventually succumbing to the Spanish.

Hatuey was captured and burned at the stake. The remainder of the Arawaks were forced into slavery. When the Spanish occupation began in 1511, the native population on the island totaled an estimated 100,000. Within 60 years the Arawaks were wiped out.

By 1560, Havana had become the most important Spanish settlement in the Caribbean. The Gulf Stream carried ships through the Bahama Channel and past Havana at up to 10 knots per hour. Its naturally protected port became the staging area for Spain's treasure fleets before the long voyage back to Seville. The value of the gold, silver, gems and artifacts that passed through the port of Havana between 1540 and 1600 exceeded an estimated 200 million ducats.

The Spanish treasure fleets attracted the attention of pirates, who by the 1530s freely roamed the Caribbean, attacking coastal cities as well as vessels at sea. In 1555, the French pirate Jacques de Sores sailed his fleet of 30 ships into Havana harbor. The lightly defended Spanish garrison was quickly overrun. The pirates went on a killing spree, plundered the city and set it aflame.

With the steady demise of the island's native population, Spain needed to replenish the labor force on Cuba. In 1524, they began importing African slaves to work the tobacco and sugar cane plantations and mills. Despite commercial limitations imposed by the mother country—policies intended to bolster its domestic economy—the Cuban economy boomed well into the 18th century.

Meanwhile, Spain's fortunes were taking a turn for the worse. In 1588, the British Royal Navy defeated the Spanish Armada, crippling the ability of King Philip to monopolize the Caribbean. Spain's European campaigns and political commitments further drained the country's treasury. The Crown clamped down on its remaining Caribbean colonies, prohibiting them from trading with foreign nations, greatly restricting their economic development.

During the Seven Years' War between Britain, France and Spain, the English attacked and captured a number of French islands. The prize of the West Indies, however, was Cuba. In 1762, the British surprised the Spanish defenders by sending their fleet north through the dangerous Old Bahama Channel. After a two-month siege, the city of Havana surrendered. The British force seized enormous booty, including 12 ships of the line and nearly 100 merchant ships. The estimated value of the capture was a phenomenal £750,000.

The British occupied Havana and Cuba for only 11 months, but it provided a huge boost to the island's sugar industry. The lifting of trade restrictions enabled Cuban sugar producers to trade freely. Sugar production surged as plantation owners attempted to keep up with demand. Traffic in Havana's port skyrocketed as ships from many nations had access to the Cuban market for the first time.

The plantation owners were also able to greatly increase the number of slaves on the island. During the 11-month occupation, the British transported over 10,000 Africans to Cuba. In 1763, the Treaty of Paris was ratified in which Britain agreed, among other things, to relinquish control over Cuba in exchange for possession of Spain's dominion over Florida.

Once back in power, the Spanish again clamped down on foreign trade with Cuba. The result was a dramatic increase in smuggling and illicit trade with the British, French and Dutch. In 1818, Spain finally capitulated and lifted all trade restrictions. As soon as Spain opened up Cuba's ports to foreign ships, it sparked an international run on Cuban sugar. This boom market would last for the next 70 years.

At that point, the Cuban plantation economy was completely dependent on the slave system. The resurgent sugar industry demanded an influx of massive amounts of labor to work the cane fields and man the sugar mills.

When the slavery system was abolished throughout the British and French Caribbean colonies in 1838 and 1848 respectively, Spain steadfastly refused to follow suit. The African slave trade collapsed with the end of the American Civil War, and even then Spain clung on to slavery. With the possible exception of Haiti, no other Caribbean country withstood more slave rebellions than Cuba. There were 13 uprisings on the island between 1713 and 1886, the year Spain abolished slavery. It was the last Caribbean country to do so.

Spain had hedged its bet, however. In the 1850s through 1870s, Spanish plantation owners began importing indentured laborers from China to supplement their African slaves. An estimated 125,000 Chinese laborers were brought into Cuba between 1853 and 1871. Shortly before Spain abolished slavery there were over 211,000 African slaves and roughly 44,000 Chinese on the island.

Cuba became increasingly restive under Spanish control. The Crown continued to deny the colony any measure of autonomy or self-rule. When Spain imposed a set of laws further restricting personal freedoms, revolt was imminent. On October 10, 1868, a group called *Grito de Yara* proclaimed Cuba's independence from Spain, thus beginning the Ten Years' War. The rebellion was led by Carlos Manuel de Céspedes, and for years neither the rebels nor the Spanish army could claim a decisive victory. The revolt was fought in the eastern half of the country, leaving the more affluent western half and Havana unscathed.

During the revolt, Spain was embroiled in its own civil war, which ended in 1874. The government in Seville then poured troops into Cuba to crush the rebellion. The Spanish army constructed a fortified ditch running the entire width of the island to contain the revolt. In the end the rebels were forced to end the conflict, but not until extracting the promises from Spain to implement political and social reforms, one of which was the abolition of slavery.

Following the end of the rebellion, the country fell into an economic depression. The war had destroyed the coffee industry. The United States had levied a heavy tariff on the importation of Cuban cigars, severely constricting exports. Spain made matters worse by confiscating estates and sugar plantations, and sharply raising taxes to recoup its costs of suppressing the rebellion. Hundreds of plantation owners declared bankruptcy and thousands of workers fell into unemployment.

The separatist movement steadily grew in size and international recognition. Civil war was declared in January 1895, and this time an extraordinary leader and gifted orator, José Marti, would direct the rebellion. Tens of thousands of Cubans joined the rebels. Arms were smuggled in from America and a fierce guerilla war was waged.

Tragically, José Marti was killed in action on May 19, 1895. By late 1897, the war had reached a stalemate, with neither side able to secure a decisive victory over the other. By then, the United States was concerned about the security of its financial investments in Cuba and preserving its strategic interests.

As a show of military resolve and to be ready to intervene to protect Americans living in Cuba, the United States sent the battleship *USS Maine* into Havana's harbor. On the night of February 15, 1898, an explosion ripped through the *Maine*, sinking the ship in minutes and killing 266 of its 354-man crew.

The Spanish were blamed for the blast and the American press clamored for war. President McKinley immediately recognized Cuba as a free, independent nation, and demanded an armistice. Spain rejected McKinley's demands and severed diplomatic relations with the United States, which propelled Congress to declare war on Spain on April 25, 1898.

American forces landed. The United States Navy blockaded Havana harbor, then summarily defeated the Spanish fleet at Santiago de Cuba. The Americans quickly overwhelmed the Spanish defensive positions and the war was over within 10 weeks. In December 1898, the Treaty of Paris was signed, in which Spain granted Cuba its independence, and ceded Puerto Rico and the island of Guam to the United States.

Over 300,000 Cubans, or roughly 20% of the population, died in the conflict that ended Spain's 400 years of colonial rule. In 1902, the Republic of Cuba was formed and Estrada Palma, the country's first democratically elected president, took office.

In September 1933, a group of military officers led by Fulgencio Batista overthrew the elected government. Batista promised the people of Cuba a government free of corruption and political retribution, promises he had no intention of keeping. In 1940, Batista pushed through the assembly a new Constitution, which included universal suffrage and workers' benefits such as minimum wage, social insurance and an eight-hour day.

After losing reelection as president, General Batista staged a coup and successfully overthrew the newly elected government. His first order of business was to permanently suspend the constitution, effectively ending democracy in Cuba. In July 1953, a small band of revolutionaries looking to spark a rebellion that would lead to the overthrow of Batista, launched an unsuccessful attack against the military barracks at the Moncada Army Base. The attack was lead by Fidel Castro.

At his much-publicized trial, Castro defended himself brilliantly. Instead of a death sentence, he and his cohorts were exiled to Mexico. Castro, along with Argentinean Ernesto "Che" Guevara, used the reprieve to train a small revolutionary army in the tropical forests of Mexico.

In December 1956, Castro and his army of 82 revolutionaries sailed back to Cuba and covertly moved into the Sierra Maestra Mountains. Castro soon perfected his guerilla war tactics and began inflicting serious damage to the government's armies, so much so that after two years of fighting, Batista fled Havana in the early hours of January 1, 1959.

A few days later, Castro rode triumphantly into Havana and took control of the government. He immediately nationalized all foreign properties and businesses and put his political adversaries in prison. Promised elections were never held, and all newspapers and radio stations were seized. Castro appointed his own judiciary, and disbanded all trade unions and professional associations.

Relations with the United States were further strained when Castro aligned his government with communism and the Soviet Union. In 1961, a group of 1,400 trained Cuban exiles landed in the *Bahia de Cochinos* (Bay of Pigs) with the intent of starting an armed insurrection and overthrowing Castro. The mission failed at a cost of 200 dead, the rest imprisoned.

This fiasco was followed months later by the Cuban Missile Crisis, in which President Kennedy and Soviet Premier Kruschev brought the world to the brink of nuclear war. At the eleventh hour, Kruschev backed down and agreed to remove the offensive weapons from Cuban soil. In 1961, Congress imposed a trade embargo with Cuba that is still in place 40 years later.

Cuba under communism has outwardly suffered greatly. With the collapse of the Soviet Union in 1990, Castro lost his principle financial and political backer. The country has faced numerous economic crises and the country's infrastructure is in a visible state of decay. Food shortages are the norm.

Despite the political and economic situation, Cuba is undergoing a resurgence in tourism. People from around the world are rediscovering the charm of the country and the warmth of the Cuban people.

RUM AND THE ISLAND OF CUBA

Although Columbus hand-carried sugar cane plants onto the island, the sugar industry on Cuba was slow in developing. Most of the other Caribbean colonies were profiting from the cultivation of sugar cane well before it took hold in Cuba. For example, in 1528 there were 30 sugar mills operating in Jamaica, 10 in Puerto Rico and none in Cuba.

That situation changed dramatically when the British occupied Cuba in 1762. They fully understood the economic potential of cultivating sugar cane and immediately eliminated all impediments to the Cuban sugar industry and production surged.

Before the British occupied Cuba, the average annual production of sugar was 2,000 tons. Shortly after the Spanish regained control of the island, annual production rose to 5,200 tons. In 1790, production nearly tripled to 14,000 tons, and by 1820, annual sugar production on Cuba increased to over 50,000 tons, an amount exceeding the total production of the entire French West Indies. By 1860, Cuba was producing more than a third of the world's sugar.

The development of the island's sugar producers dictated the fortunes of the Cuban rum industry. The Spanish brought the art of distillation to Cuba. From the 1500s through the middle of the 17th century, all of the spirits distilled on the island were consumed locally or traded with pirates.

The rum—referred to then as *ron peleon*—was fiery, harsh and unrefined. It was distilled on sugar plantations from molasses, which was essentially a by-product of sugar production. Distilling rum was a profitable side venture for most plantation owners, so nearly every plantation had facilities for the production of rum.

The molasses would be mixed with fresh water and yeast to precipitate fermentation. The fermented wash would then be distilled in small copper pot (alembic) stills. The spirits were left totally intact and drunk exactly as they came out of the still, unfiltered, unaged and undiluted. There was little technological advancement in distillation on the island until the middle of the 19th century.

In February 1862, Don Facundo Bacardi opened a distillery in Santiago de Cuba called Bacardi y Compañía. He began distilling rum from a mash of fermented molasses in a copper and cast iron alembic still. Bacardi pioneered the technique of using charcoal filtration to remove congeners, particulate and impurities, as well as the color from barrel-aged rum. *Bacardi Carta Blanca* was the first white rum in the world, and soon became the most popular and successful brand in Cuba (refer to Chapter 3).

Santiago was also the birthplace of the famed Cuban rum, Ron Matusalem. Two brothers, Benjamin and Eduardo Camp, emigrated from Spain to Cuba in pursuit of opening their own rum distillery. It was their dream to use their knowledge and expertise, combined with the pure molasses to make the finest Cuban *aguardiente de caña*—the Spanish designation for rum, or the distillate of sugar.

In 1872, the brothers opened the Camp & Brothers, S.A. in a small building in Santiago. They began distilling Ron Matusalem and

within a few years the distillery was producing a range of rums, including a light, dry rum and an overproof. They also began employing Spain's famed Solera aging system.

The Solera system was originated by the Spanish and used in the production of sherry. The system involves the use of a series of oak casks arranged in tiers. The barrels on the top tier contain the youngest rums. The casks on the middle tier contain older rums and the barrels on the bottom tier are filled with the oldest rums. When deemed appropriate, the master blender will remove half the contents of the barrels from the lowest tier for bottling. The emptied barrels are then filled to capacity with rum from the middle tier. Young rums from the barrels on the highest tier are used to fill the casks on the middle tier.

In the Solera system the older rums "educate" the younger rums, enhancing their taste and character. Another advantage of Solera aging is that it ensures that the blended rums will be consistent from one to the next.

The name Ron Matusalem was chosen as a reference to Methuselah, the Old Testament patriarch said to have lived 969 years. The brand's añejo rums were advertised with the tag line, *"Ron Matusalem. Esto es mas viejo que Matusalem."* (Ron Matusalem. It's older than Methusaleh."

Prior to the 20th century, the distillery began distilling rum using the Coffey continuous still, which enabled the distillery to produce increasingly lighter spirits. In 1881, nine years after opening for business, Ron Matusalem won its first medal at an international competition. The brand earned two more medals—both gold—at competitions; the first in 1904 at the St. Louis Exposition and again in 1911 in Havana.

In 1912, Benjamin Camp returned to Spain. His brother, Eduardo Camp than became partners with Evaristo Alvarez, and the name of the distillery was changed to Alvarez, Camp y Compañía.

In 1959, Fidel Castro seized control of the Cuban government. A year later, faced with the loss of Cuba as they knew it, the Alvarez family left the island and relocated the family-owned and operated business to the United States. Today, Ron Matusalem is made from a blend of Solera aged West Indies rums. It is produced and bottled in the Bahamas or Lake Alfred, Florida. Rum marketed in Europe is produced at Distillerie Smeets in the Netherlands.

It is the fervent desire and dream of the Alvarez family to return the company to the country of its origin.

THE RUMS OF RON MATUSALEM

RON MATUSALEM GRAN RESERVA®

Introduced in 1997, GRAN RESERVA is Ron Matusalem's crowning achievement. One of the singular features of their luxurious, topshelf rum is that it is built around a core "blender rum." This rum has been Solera aged approximately 15 years and is comprised of rums between 8- and 32-years old. Various other rums are then added to the core blender. These barrel-aged rums are produced by several West Indies distilleries and range in age between 3 and 4 years. The result is the most sublime marriage between these younger, exuberant rums and the mature and stately blender.

Matusalem Gran Reserva has an amber hue and a satiny texture. The first course is the generous and well-developed bouquet, a lavish offering of vanilla, caramel, plums and molasses. You immediately get a keen sense of its grace and finesse as it enters the mouth. The rum has a complex palate that barely generates any heat as its dry, toasty flavors take center stage, before slowly ebbing away in a long and satisfying finish. It is marketed at 40% abv (80 proof).

Sipping the Matusalem Gran Reserva neat is a marvelous experience, one that would appeal to the aficionado and novice alike. It is an elegant rum that's exceedingly easy to drink. Gran

Reserva won the gold medal in the premium rum category at RumFest 2000, and was named "Best Rum in America" in 1999 and 2000 by the American Tasting Institute.

RON MATUSALEM LIGHT DRY (CARTA PLATA)®

The rum style of choice in Cuba is light, dry and crystal clear, the type of spirit that can only be produced in a continuous still. This traditional spirit is skillfully represented in RON MATUSALEM LIGHT DRY (CARTA PLATA), one of the best selling rums in Cuba.

This popular Matusalem rum is made from a blend of molasses-based, continuous-distilled rums. The blend is barrel-aged in used American oak bourbon barrels for a minimum of two years. After aging, the rum leaves the barrel with a rich, golden hue. It is then filtered through activated charcoal to remove impurities, particulate and all of the color it obtained maturing in the barrel. The white rum is marketed at 40% abv (80 proof).

Ron Matusalem Light Dry is appropriately named. The rum is clear, clean and has a lithe, wispy body. Its alluring bouquet is subtly perfumed with floral aromas, an accurate precursor to what lies ahead. The rum enters the palate softly, then steadily grows in intensity and heat, peaking at just the right moment. On the palate the rum is essentially dry, with only a trace of sweetness. It has a delicate, fruity array of flavors and a warm, medium-length finish.

Ron Matusalem Light Dry earned gold medals at the RumExpo 1999 and RumFest 2000, events held annually in Barbados. This has scores of applications behind the bar.

RON MATUSALEM GOLDEN DRY (CARTA ORO)®

There are times when making cocktails that only a gold-colored rum will do. These are the occasions for which RON MATUSALEM GOLDEN DRY (CARTA ORO) RUM was created.

This version of Matusalem is made from a blend of molasses-based, continuous-distilled rums. The blend is Solera aged a minimum of five-years. After aging, the rum leaves the barrel with its trademark golden color. It is then filtered through activated charcoal to remove impurities and particulate only, leaving its golden/honey hue intact. It is bottled at 40% abv (80 proof).

Ron Matusalem Golden Dry is brilliantly clear with a wonderfully light and airy body. It has a delicate, floral/fruity bouquet that does a superb job preparing you for the pleasures that lie ahead. It has a more refined presence on the palate and doesn't generate the same intensity in the mouth as the white version. The rum is well balanced, offering hints of sweetness between tastes of molasses, cocoa and caramel. The rum has a light, medium-length finish.

The mission of Ron Matusalem Golden Dry is clear. This gold rum was born and bred for use in cocktails. It has the body, taste and character that mixologists are searching for.

RON MATUSALEM CLASSIC BLACK®

This is a fun, attention-grabbing product to have in your drink-making repertoire. Not only is the dark, richly textured rum an excellent choice for such drinks as daiquiris and piña coladas, it can also create a dramatic presentation when floated on top of tall, iced libations.

RON MATUSALEM CLASSIC BLACK RUM is made from a blend of molasses-based, continuous-distilled rums. The blend is Solera aged a minimum of seven-years. It is then filtered through activated charcoal to remove impurities and particulate only, leaving its famed deep copper/honey brown hue intact.

Matusalem Classic Black is a lush, full-bodied rum. It has a seductive bouquet brimming with the warm, creamy aromas of vanilla, coconut, molasses and toffee. The rum is jam packed with toasty, well-balanced flavors that dance over the palate without a trace of excess heat. There is also an intriguing, bourbon-like quality to its taste. The rum has a lingering and flavorful finish. It is marketed at 40% abv (80 proof).

Matusalem Classic Black is a lot of rum for the price. It earned a gold medal at RumExpo 1999. Then at RumFest 2000 it won a gold medal and was named the "Judges Choice" in the dark rum category.

RON MATUSALEM RED FLAME®

RON MATUSALEM RED FLAME RUM is made from a blend of molasses-based, continuous-distilled rums. The blend is barrel-aged in used American oak bourbon barrels for a minimum of two years. After aging, the rum is filtered through activated charcoal to remove impurities and particulate only, leaving its golden/honey hue intact. It is marketed at 75.5% abv (151 proof).

While the barrel aging has somewhat tempered this overproof rum, it is still a heady dram with a high-octane character and sizzling palate. Herein lies the explanation behind its name.

The true charm and inherent good taste of Matusalem Red Flame comes out when mixed, which is how it is intended to be consumed. Instead of the rum being diluted with purified water at the distillery, you're essentially doing the diluting for them when you add it to a tall, mixed drink. It is ideally suited for such exotic concoctions as the Zombie and Mai Tai.

OTHER CUBAN RUMS

There were several established distillers on the island before Castro took over on January 1, 1959. In addition to Bacardi y Compañía, and Alvarez, Camp y Compañía (Ron Matusalem), the Arechabaia, Cadenas and Matanzas distilleries were all in distribution to some degree. After Castro's takeover, free enterprise gave way to communism and the nationalization of industry. Both the Matusalem and Bacardi families left Cuba in 1960.

Havana Club is the only major brand of rum produced in Cuba today. They are molasses-based, continuous-distilled rums aged a minimum of 18-months in American white oak vats. Havana Club produces a range of rums including HAVANA CLUB SILVER DRY (18-months and 37.5% abv), HAVANA CLUB 3-YEAR (40% abv), HAVANA CLUB 5-YEAR (40% abv) and HAVANA CLUB AÑEJO RESERVE (7-years and 40% abv).

Archival photographs and registered trademarks in this chapter may not be reproduced without the written consent of Rum Matusalem.

THE TRADITIONAL ROYAL NAVY TOASTS

MONDAY:	Our Ships at Sea
TUESDAY:	Our Men
WEDNESDAY:	Ourselves (As no one is likely to concern themselves with our welfare)
THURSDAY:	A Bloody War and Quick Promotion
FRIDAY:	A Willing Soul and Sea Room
SATURDAY:	Sweethearts and Wives, May They Never Meet
SUNDAY:	Absent Friends and Those at Sea

Chapter 12

Naval Rums, Pusser's and Her Majesty's Navy

In the early 1500s, the shipping lanes in the Caribbean Sea were the most dangerous, hotly contested waters in the world. Through its narrow island passages and channels sailed the plundered riches of the New World, treasures so fabulous that they threatened to change the course of history.

The monarchies of Spain, France and England were at war, as they had been for the previous century. But it takes a great deal of money to wage war, and the nation with the most money can do so the longest. The most promising strategy at the time for generating wealth was to conquer other lands—preferably those without the capacity to effectively resist—and to seize their resources, the most negotiable of which was gold.

While England and France were occupied elsewhere, Spain captured the mother lode. Columbus' voyages of discovery yielded unimaginable wealth. In one brilliant stroke, Spain claimed the entirety of the New World, from the Caribbean basin to Mexico, Central America and South America. The indigenous people were scarcely a match for the Spanish Armada and the Conquistadors.

At first there was little that England and France could do but watch as the Spanish Crown cashed in. Then in 1522, the King of France commissioned an Italian named Giovanni da Verrazanno to attack the Spanish treasure fleets and capture their riches for France. The mission was enormously successful as the Florentine pirate seized two Spanish galleons loaded with gold from Mexico, and a third filled with sugar, pearls and hides from Hispaniola.

England soon followed suit and profited handsomely. In fact, the most feared pirate of his time was Sir Francis Drake. Funded by Queen Elizabeth, Drake attacked the Spanish shipping lanes at will. It is believed that Drake turned over to the Crown roughly 15% of the booty he seized and that his expeditions yielded dividends of £47 Sterling for every one invested.

State sanctioned piracy proved to be a highly effective and lucrative strategy. What England and France hadn't counted on was the rapid growth in the pirate ranks. The lure of riches, violence and living outside authority's reach attracted cutthroats, fugitives and renegades from Europe, Africa and the Caribbean colonies. Within a few years, piracy in the Caribbean was past the point where either England or France could control it.

By the 1660s, thousands of pirates were operating out of Port Royal (Jamaica), Tortuga, St. Croix and Curaçao. In 1666, pirate Henry "Captain" Morgan started raiding coastal towns. With ten ships and a force of 700 men, Morgan sacked the city of Puerto Principe in Cuba. He then stormed the well-fortified and heavily armed garrison of Porto Bello, Panama, holding it until he was paid a £10,000 ransom for the return of the city.

Several years later, Morgan and his pirates sacked the Cuban towns of Gibraltar and Maracaibo, seizing huge amounts of loot, as well as extracting a sizeable ransom from the Spanish for the return of the city. In 1673, pirates plundered Trinidad yielding 100,000 "pieces of eight." Then they seized what was at the time the wealthiest city in the "New World," Vera Cruz, Mexico, carrying off what in today's dollars amounted to $6,000,000.

The superpowers tried every tactic they could think of to stem their growing losses due to piracy. A few of the enticements did work at luring buccaneers into changing professions, but by the turn of the 18th century, piracy on the Caribbean Sea was still rampant.

Exacerbating the situation, France and Spain continued to enlist the services of buccaneers to fulfill their strategic missions against the British and their colonies. In 1706, pirates under the command of French officer Pierre d'Iderville plundered St. Kitts and Nevis. A few years later, a French-led force of 3,500 buccaneers sacked Antigua and Montserrat.

It was the British Royal Navy that would eventually turn the tide. The Admiralty established the first naval stations in the Caribbean, at Port Royal, Jamaica in 1692 and the second at English Harbour, Antigua in 1743. While the other superpowers had to shuttle their fleets between Europe and the Caribbean, remaining in the area no more than six-months at a time, the British maintained a permanent presence. The Royal Navy began to regularly patrol off the coasts of its colonies.

When not fighting in concert with the French or Spanish, the pirate fleets began to lose their effectiveness. Despite having great strengths in ships and men, the pirates' chief problem was greed and the inability to fight as a cohesive force. Infighting among the pirate captains led them to pursue their own self-interests. In the face of the heightened presence of the British Royal Navy, most of the remaining buccaneers sought less dangerous waters, usually the South Seas.

The Royal Navy had grown into the most formidable fighting force in the world. No individual nation's navy could match it. The only viable strategy remaining for France, Spain and the Netherlands was to ally themselves and their navies against the growing British threat.

The 18th century was a succession of European wars fought on a global scale. It began with the War of the Spanish Succession (1702-14), which pitted England, Austria and the Netherlands against France and Spain. England and France fought again during the War of the Jenkin's Ear (1739-48), the Seven Years' War (1756-63), the War for American Independence (1776-83) and the War of the Saints (1782-1803).

Throughout the wars, the islands of the Eastern Caribbean were repeatedly invaded and occupied, only to be ceded back to the original colonial power through treaty. The century extracted a heavy toll on the warring superpowers and their colonies. In addition to the loss of life, the widespread destruction of property continued to cripple development of the island nations.

In the end, the only real tangible winner was the British Royal Navy, which emerged from the century with complete control of the world's seas, including the Caribbean. The advent of the 19th century found the United Kingdom reaching from Singapore, Australia and India to the East, Canada in North America, Jamaica, Bermuda, and the British Virgin Islands in the Caribbean, and much of Africa.

The sinew that bound the United Kingdom together and permitted England to maintain its global empire was the invincibility of the British Royal Navy.

RUM AND THE ROYAL NAVY

The life of the average seaman aboard a British warship during the 17th and 18th centuries was a mix of drudgery and backbreaking labor, all the while faced with the constant threat of violent death. To break the tedium and stress, sailors were given a daily ration of beer. Unfortunately, the barrels of beer fared poorly on long voyages— especially in tropical climes—and the brew quickly soured and became unpalatable.

'Grog' – Pusser's Rum & water – being issued from the grog tub on board HMS ENDYMION in 1905.

The first reference to rum being served onboard a Royal Navy Ship places the event in 1655. Vice-Admiral William Penn had just captured Jamaica from the Spanish and he rewarded his crews by providing them with local rum. It is said the crews immediately took to the robust pot-distilled Jamaican rum.

By the early 1680s, it was standard practice for a Royal Navy Purser to supplement the onboard provisions with West Indies rum. Plantation owners sold the rum to the navy at favorable prices to encourage their frequent return. The mere presence of the Royal Navy was enough to keep pirates away.

In 1687 the Admiralty officially adopted a pint of rum as the daily ration for crews in the West Indies, and by 1731, a pint of strong, undiluted rum was being doled out throughout the Royal Navy. One unfortunate side effect was that many sailors became too impaired to carry out their responsibilities, some of which were too hazardous to perform intoxicated. So while it made life more bearable for the men of the Royal Navy, it was noted that the "incidence of accidents in the rigging and losses overboard increased."

In 1740, Admiral Edward Vernon ordered that the daily ration of "Pusser's" rum be diluted 2:1 with water and that the rations of rum were to be issued twice daily—a half-pint in the morning and in the evening. As a reward for good behavior, lime juice and sugar were added to the rum to make it more palatable. Vernon received commendation from the Admiralty for his order citing it as "perhaps the greatest improvement to discipline and efficiency ever produced with one stroke of the pen." Not surprisingly, Vernon's order didn't receive similar reviews from the sailors of the Royal Navy.

Admiral Vernon was nicknamed "Old Grog," because of the grogham boat-cloak he wore on deck. So out of contempt for the new water-diluted rum, the daily rations became known as "grog." In 1850, the Admiralty Board ordered that the rum rations be further weakened to a water-to-rum ration of 4:1.

England's greatest naval hero, Admiral Horatio Viscount Nelson, was mortally wounded in 1805 at the Battle of Trafalgar. His brilliant tactics led to the defeat of the combined French and Spanish fleets. Nelson's body was returned to England in a cask of Pusser's rum, the alcohol to serve as a preservative until he could be buried with full honors at St. Paul's Cathedral. As the story goes, during the voyage the sailors onboard secretly emptied the cask of rum so as to drink "Nelson's Blood," which became the name of another classic drink.

The daily rationing of rum was one of the Royal Navy's longest standing traditions. The practice remained in effect until July 31, 1970, a date that has become known as "Black Tot Day." The Admiralty Board then canceled longstanding purchasing agreements with the West Indies rum distillers. Most of these relationships had been in place since 1810, the year that the official blend of the dark rums was adopted.

In 1979, an American ex-Marine named Charles Tobias approached the Royal Navy with a plan to begin marketing Pusser's Rum. At first the notion was met with profound skepticism by the Admiralty. But Tobias persisted, and offered to donate a sizable portion of the proceeds to the Royal Navy Sailor's Fund. The

Admiralty Board eventually consented, giving Tobias access to the official Pusser's Rum recipe and granting him permission to incorporate the Royal Ensign on the label.

That same year Tobias launched Pusser's Rum. It is made according to the exact specifications adopted in 1810 by the Admiralty. Pusser's is a blend of six alembic-distilled, barrel-aged rums produced in Trinidad, Guyana and Tortola. The blending and bottling takes place in Tortola in the British Virgin Islands.

At first, Pusser's Rum was marketed solely in a small bar on Main Street in Road Town, Tortola. Tobias opened the bar as a way of getting people to sample the rum. The success of that venture led Tobias to open a much larger bar called the Pusser's Road Town Pub and a restaurant called Pusser's Landing at West End, Tortola.

THE RUMS OF PUSSER'S

PUSSER'S RED LABEL BRITISH NAVY®

The romance begins the moment you pick up a bottle of PUSSER'S RED LABEL BRITISH NAVY RUM. It looks like something that belongs on a ship of the line. There's even something disciplined about its no-nonsense label, which bears the Royal Ensign and states its name, strength and port of call. The whole package is strong, concise and dripping of tradition.

Pusser's Red Label is a blend of six, molasses-based, pot-still rums, produced at several undisclosed West Indies distilleries. The label identifies it as being a product of Guyana, Trinidad and the British Virgin Islands. While there is no age statement, there is no doubt that these are barrel-aged rums. Pusser's Red Label is bottled at 40% abv (80 proof). Any other hard intelligence about the rum is a carefully guarded military secret.

Pusser's Red Label has a chardonnay/golden hue and a light, well-rounded body. The bouquet, while restrained, has an engaging whiskey-like character with aromas of honey and vanilla. Don't brace yourself for a slap-in-the-face experience. The rum is almost reserved as it enters the palate, then the exceptionally dry, woody flavors take over and builds in intensity, stopping well short of hot. The finish is very long and pleasantly warming.

There had to be some cold and lonely watches when this rum, even diluted with stale water, made life more bearable.

PUSSER'S BLUE LABEL BRITISH NAVY®

Everything about this rum smacks of authenticity. Pusser's is "The Original Rum of the Royal Navy." From stem to stern, PUSSER'S BLUE LABEL BRITISH NAVY RUM is a singular spirit with qualities unlike those found in other rums. It's easy to imagine this rum being doled out in daily rations on the decks of Her Majesty's Ships.

Pusser's Blue Label is a blend of six, molasses-based, pot-still rums, produced at different West Indies distilleries. The label identifies it as being a product of Guyana, Trinidad and the British Virgin Islands. Their bottle makes no claim as to the age of the rums in the blend, nevertheless, there is abundant evidence that they have spent a considerable amount of time in wood. The rum is bottled at 47.75% abv (95.5 proof).

The Pusser's Blue Label has a lustrous honey/amber hue with brilliant red-orange highlights. It's deep, rich color will make you want to take a moment. The huge bouquet alerts the senses that this is not business as usual. It immediately fills the glass with an array of aromas, including sugarcane, molasses and toasted oak, followed by vegetal notes. The rum has a light, sinewy body that storms the mouth with a salvo of fresh, earthy flavors. The protracted finish presents layers of woody flavors steeped in tannin.

This energetic rum will leave your lips tingling and your mouth wanting more. The elevated alcohol contributes to the heady, Pusser's Blue Label experience. After a dram or two, it's hard not to subscribe to Admiral Vernon's point of view. A touch of water is a good thing.

OTHER NAVAL RUMS

When the Admiralty abandoned the practice of a daily ration of rum, it had stores of spirits aging in vast underground warehouses near Bath. Since July 31, 1970, this naval rum has been reserved exclusively for Royal functions.

Importer Mark Andrews of the Great Spirits Company approached the Admiralty about a special release of this historic rum. After long negotiations, Andrews received dispensation to market BRITISH ROYAL NAVY IMPERIAL RUM. This magnificent, limited release rum is a blend of alembic spirits distilled in the West Indies, aged in American oak barrels and casked at 54% abv (108 proof). The rum is marketed in an authentic, 4.54-liter demijohn flagon with a stainless steel label affixed to the woven wickerwork. It also comes with an elegant crystal decanter from which to serve the rum.

British Royal Navy Imperial Rum has a prominent bouquet with notes of smoky, toasted oak, bread yeast, molasses, and vanilla. Its lush, full body immediately engages the palate with a rush of tightly compacted flavors, notably malt, caramel, and vanilla. Its long, warm finish is reminiscent of an aged malt whisky.

Another naval rum worth sampling is LAMB'S NAVY RUM, which is produced by Alfred Lamb's of London. It is a blend of molasses-based, pot- and column-distilled rums from distilleries in Jamaica, Guyana, Barbados and Trinidad. It is dark, aromatic and fruity.

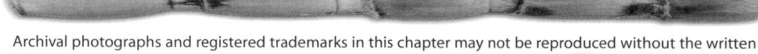

Archival photographs and registered trademarks in this chapter may not be reproduced without the written consent of Pusser's Limited.

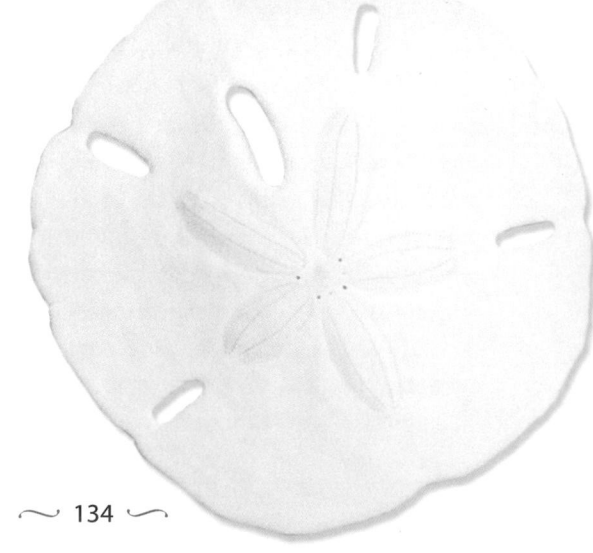

Chapter 13

Caribbean Rums Off the Beaten Path

Beyond the boundary of well-known rum brands lies a fascinating and exciting cadre of smaller rum producers. Their limited distribution and marketing budgets have kept them off grocery store shelves and out of the popular mainstream. They are, however, well known in the rum community and objects of fascination for connoisseurs, enthusiasts and aficionados around the world.

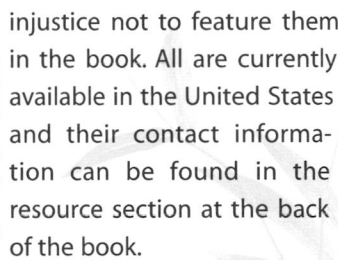

This chapter includes the profiles of six such producers. Collectively these rums are so exquisite that it would be an injustice not to feature them in the book. All are currently available in the United States and their contact information can be found in the resource section at the back of the book.

While the majority of Americans haven't heard of these highly acclaimed brands, they soon will. These rums have everything one could ask for from a spirit. They come from fascinating ports of call, have engaging legacies and are brimming with character. Add to the mix that none of these rums are even remotely alike and you have all the makings of a box office hit.

Be prepared to jump on the bandwagon before it gets too crowded.

RHUM DILLON

A magnificent plantation and sugar cane refinery were built in 1690 by Frenchman Claude de Girardin de Montgeralde. Located near the port of Fort de France, Martinique, the Girardin Sugar Plantation became one of the most significant on the island. On the grounds of the plantation was a still house that produced rhum agricole, a spirit distilled from fresh sugar cane juice, rather than molasses or other sugar cane by-products.

During the American War of Independence, French Colonel Arthur Dillon fought alongside Lafayette in the defense of the United States. In 1779, Dillon was sent to the French colony of Martinique, and shortly after his arrival, purchased the Girardin Sugar Plantation.

The distillery was forced to cease operations due to extensive damage in 1891 when a hurricane devastated Martinique and again in 1902 after the eruption of Mont Pelée. The distillery's machinery was updated and soon production began anew. In 1920, the alembic still that had been in use at the Dillon Distillery since 1869 was replaced with two copper column stills imported from France. The stills, which significantly increased rhum production, remain in use to this day. The plant's cane crushers, installed in 1934, also remain in use.

The city of Fort de France has grown considerably, now literally reaching the doorsteps of the Dillon Distillery. Long gone are the plantation's vast fields of sugar cane. Dillon purchases its sugar cane from growers around the island. The cane is crushed at the plantation's mill house and the fresh running juice is filtered and then transferred to the operation's 22 stainless steel fermentation tanks.

The sugar cane juice is diluted with spring water, then yeast is introduced to precipitate fermentation, a process that lasts for 48 hours. The Dillon Distillery relies on the single column distillation process. The tall, copper stills produce a distillate that is 70% abv.

All of the rhum distilled by Dillon is aged a minimum of three months in American white oak barrels. The Dillon warehouses contain roughly 2000 barrels of rhum aging at any point in time. As is accepted practice throughout Martinique, distillers annually weigh the barrels and determine how much of the rhum aging inside has been lost through evaporation. The average annual loss is approximately 8%. The producers then replace the losses with rhum of the same type and vintage, a process referred to as *houillage*.

The Dillon Distillery releases several versions of rhum agricole. A small portion of their production is devoted to DILLON RHUM PAILLE®, 50% abv, a rhum aged for a minimum of 1-year and DILLON GRAND RHUM BLANC®, a white rhum aged for a minimum of three-months, then filtered through activated charcoal to remove coloring and impurities. The Rhum Blanc is bottled at 50%, 55% and 62% abv.

The distillery bottles a fifteen-year old masterpiece labeled DILLON TRÈSVIEUX RHUM®. The Dillon also markets vintage-dated versions of the TrèsVieux. The rhum is highly aromatic, spicy on the palate and imbued with a lingering finish. Both versions are bottled at 45% abv.

Rhums from Dillon are shipped to Bardinet in Bordeaux, France, and blended with agricole rhum distilled on Reunion Island, Philippines, to create BARDINET NEGRITA and OLD ST. NICK.

The best selling label from the Dillon Distillery is known as DILLON DARK RHUM® in the United States, and DILLON RHUM VIEUX CARTE NOIRE® on Martinique. It is aged a minimum of 6-years in American white oak barrels. The rhum is copper/bronze colored, light-bodied and has a distinctively agricole nose, a fresh, herbaceous offering of chocolate, cola, and grass.

Dillon Dark Rhum drinks much older than six-years. The rhum gradually builds in intensity, reaching a crescendo right before it slips into a warm, flavorful finish. There is a kinetic charge in the rhum that is a pleasure to experience. Its energy almost crackles on the palate. Sip Dillon Dark Rhum neat before you start playing with it. The rhum is marketed at 40% abv (80 proof).

In 1967, the Bardinet Company purchased Dillon Distillery, ending seven generations of family control. Worry not, while annual production has reached 2,000,000 liters, strict adherence to quality control keeps the Rhum Dillon a qualitative step ahead.

J. BALLY RHUM

About 12 miles northwest of Fort de France and the Dillon Distillery along the coastal highway N2 is the city of Carbet, where Christopher Columbus first stepped foot on the island of Martinique on June 15, 1502. The city is home to one of the most famous distilleries on the island, J. Bally.

Jacques Bally emigrated from France to Martinique at the end of the 18th century in pursuit of producing rhum using similar aging techniques employed to mature cognac. He settled in Carbet in a house built in 1733 named Habitation Lajus. It was here that he began distilling rhum agricole from sugar cane grown on his estate. The fresh sugar cane juice was distilled in a copper, single column continuous still.

The violent eruption of Mont Pelée in 1902 destroyed the then capital of Saint-Pierre and killed the city's entire population of 30,000 people. Located a scant 2 miles south, Carbet was laid to rubble from the blast. The eruption destroyed nearly every distillery and warehouse on the island. While damaged, the J. Bally Distillery and Habitation Lajus remained standing.

In 1917, Bally began aging his agricole rhums in Limousin oak barrels that had been used to age cognac. The result was sensational, creating a line of aged rhums with a distinctive brandy finish, something singular for Martinique rhum.

The eruption of Mont Pelée wiped out all but a small amount of the island's aging rhum. Placing a premium on bottling vintage rhum, Bally set aside barrels of specific vintages. The vintages were selected based on favorable weather conditions and the quality of the sugar cane harvested. The firm has the oldest stocks of Martinique rhum with vintages dating back to 1924.

In 1997, the single cane rums from J. Bally earned the French government's prestigious designation as an Appellation

d'Origine Contrôlée (AOC). The designation acknowledges the firm's strict adherence to quality and the preservation of traditional methodology and ingredient use.

The company bottles several versions of J. Bally Rhum Agricole. All of the rhums are produced from fresh sugar cane juice distilled within 24-hours of harvesting in a copper, single column continuous still located at Distillerie Simon. The distinctive square bottles and pyramid shaped decanters have been in use exclusively since the firm began and were designed by Jacque Bally himself.

Unaged J. BALLY RHUM BLANC®, 50% abv (100 proof), is colorless, crystal clear and light-bodied. It has an expansive bouquet loaded with the fresh aromas of ripe fruit, grassy sugar cane and young alcohol. Considering its age and elevated alcohol the rhum is remarkably supple, although it does generate ample warmth and leaves the lips tingling. On the palate, the Rhum Blanc tastes fruity, devoid of bitterness and dry as an eau-de-vie brandy. The finish is quite warm and lingering.

Next in line is the straw-colored J. BALLY RHUM PAILLE®, which is barrel-aged for a minimum of 12-months. It is bottled at 50% abv and has limited distribution.

The distillery markets two 45% abv, age-designated rhums. The 7-year old version of J. BALLY RHUM VIEUX® has a lustrous, amber color and satiny smooth body. The rhum is aromatic with vanilla, cinnamon and notes of brandy. It slips over the palate lightly, then unfolds in a long finish with the warm oaky flavors of toffee, spice and ripe fruit.

The J. BALLY RHUM VIEUX 12-ANS D'AGE® is considerably darker than the younger release. The rhum has a greenish tint around the edges that confirms the long aging in wood and an elegant bouquet with notes of honey, wine and oak. The palate is a delightfully complex affair with a fascinating texture and an array of dry, spicy flavors. The tasty, glowing finish is exceptionally long and much appreciated.

A share of the distillery's international renown is certainly due to its extraordinary collection of rare vintage rhums. At the time of this writing there are about a dozen vintages—or *millésimes*—available in the United States. The earliest is the J. BALLY RHUM VIEUX MILLÉSIME® 1924. Other vintages include: 1929; 1955; 1960; 1970; 1975; 1979; 1982; 1985; 1986; 1989 and 1990. All were bottled at 45% abv (90 proof).

Drinking one of these rare, aged rhums is like sampling a slice of history. The five vintages tasted for this book were 1979, 1982, 1987, 1989 and 1990. While the vintages varied somewhat in character, each was wonderfully aromatic, satiny smooth, and brimming with an array of elegant flavors. Keep an eye out for these sophisticated rhums, they're well worth the search.

GOSLING'S BLACK SEAL® RUM

GOSLING'S BLACK SEAL RUM is the national spirit of Bermuda. This British colony is comprised of a group of islands situated in the Atlantic Ocean, 580 miles east of North Carolina and approximately 1200 miles north of the Caribbean Sea. While technically not from one of the Caribbean islands, Gosling's is a popular and delicious blend of rums made by Caribbean producers, which is good enough for us.

The Bermuda islands were still unpopulated at the turn of the 17th century. It wasn't until 1612 that the British ship *Plough* arrived carrying the islands' first settlers. By the 1620s, Bermuda had a population of around 2,000 people. With the outbreak of the British Civil War, many of the settlers fled Bermuda for the Bahamas and relief from the escalating religious conflict and subsequent persecutions.

Nearly all attempts at agriculture failed in the arid climate and thin soil of the Bermuda islands. Because of their strategic position, however, trade and commerce flourished, which eventually precipitated dramatic increases in the population. Bermuda had quickly become a British stronghold in the New World.

In the spring of 1806, English wine and spirits merchant James Gosling set out from England aboard the clipper *Mercury* with £10,000 of merchandise bound for Virginia. The voyage was a difficult one. Ninety-one consecutive days of calm left the crew and passengers in dire straits. The ship eventually made port in

St. George's, Bermuda, where Gosling and his family decided to set-up shop rather than press on to America.

James Gosling opened a shop on the King's Parade, St. George's in December 1806. In 1824 the enterprise was moved to Front Street in the new capital of Hamilton. By that time, Ambrose Gosling—James' brother—had joined the firm, and in 1857 the name of the business was changed to Gosling Brothers. To this day the company remains the oldest surviving business in Bermuda.

The company imported its first barrels of Caribbean rum into Bermuda in 1860. Numerous different blends were tried until one was formulated and deemed ideal. The result was a well-aged, extremely dark rum, which the firm dubbed "Old Rum."

For over 50 years the rum was sold only by draught, with local patrons bringing in their own bottles to be filled. The rum continued to be sold exclusively out of the barrel until the First World War, when the company began filling champagne bottles reclaimed from British Officer's mess. The corks were secured in place with the use of black sealing wax, prompting people to refer to the brand as "Black Seal." It wasn't until many years later that Gosling Brothers adopted the image of the barrel juggling "black seal" on its labels.

To this day, Gosling's Black Seal Rum is created according to the original family recipe from a premium blend of 3-6 year old rums. It has a dark amber/brown color with prominent red highlights. The color is absolutely intriguing and serves as an enticement for things to come. Its compact bouquet features the aromas of coffee, sugar cane, caramel and toasted oak.

Gosling's Black Seal Rum makes its presence known upon entry. Its palate is a medley of roasted and spicy flavors that completely fill the mouth before slipping away in a warm, lingering finish. The rum is exceptionally well balanced, with an enjoyable dose of bitterness to balance out its inherent sweetness. Black Seal is 40% abv (80 proof).

It is understandable why the brand is the best selling spirit in Bermuda. While a pleasure to drink neat, Gosling's Black Seal Rum is a delight to mix in cocktails. It is at the core of such classics as the Dark'n Stormy® and Rum Swizzle. But there seems to be no creative limits on what can be done with the rum in the hands of a skilled mixologist.

COCKSPUR BARBADIAN RUMS

The brand COCKSPUR BARBADIAN RUM was established in 1884 by a Danish sea captain named Valdemar Hanschell, who moved to the island of Barbados to open a ship's chandlery and liquor store. For its first 90 years, demand for the brand consistently far exceeded supply. Cockspur was released in limited quantities primarily because high quality, unaged rums were difficult for the small company to secure.

Prospects for the brand improved in 1973. A series of business purchases eventually put the Hanschell Inniss blending and bottling facilities near Bridgetown in partnership with famed West Indies Rum Refinery, located just north of the city. Among its many attributes, the distillery sits atop its own coral filtered spring, assuring itself of a consistent supply of pure water.

The West Indies Rum Refinery ferments its molasses for five-days and uses a proprietary, molasses-cultured yeast to precipitate fermentation. The yeast strain is safeguarded under lock and key. The distillery is equipped with both an alembic still and four-column, continuous still, making the West Indies Rum Refinery an ideal source for light-bodied rums, as well as fuller-bodied, pot still spirits.

After distillation, rums of different ages and compositions used to produce the Cockspur blends are casked in used American oak bourbon barrels. The staves are scraped by hand at the distillery to remove the charred wood from the inside of the barrels. The various rums are transferred to Hanschell Inniss for blending and bottling.

There are four versions of Cockspur Barbadian Rum. The COCKSPUR FIVE STAR FINE® RUM is produced in both a gold and white style, the latter being filtered to remove all traces of color. The blend is comprised of light-bodied, continuous distilled rums and heavier, fuller-bodied alembic distilled rums. It has a minimum age of two-years.

The golden version of Cockspur Five Star has a medium body and a soft, subtle bouquet of ripe fruit and brown sugar. The palate is dry and slightly smoky with the flavors of chocolate, toffee and honey. The rum has a finish of moderate-duration. Cockspur Five Star is marketed at 37.5%, 40% and 43% abv.

The mid-range brand is COCKSPUR OLD GOLD RESERVE®. It is a blend of pot still and continuous still rums aged up to five years. The brand has limited distribution and is bottled at 43% abv (86 proof).

COCKSPUR V.S.O.R. (VERY SUPERIOR OLD RESERVE) FINE® RUM is the company's luxury brand, which is an apt description of this rum. The Cockspur V.S.O.R. is comprised of a blend of light-bodied, continuous distilled rums and fuller-bodied, alembic distilled rums that have been aged a minimum of ten years in American oak bourbon barrels. The brand is produced in limited quantities.

Cockspur V.S.O.R. has a deep golden/amber appearance and a prominent greenish tint around the edges derived from extended aging in oak. The bouquet fills the glass with an alluring offering of spice, caramel and honey. The rum has a medium body and satiny texture. On the palate the rum presents an array of warm, toasty flavors that slowly build in intensity before gracefully tapering off into a sublime, slightly citrus finish.

This is a rum that should be enjoyed neat. Keep the ice in the freezer and leave the water in the well. Once you become old friends with the V.S.O.R., then and only then should you use it in drink making.

CONCH REPUBLIC RUMS

The Florida Keys is a chain of small coral and limestone islands or reefs extending about 225 miles southwest from Cape Florida. The principle islands include Key Largo, Islamorada, Matecumbe, and Key West. The Keys are now largely inhabited and have become something of a tourist destination, where for many the highlight of the day is to relax as the sun slowly melts into the Caribbean.

The people who live in the Florida Keys refer to themselves as "Conchs," and have a fierce desire to preserve their way of life. In the spring of 1982, federal agents set-up a roadblock along U.S. Highway 1, which connects Miami with the Keys, ending at Key West. The roadblock was intended to intercept illegal trafficking, but what it did was spark a confrontation between residents of Key West and federal officials.

The following day, April 23, 1982, the Key West City Council passed a resolution proclaiming that Key West and the Florida Keys

were seceding from the United States. Their new nation would from then on be referred to as the Conch Republic. The "Declaration of Independence" was enacted and sent to Washington. Demands were made to remove the roadblock and that a permanent border crossing would be erected.

As if that wasn't enough, the new nation declared war on the United States. To show that they hadn't lost all connection with reality, the officials promptly surrendered and petitioned for foreign aid. Such was the beginning of the Conch Republic.

To celebrate the birth of the new republic, the Old Florida Rum Company released a line of new rums in 1982 named after the Conch Republic. The famed distillery, now owned by Todhunter International, is the oldest distillery in Florida and the last remaining rum distillery in the continental United States. Located at Lake Alfred in the central part of the state, the distillery obtains its high-grade molasses from local sugar mills. The molasses is fermented over three days and then double distilled; once in a single column, continuous still, then again in a large, four column, continuous still.

There are four versions of Conch Republic Rum. ISLAMORADA LIGHT® RUM and MATECUMBE DARK® RUM are made in a similar manner. The two brands are an equal blend of light-bodied, continuous distilled rums produced at the Lake Alfred distillery, and rums distilled at the Cruzan Distillery in St. Croix, U.S. Virgin Islands. All of the rums used in the blend are aged between 2-3 years in charred American oak barrels.

After aging, some of the golden, medium-bodied rum is sent directly to bottling where it becomes Conch Republic Matecumbe Dark. The rum that becomes Islamorada Light is then sent through a series of charcoal filters that render it brilliantly clear.

The marriage of the two countries' rums is a superb match. The vanilla and honey bouquet is slightly sweet, and it makes you think that the rum might be sedate for its age. Worry not. They are energetic spirits that enter the palate and start working. Like other young premium rums, these two are delightfully flavorful and warming. Both the Islamorada Light and Matecumbe Dark are marketed at 40% abv (80 proof).

Introduced in 1996, CONCH REPUBLIC DURDY WHITE® RUM is a 100% Florida rum. All of the rums used in its blend are distilled by the Old Florida Rum Company at the Lake Alfredo distillery. It is a blend of continuous distilled rums and alembic distilled rums that have been aged four to eight years in charred, American oak bourbon barrels. Durdy White is bottled directly from the cask without charcoal filtration and marketed at 40% abv (80 proof).

Despite its name there is nothing white about this rum. Durdy White is actually a tantalizing yellow/gold with a greenish tint around the edges. The pot still rums endow it with the aromas of apples, vanilla and baking spices, while the column still rums keep the bouquet light and balanced. This Conch Republic rum has spirit and backbone with flavors that sizzle on the palate. It's bold, full of character and a treat to drink.

The final member is the CONCH REPUBLIC ATOCHA GOLD SPICED® RUM. The rum was created in 1998 as a collaboration with Mel Fisher, renowned treasure hunter and longtime denizen of the Conch Republic. It was just off the coast of the Florida Keys that Fisher and his team recovered the fabulous treasure from the Spanish galleon Nuestra Senora de Atocha. The ship's hold was strewn with dozens of silver bars, jewels, priceless artifacts and chests of gold coins.

Long a devotee of the Conch Republic rums, Fisher expressed a desire to work with the people at the Old Florida Rum Company in developing a spiced rum. The Atocha Gold is made according to the recipe Mel eventually created, one that naturally includes a liberal dose of 24-karat gold flakes.

The Conch Republic Atocha Spiced Rum is a lively combination of spices with a voluminous bouquet and scintillating palate. The gold flakes floating in the rum are certainly an attention getter.

CADENHEAD'S COLLECTION OF RUMS

In the strictest definition of the word, the rums in CADENHEAD'S COLLECTION are unique, each authentic and never duplicated. These independently bottled rums have gained international celebrity as being among the most exclusive rums in the world.

The firm of William Cadenhead Ltd., Wine and Spirit Merchants, was founded in 1842 in Aberdeen, Scotland. The business originally imported malt whiskies from Scotland and Demerara rum from Guyana. The company advertised extensively on the back of buses, theatre curtains, and concert programs, with the tagline, "By Test the Best."

After the founder, George Duncan, passed away in 1858, the firm passed through the hands of numerous generations of family; beginning with brother-in-law, William Cadenhead, passing down to a nephew, and eventually to the man's sisters, who while well-intentioned, allowed the business to fall into financial straits.

In October 1972, Christie's Auction House in London held the largest sale of wines and spirits to date. It was a huge affair that left William Cadenhead Ltd. with money in the bank and empty warehouses. A short time later the company was bought by one of the legendary whisky-producing families in Scotland, the Mitchells of Campbeltown.

The firm, J & A Mitchell & Co Ltd., owns and operates the famed Springbank Distillery, the oldest family-owned Scotch distillery, and

is one of the last two remaining Campbeltown malt whisky distillers. The Mitchells are sticklers for authenticity. They take no shortcuts and do not yield to market pressures, which is why inevitably some of their whiskies are sold out even before they're released.

Since 1972, William Cadenhead Ltd. has grown again into the world's preeminent independent bottler of single cask Caribbean rums and Scotch whiskies.

What makes Cadenhead's rums unique? The firm seeks out barrels of select rums from smaller, quality distillers in Jamaica,

Barbados and Guyana. The rums are shipped from the Caribbean, where evaporation losses during aging often exceed 8% per year, to the cool, damp climate of Scotland, where losses are less, enabling the rum to remain in the barrel for much longer periods of time.

Cadenhead's produces two types of aged rums. The first are CASK STRENGTH® rums, which are bottled unfiltered, undiluted and unaltered in any way. The cask strength rums range in strength from 70.4% abv (140.8 proof) to 74.1% abv (148.2% proof). They are comparable to dipping the bottle in the cask and putting a cork in it. The second type of Cadenhead's rum is their proprietary brand, GREEN LABEL®, which has been an integral part of the collection since the early 1900s. These rums are similar to the cask strength releases, in as much as they are unfiltered, unaltered and bottled from a single cask. The one point of difference being that the Green Label rums are diluted with pure water to reduce them from cask strength to 46% abv (92 proof).

The Cadenhead's Collection concentrates on the rums of smaller producers from Jamaica, Barbados and Guyana, a tiny country on the northern coast of South America. Demerara rum is distilled in Guyana from sugar cane grown next to the Demerara River. William Cadenhead Ltd. has the most extensive stocks of old, barrel-aged Demerara rums in the world.

The selection of rums in the Cadenhead's portfolio changes frequently. When a cask is emptied, that individual rum is simply no longer available. No two barrels of rum age exactly alike, even when they're resting next to each other in the Campbeltown warehouses. These bottlings are like slices of life never to be repeated.

At the time of this writing, there are nine different Cadenhead's Green Label rums. The portfolio includes: a 12-year old Barbados; a 10-, 22-, 24- and 25-year old Demerara;

a 9-year old Guyanan, and a 10-, 18- and 22-year old Jamaican. Their price tags range from $60 to $150 (US).

The current lineup of single cask rums numbers seven. The release from Barbados was distilled in an alembic still at the Blackrock Distillery. This particular barrel—identified by the letters WIRR—went into bond in 1986 and was bottled at 74.1% abv in 1998.

The two, single cask Demerara rums in the collection were distilled in alembic stills in Port Morant at the Dutch Uitvlugt Distillery. The barrel of 32-year old Demerara rum, 72.1% abv, went into bond in 1964 and was bottled in June 1997.

The Jamaican single casks were distilled in continuous stills at the Long Pond Estate and bottled at four different ages and vintages: 10-years/1987 (73.7% abv); 10-years/1986 (73.6% abv); 20-years/1974 (73% abv) and 22-years (70.4% abv).

The single cask rums are an extravaganza for the senses. They're big, powerful and enormously heady. The key to appreciating their marvelous character without being overpowered by the alcohol is to first add a healthy dose of spring water. It softens the impact of the alcohol and allows the rum's flavors to come to the forefront.

The Cadenhead's single cask rums range in price from $100 to $225 (US). Go ahead and splurge, they're worth it.

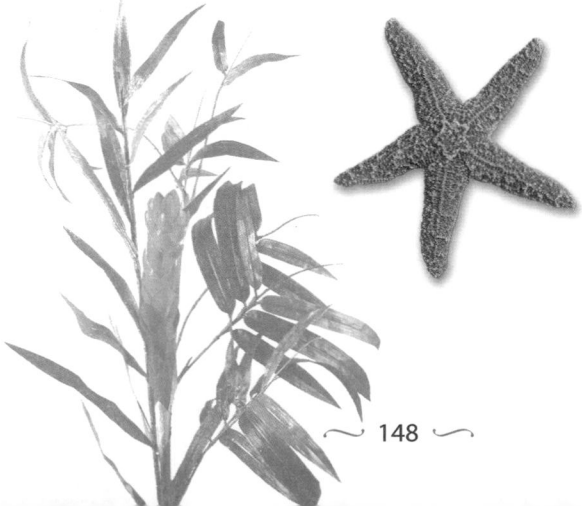

Chapter 14

The Worlds Best Collection of Rum Drink Recipes

Rum is perhaps the most dynamic and distinct spirit in the world. It is made in exotic places, graced with brilliant hues, rich aromas, and captivating flavors. Part of rums immense popularity lies in its diversity. Rums are made in a broad range of styles, from clear, light-bodied, semi-dry to dark, full-bodied and full-flavored.

But the shared attributes that put rum on the map are their mixability and universally popular flavor. Rum is extremely versatile, equaling vodka in that respect. But unlike vodka, rum has an irresistible taste and a savory aroma that lifts it head and shoulders above any other light liquor. In most cocktails, vodka's characteristics go unnoticed, and it adds little flavor to the drink. Rum is nearly always a primary flavor and adds greatly to a drink's ability to captivate.

Equally important, rum is fun and enjoyable. It has a reputation that few other products enjoy. So jump in with both feet and catch a rum state of mind.

There is a misconception that rum is sweet, and therefore not in keeping with contemporary tastes. While it's true that rum is distilled from sugar cane juice or molasses, the finished spirit doesn't taste sweet. The likely reason that people think rum is sweet is that it is frequently mixed with cola or fruit juices.

Thus the reason to master the daiquiri. Not the sweet, syrupy drink that many establishments serve, but rather the classic daiquiri. The daiquiri that was popular in Cuba back in the '20s and '30s, when the island was renowned for having the most capable, professional bartenders in the world. The daiquiri was one of the drinks made famous by Ernest Hemingway. Its popularity received a huge boost when it came out that the daiquiri was President Kennedy's favorite cocktail.

The daiquiri is the quintessential rum libation. It is a perfect balance between sweet and tart, and loaded with flavor. The original daiquiri was made with light rum, sugar and fresh lime juice, shaken and then strained into a chilled cocktail glass. The classic hand-shaken daiquiri is an excellent way to enjoy a wide array of rums.

The daiquiri is also an extremely versatile drink, capable of being modified in a number of different ways. For example, at the legendary La Floridita Hotel in Havana, the signature of the house is the La Floridita Daiquiri, which adds a quarter ounce of Cointreau to the original recipe. The Charles Daiquiri is made with light and dark rum, Cointreau, fresh lime juice, and sugar. The Florida Daiquiri is made with a splash of grapefruit juice, the Pink Daiquiri with a dash of grenadine. Tweak the recipe as you wish. Keep the ingredients to a minimum, maintain a clean taste, and create your own classic daiquiri.

Light rum is traditionally used as the basis for fruit daiquiris because its subtle flavor will not overwhelm the taste of the fresh fruit. On the contrary, using a dark, full-bodied rum such as Bacardi Select or Appleton Estate V/X, in a strawberry daiquiri adds a thoroughly delightful, caramel essence to the drink. Dark rums are also excellent in banana or raspberry daiquiris. Adding spiced rum will lace a fruit daiquiri with flavors of clove, allspice and cinnamon.

Dark rum is also ideal for drizzling on top of a fruit daiquiri. It adds a great flavor and enhances the drink's presentation. Drizzles are especially effective on light-colored, light-flavored drinks, such as banana, pineapple or peach daiquiris.

Swirl daiquiris are another creative way to enjoy different rums. Swirls are frozen drinks prepared simultaneously in different blenders. The concoctions are then layered or swirled together in a house specialty glass. Each component can feature a different type of rum. For instance, one layer could be a raspberry daiquiri made with Mount Gay Eclipse, an aromatic, amber rum from Barbados, and the other a banana daiquiri made with Bacardi Select. Serve with a drizzle of Appleton V/X Jamaican rum over a dollop of whipped cream for a superb summer specialty.

To help get your creative juices flowing, we've assembled 23 delicious variations on the daiquiri. In your enthusiasm to taste the best and brightest daiquiris, don't overlook the original. There's a reason it's the original, after all.

RUM CLASSICS ABOUND

In 1954, Bartender Ramon (Monchito) Marrero created the piña colada at the Caribe Hilton Hotel in San Juan, and ever since it has remained among the most enduring of rum classics. It is a drink filled with possibilities.

While often made with light rum, the piña colada is perfectly suited for full-bodied, full-flavored rums. The character of Bacardi Select, Mount Gay Eclipse, or Appleton Estate V/X provides an excellent counterpoint to the coconut-pineapple flavor in the piña colada. For additional pizzazz, add some Conch Republic Spiced Rum or Cruzan Coconut Rum to your coladas.

Piña coladas also marry beautifully with liqueurs. Among the popular favorites are the Kahlúa Colada, Green Eyes Colada (Midori), Italian Colada (Disaronno Amaretto), and the Toasted Almond Colada (Kahlúa and Amaretto). The Kokomo Joe is a colada made with crème de banana, orange juice, and a banana. Another delicious specialty is the Sea Side Liberty, which features Mount Gay Eclipse, Cruzan Coconut Rum, Kahlúa and a float of Appleton Estate V/X Jamaican Rum.

Specialty coladas derive their flavor in a number of different ways. The Stramaretto Colada uses a blend of fresh strawberries and Disaronno Amaretto. The Monkalada Piña Colada and Holiday Isle Piña Colada are prepared with ice cream. Others are flavored with different blends of fruit juices.

Swirls are a creative possibility with piña coladas. For example, one layer could be made with dark rum and fresh fruit, the other could be prepared with light rum and a liqueur, such as Kahlúa, Midori, or Disaronno Amaretto. Add a float of dark savory rum and a fresh fruit garnish and you've created a swirled colada. The key is for the different colored layers to complement the flavor of the other. One popular swirl is the Pain in the Butt, which is a piña colada and strawberry daiquiri stacked on top of each other in the same glass.

As one would expect of "The World's Best Collection of Rum Drink Recipes," we've included a number of great piña colada recipes, 29 to be exact. That should be enough recipes for you to get the idea.

Another classic rum drink experiencing a popular resurgence is the mojito, a libation born in the heart of Havana at the Bodeguita del Medio. The drink is about as lively and refreshing as any ever concocted. It's made by first muddling fresh lime juice, sugar and mint sprigs inside a glass. Ice, light rum and club soda are then added. Garnish with a lime wedge and you've constructed a mojito.

It is an effervescent drink, so the quality of the rum plays a significant role. The mojito is ideally paired with an upper echelon white rum, something along the lines of Bacardi Carta Blanca, Matusalem Light & Dry, Cruzan Estate Light, or Angostura's Old Oak White. The character of the rum will shine through, so it's advisable not to cut corners.

Rum cocktails are experiencing a popular resurgence. They're sophisticated, elegant and excel at showcasing the quality products used in their recipes. The collection of rum recipes contains some of the finest cocktails ever conceived.

For example, our favorite derivation of the ultra-popular cosmopolitan is the Limón Cosmopolitan, made with the all-too-delicious, citrus-infused Bacardi Limón rum. The Limón Cosmo has more dimension and a more intriguing flavor than the original. The Havana Sidecar is another cocktail that should be sampled at your earliest possible convenience. There are two versions, one features Bacardi 8, the other Matusalem Golden Dry. Both are silky smooth and quite delicious.

The Larchmont is also worth visiting. It is made with añejo rum, Grand Marnier and lime juice. We've included three versions—made with añejos Pyrat Cask 23, Bacardi 8 and Cruzan Single Barrel—primarily because they were so good that no amount of scrutiny could determine which version to feature, so we included all three.

There are seven rum martinis included in our recipe collection. We advise sampling the lot, however, don't miss the Pyrat Martini, made with Pyrat Cask 23 Rum and a healthy splash of Godiva Chocolate Liqueur. Save an occasion for the Havana Martini, which features Bacardi 8 and a dose of tawny port.

Another cocktail of note is the Bacardi Cocktail. The cocktail dates back to 1934 and is made with Bacardi Carta Blanca, sweet 'n' sour and grenadine. Interestingly enough, the New York Supreme Court ruled in 1936 that the cocktail must be made with Bacardi rum or it can't be called a Bacardi Cocktail. Try one with your attorney, it's delicious.

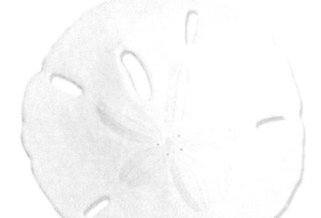

Rum Drink Recipes
From A to Z

A

"The World's Best Collection of Rum Drink Recipes" contains over 400 of the finest rum concoctions known to man and woman alike. Start at the top of the list and let us know what you think.

ACAPULCO
House specialty glass, ice
1 oz. Tequila
1 oz. Bacardi Light Rum
1 oz. grapefruit juice
3 oz. pineapple juice
Shake and strain
Pineapple garnish

ACAPULCO GOLD
Highball glass, ice
Build in glass
3/4 oz. Bacardi Gold Rum
3/4 oz. Peach Schnapps
Fill with orange juice

A DAY AT THE BEACH
House specialty glass, ice
1 oz. Bacardi Light Rum
1 oz. Cruzan Coconut Rum
1/2 oz. Disaronno Amaretto
1/2 oz. grenadine
4 oz. orange juice
Shake and strain
Pineapple and orange garnish

AFTER TAN
House specialty glass, chilled
3/4 oz. Cruzan Coconut Rum
3/4 oz. Cruzan Orange Rum
1/2 oz. Dark Crème de Cacao
2 scoops vanilla ice cream
Blend with ice; pour into glass
Whipped cream garnish
Float 1/2 oz. Crème de Noyaux

ALIEN SECRETION
Bucket glass, ice
1 oz. Malibu Rum
1 oz. Midori
Fill with pineapple juice

ALPINE GLOW
House specialty glass, ice
1 1/2 oz. Bacardi Gold Rum
1 1/2 oz. Brandy
1/2 oz. Triple Sec
1/2 oz. grenadine
2 oz. sweet 'n' sour
Shake and strain
Float 3/4 oz. Gosling's Black Seal Rum
Lemon twist garnish

AMARETTO CRUISE
House specialty glass, chilled
1 1/4 oz. Bacardi Gold Rum
1 oz. Disaronno Amaretto
3/4 oz. Mount Gay Eclipse Rum
1/2 oz. Peach Schnapps
1 oz. sweet 'n' sour
1 oz. half & half cream
2 oz. orange juice
2 oz. cranberry juice
Blend with ice; pour into glass

AMERICAN GRAFFITI
Bucket glass, ice
1 1/4 oz. Bacardi Light Rum
3/4 oz. Mount Gay Eclipse Rum
1/2 oz. Sloe Gin
1/2 oz. Southern Comfort
1/4 oz. Rose's Lime Juice
1 1/2 oz. pineapple juice
1 1/2 oz. sweet 'n' sour
Shake and strain
Orange garnish

ANCIENT MARINER (1)
Brandy snifter, ice
Build in glass
1 1/4 oz. Bacardi 8 Rum
1 oz. Grand Marnier

ANCIENT MARINER (2)
Brandy snifter, ice
Build in glass
1 1/4 oz. Pyrat Cask 23 Rum
1 oz. Grand Marnier

ANDALUSIA
Brandy snifter, pre-heated
Build in glass
1 1/2 oz. Bacardi 8 Rum
1/2 oz. V.S. Cognac
1/2 oz. Dry Sherry
(1-2 dashes Angostura
    Bitters optional)
Lemon twist garnish

APPLE BRANDY COOLER
House specialty glass, ice
1 oz. Bacardi Light Rum
1 oz. Brandy
4 oz. apple juice
Shake and strain
Float 1/2 oz. Cockspur V.S.O.R. Rum
Lime garnish

APPLETON BLAST
House specialty glass, ice
Build in glass
1 1/2 oz. Appleton Estate V/X Rum
1/2 oz. Disaronno Amaretto
1/2 oz. Peach Schnapps
Fill with cranberry juice
Orange garnish

APPLETON BREEZE
House specialty glass, ice
Build in glass
1 1/2 oz. Appleton Special Rum
1/2 oz. Rose's Lime Juice
3 oz. cranberry juice
3 oz. grapefruit juice
Lime garnish

APPLE WORKS
Coffee mug, heated
Build in glass
1 1/4 oz. Bacardi Light Rum
3/4 oz. Mount Gay Extra Old Rum
1/2 oz. Apple Brandy
1/2 fill warm cranberry juice
1/2 fill warm apple cider
Cinnamon stick garnish

ARIANA'S DREAM
House specialty glass, chilled
1 oz. Bacardi Light Rum
1 oz. Alize Passion Red
1 oz. White Crème de Cacao
3 oz. orange juice
Blend with ice; pour into glass
Strawberry and orange garnish

ARTIFICIAL INTELLIGENCE
House specialty glass, ice
3/4 oz. Mount Gay Eclipse Rum
3/4 oz. Bacardi Select Rum
3/4 oz. Appleton Estate V/X Rum
3/4 oz. Cruzan Coconut Rum
1 oz. fresh lime juice
3 oz. pineapple juice
Shake and strain
Float 3/4 oz. Midori
Orange, lime and lemon garnish

BACARDI COCKTAIL
Cocktail glass, chilled
1 1/2 oz. Bacardi Light Rum
2 oz. sweet 'n' sour
3/4 oz. grenadine
Shake and strain

B

BACARDI TROPICO DREAM
House specialty glass, chilled
1 3/4 oz. Bacardi Gold Rum
1 1/4 oz. Tropico
3/4 oz. Disaronno Amaretto
1/2 oz. Rose's Lime Juice
1 1/2 oz. sweet 'n' sour
2 oz. orange juice
Blend with ice
Lime, orange and lemon garnish

BAHAMA MAMA (1)
House specialty glass, ice
1 1/2 oz. Bacardi Light Rum
3 oz. pineapple juice
Shake and strain
Float 1/2 oz. Appleton Estate V/X Rum
Float 1/2 oz. Gosling's Black Seal Rum

BAHAMA MAMA (2)
House specialty glass, ice
1 1/4 oz. Bacardi Light Rum
1/2 oz. Bacardi 151° Rum
1/2 oz. Cruzan Coconut Rum
1/2 oz. Kahlúa
1/2 oz. Rose's Lime Juice
1 1/2 oz. sweet 'n' sour
3 oz. pineapple juice
Shake and strain
Lime, orange and lemon garnish

BAILEY'S MALIBU RUM YUM
Rocks glass, chilled
1 oz. Bailey's Irish Cream
1 oz. Malibu Rum
1 oz. half & half cream
Shake and strain

BANANA COW
House specialty glass, chilled
1 1/2 oz. Angostura Royal Oak
Extra Old Rum
1 oz. Cruzan Banana Rum
1 oz. Cruzan Orange Rum
1/2 oz. grenadine syrup
1/2 oz. half & half cream
2 scoops vanilla ice cream
Blend with ice; pour into glass
Banana slice garnish

BANANA DAIQUIRI
See DAIQUIRI, BANANA

BANANA FRUIT PUNCH
(Makes Two)
House specialty glass, chilled
2 1/2 oz. Bacardi Gold Rum
1 3/4 oz. Mount Gay Eclipse Rum
4-5 slices cored, peeled pineapple
3 ripe bananas
5 oz. orange juice
4 oz. sweet 'n' sour
2 oz. fresh lime juice
1/2 tsp. grated nutmeg
Blend with ice; pour into glasses
Float each with 3/4 oz.
Cockspur V.S.O.R. Rum
Pineapple and cherry garnish

BANANA MILKSHAKE
House specialty glass, chilled
1 1/2 oz. Bacardi Gold Rum
3/4 oz. Gosling's Black Seal Rum
2 ripe bananas
1 oz. honey
1 cup milk
2 scoops vanilla ice cream
Blend with ice; pour into glass
Whipped cream garnish
Drizzle chocolate syrup

BANANA MONKEY
Cocktail glass, chilled
2 oz. Angostura Royal Oak Extra Old Rum
1 oz. Mount Gay Eclipse Rum
1 oz. Crème de Banana
1 oz. fresh lime juice
3/4 oz. grenadine
Shake and strain
Lime garnish

BANANAS BARBADOS
House specialty glass, chilled
1 oz. Mount Gay Eclipse Rum
1 oz. Mount Gay Extra Old Rum
1/2 oz. Crème de Banana
2 oz. sweet 'n' sour
Dash vanilla extract
1 ripe banana
Blend with ice; pour into glass
Float 1 oz. Mount Gay Extra Old Rum

B

BEACH BLONDE
House specialty glass, ice
1 1/2 oz. Bacardi Light Rum
1 oz. Disaronno Amaretto
3/4 oz. grenadine
3/4 oz. Rose's Lime Juice
2 1/2 oz. orange juice
Shake and strain
Float 3/4 oz. Cockspur V.S.O.R. Rum
Fill with Seven-Up

BEACHCOMBER
Cocktail glass, chilled
1 1/4 oz. Bacardi Light Rum
3/4 oz. Mount Gay Eclipse Rum
1/2 oz. Triple Sec
1/2 oz. grenadine
1 oz. sweet 'n' sour
Shake and strain
Lime garnish

BERMUDA TRIANGLE (1)
Bucket glass, ice
Build in glass
1 1/2 oz. Gosling's Black Seal Rum
1 oz. Peach Schnapps
1/2 oz. Meyer
Fill with orange juice
Orange garnish

BERMUDA TRIANGLE (2)
Bucket glass, ice
Build in glass
1 1/2 oz. Gosling's Black Seal Rum
2 oz. cranberry juice
2 oz. orange juice
Orange garnish

BETTY GRABLE
Coffee mug, heated
Build in glass
1 1/4 oz. Bacardi Select Rum
1/2 oz. Disaronno Amaretto
1/2 oz. Chambord
Fill with hot apple cider
Cinnamon stick swizzle
Whipped cream garnish

BIG BACARDI BAMBOO
House specialty glass, ice
1 oz. Bacardi Gold Rum
1 oz. Bacardi 151° Rum
3/4 oz. Chambord
1 oz. pineapple juice
1 oz. orange juice
1 oz. fresh lime juice
Shake and strain
Float 3/4 oz. Grand Marnier
Orange garnish

BIG BLUE SHOOTER
Rocks glass, chilled
1 1/4 oz. Pyrat Pistol Rum
1 oz. Malibu Rum
3/4 oz. Captain Morgan Spiced Rum
3/4 oz. Blue Curaçao
3 oz. pineapple juice
Shake and strain
Lime garnish

BIG CHILL
House specialty glass, chilled
1 1/2 oz. Bacardi Select Rum
1 oz. Cruzan Coconut Rum
3/4 oz. Rose's Lime Juice
1 oz. pineapple juice
1 1/2 oz. cranberry juice
1 1/2 oz. orange juice
Blend with ice; pour into glass
Float 3/4 oz. J. Bally Rhum
    Vieux 7-Year
Pineapple and cherry garnish

BLACKBEARD'S TREASURE
House specialty glass, chilled
1 1/2 oz. Captain Morgan Spiced Rum
1 oz. Mount Gay Eclipse Rum
1 oz. Chambord
2 oz. raspberry puree
2 oz. sweet 'n' sour
Blend with ice; pour into glass
Pineapple and cherry garnish

BLACK JAMAICAN
Rocks glass, ice
Build in glass
1 1/2 oz. Appleton Estate V/X Rum
1/2 oz. Tia Maria

BLACK MARIA
Coffee mug, heated
Build in glass
  1 1/2 oz. Bacardi Select Rum
  1 1/2 oz. Tia Maria
  3/4 oz. Dark Crème de Cacao
  4 oz. hot coffee
  Whipped cream garnish

BLACK MASS
Presentation shot glass, chilled
Layer in glass
  1/3 fill XO Café Coffee Liqueur
  1/3 fill Sambuca
  1/3 fill Matusalem Classic Black Rum

BLACK ORCHID
Bucket glass, ice
  1 oz. Bacardi Select Rum
  1 oz. Blue Curaçao
  1 1/2 oz. grenadine
  1 1/2 oz. cranberry juice
Shake and strain
  Float 3/4 oz. Gosling's Black Seal Rum
Orange garnish

BLAST-OFF PUNCH
House specialty glass, ice
  3/4 oz. Bacardi Light Rum
  3/4 oz. Bacardi Gold Rum
  3/4 oz. Blue Curaçao
  1/2 oz. Cruzan Orange Rum
  1 1/2 oz. sweet 'n' sour
  1 1/2 oz. orange juice
Shake and strain
Float 3/4 oz. Mount Gay Extra Old Rum
Lime, orange and lemon garnish

BLIZZARD
House specialty glass, chilled
  1 1/4 oz. Matusalem Classic Black Rum
  3/4 oz. Brandy
  3/4 oz. Cruzan Rum Cream
  3/4 oz. half & half cream
  2 scoops chocolate ice cream
  Blend with ice; pour into glass
  Float 3/4 oz. XO Café Coffee Liqueur
  Whipped cream and nutmeg garnish

BLOODY WRIGHT
Bucket glass, ice
(Salted rim optional)
Build in glass
  1 1/2 oz. Cruzan Estate Light Rum
Fill with Bloody Mary mix
Lime and celery garnish

BLUE BAYOU
House specialty glass, chilled
  1 1/2 oz. Bacardi Light Rum
  1 oz. Blue Curaçao
  3/4 oz. half & half cream
  2 scoops French vanilla ice cream
Blend with ice; pour into glass
Orange and cherry garnish

BLUE HAWAII
House specialty glass, chilled
  1 1/2 oz. Cruzan Estate Light Rum
  1 oz. Blue Curaçao
  3/4 oz. White Crème de Cacao
  3/4 oz. half & half cream
  2 scoops vanilla ice cream
Blend with ice; pour into glass
Orange and cherry garnish

BLUE HAWAIIAN
Collins glass, ice
  1 1/2 oz. Bacardi Light Rum
  1 oz. Mount Gay Eclipse Rum
  1 oz. Blue Curaçao
  1 1/2 oz. sweet 'n' sour
  1 1/2 oz. pineapple juice
  1 1/2 oz. coconut syrup
Shake and strain
Orange and pineapple garnish

BLUE LAGOON
Bucket glass, ice
Build in glass
  1 1/2 oz. Cruzan Coconut Rum
  3/4 oz. Cruzan Pineapple Rum
  Fill with pineapple juice
  Float 3/4 oz. Blue Curaçao

BLUE MARLIN
Cocktail glass, chilled
1 1/2 oz. Appleton Estate V/X Rum
1 1/4 oz. Mount Gay Eclipse Rum
3/4 oz. Blue Curaçao
1/2 oz. Citrónge Orange Liqueur
1 oz. fresh lime juice
Shake and strain
Lime garnish

BOG FOG
Highball glass, ice
Build in glass
1 1/4 oz. Bacardi Light Rum
1/2 fill cranberry juice
1/2 fill orange juice

BOINA ROJA
House specialty glass, ice
1 1/2 oz. Bacardi Light Rum
3/4 oz. Bacardi Gold Rum
1/2 oz. grenadine
1 oz. fresh lime juice
1 1/2 oz. sweet 'n' sour
Shake and strain
Mint sprig and cherry garnish

BORINQUEN
House specialty glass, chilled
1 1/2 oz. Cruzan Estate Light Rum
1 oz. Rhum Barbancourt 5-Star
3/4 oz. Rose's Lime Juice
2 oz. orange juice
2 oz. passion fruit syrup
2 oz. fresh lime juice
Blend with ice; pour into glass
Float 3/4 oz. Matusalem
    Red Flame Rum
Pineapple and cherry garnish

BOSSA NOVA
House specialty glass, ice
2 oz. Bacardi Limón Rum
1 1/2 oz. fresh lime juice
2 oz. sweet 'n' sour
2 oz. passion fruit juice
Shake and strain
Float 1 oz. Bacardi Select Rum
Orange and lime garnish

BURGUNDY BISHOP
Bucket glass, ice
Build in glass
1 1/2 oz. Bacardi Light Rum
2 oz. sweet 'n' sour
3 oz. Dry Red Wine
Shake and strain
Orange, lime and lemon garnish

BUSH TICKLER
House specialty glass, chilled
1 1/2 oz. Bacardi Select Rum
1 oz. Mount Gay Eclipse
3/4 oz. Dark Crème de Cacao
1/2 oz. half & half cream
2 oz. coconut syrup
3 oz. pineapple juice
Blend with ice; pour into glass
Float 3/4 oz. Kahlúa
Pineapple garnish

BUSHWACKER
House specialty glass, chilled
1 1/4 oz. Bacardi Light Rum
1 oz. Gosling's Black Seal Rum
3/4 oz. half & half Cream
2 1/2 oz. coconut cream syrup
Blend with ice; pour into glass
Float 3/4 oz. Kahlúa
Pineapple garnish

CAFÉ FOSTER
Coffee mug, heated
Build in glass
1 1/2 oz. Bacardi Select Rum
3/4 oz. Godiva Chocolate Liqueur
3/4 oz. Crème de Banana
Fill with hot coffee
Whipped cream garnish

CAFÉ KINGSTON
Coffee mug, heated
Build in glass
1/2 oz. Appleton Estate V/X Rum
1/2 oz. Angostura Caribbean
    Rum Cream
1/2 oz. Tia Maria
1/2 oz. Hershey's chocolate syrup
Fill with hot coffee
Whipped cream garnish
Sprinkle shaved chocolate

C

CAFÉ REGGAE
Coffee mug, heated
Build in glass
3/4 oz. Bacardi Gold Rum
1/2 oz. Tia Maria
1/2 oz. Dark Crème de Cacao
Fill with hot coffee
Whipped cream garnish
Drizzle 3/4 oz. Pusser's British Navy Rum

CAIPIRISSMA
Rocks or old fashion glass
Build in glass
4 large lime wedges
3/4 oz. simple syrup
Muddle contents
2 1/2 oz. Bacardi Light Rum
Add crushed ice
Lime garnish

CALYPSO COFFEE
a.k.a. SPANISH COFFEE
Coffee mug, heated
Build in glass
1 oz. Bacardi Light Rum
1 oz. Tia Maria
Fill with hot coffee
Whipped cream garnish
Sprinkle shaved chocolate

CALYPSO HIGHWAY
House specialty glass, ice
1 oz. Bacardi Select Rum
1 oz. Crème de Banana
3/4 oz. Blue Curaçao
2 dashes vanilla extract
1 oz. coconut syrup
2 oz. pineapple juice
2 oz. orange juice
Shake and strain
Float 1/2 oz. Bacardi 151° Rum
Pineapple and cherry garnish

CANNONBALL
Bucket glass, ice
Build in glass
2 oz. Pusser's British Navy Rum
1/2 oz. Rose's Lime Juice
1 oz. cranberry juice
1 oz. pineapple juice
1 oz. orange juice
Lime garnish

CAPPA 21
Cappuccino cup, heated
Build in glass
1 1/2 oz. Bacardi Select Rum
1/2 oz. Tia Maria
1/2 oz. Brandy
Square of Ghirardelli chocolate
3/4 fill with hot espresso coffee
Spoon on frothed milk
Shaved chocolate garnish

CAPTAIN'S COFFEE
Coffee mug, heated
Build in glass
1 1/2 oz. Pusser's British Navy Rum
1 oz. XO Café Coffee Liqueur
Fill with hot coffee
Whipped cream garnish optional
Drizzle 1/2 oz. XO Café Coffee Liqueur

CARIBBEAN BERRY
House specialty glass, chilled
3/4 oz. Bacardi Gold Rum
3/4 oz. Disaronno Amaretto
1/2 oz. Crème de Banana
1/2 cup strawberries
1 1/2 oz. sweet 'n' sour
Blend with ice; pour into glass
Float 3/4 oz. Gosling's Black Seal Rum
Strawberry and banana garnish

CARIBBEAN CHAMPAGNE
Champagne glass, chilled
Build in glass
3/4 oz. Bacardi Light Rum
3/4 oz. Crème de Banana
Fill with Champagne
Banana and cherry garnish

CARIBBEAN CRUISE (1)
House specialty glass, ice
1 1/2 oz. Bacardi Select Rum
3/4 oz. Gran Gala Triple Orange Liqueur
1 1/2 oz. sweet 'n' sour
1 1/2 oz. orange juice
Shake and strain
Float 3/4 oz. Angostura Royal Oak
Extra Old Rum
Orange garnish

C

CARIBBEAN CRUISE (2)
House specialty glass, chilled
1 oz. Appleton Estate V/X Rum
1 oz. Mount Gay Eclipse Rum
3/4 oz. Kahlúa
1/2 oz. half & half cream
2 oz. coconut syrup
3 oz. pineapple juice
Blend with ice; pour into glass
Float 3/4 oz. Cockspur V.S.O.R. Rum
Pineapple and cherry garnish

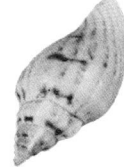

CARIBBEAN DREAM
Coffee mug, heated
Build in glass
1 oz. Mount Gay Eclipse Rum
1/2 oz. Myers's Jamaican Rum
1/2 oz. Crème de Banana
1/2 oz. White Crème de Cacao
Fill with hot coffee
Whipped cream garnish

CARIBBEAN GRIDLOCK
House specialty glass, chilled
3/4 oz. Appleton Estate V/X Rum
3/4 oz. Bacardi Light Rum
3/4 oz. Mount Gay Eclipse Rum
3/4 oz. Rose's Lime Juice
2 oz. sweet 'n' sour
2 oz. orange juice
Blend with ice; pour into glass
Float 3/4 oz. Gosling's Black Seal Rum
Orange, lime and lemon garnish

CARIBBEAN ROMANCE
House specialty glass, ice
1 1/2 oz. Bacardi Light Rum
1 oz. Disaronno Amaretto
1 1/2 oz. orange juice
1 1/2 oz. pineapple juice
1/2 oz. grenadine
Shake and strain
Float 3/4 oz. Mount Gay Extra Old Rum
Orange, lime and lemon garnish

CARIBE SURFSIDER
House specialty glass, chilled
3/4 oz. Bacardi Light Rum
3/4 oz. Bacardi Gold Rum
1/2 oz. Crème de Banana
1/2 oz. Blackberry Brandy
3/4 oz. grenadine
3/4 oz. fresh lime juice
1/2 cup strawberries
2 oz. sweet 'n' sour
Blend with ice; pour into glass
Pineapple and strawberry garnish

CECIL'S DREAM
House specialty glass, chilled
1 oz. Bacardi Light Rum
1/2 oz. Disaronno Amaretto
1/2 oz. White Crème de Cacao
1/2 oz. simple syrup
3 oz. pineapple juice
Blend with ice; pour into glass
Float 3/4 oz. Dillon Dark Rhum
Pineapple garnish

CHOCOLATE COVERED BANANA
House specialty glass, chilled
1 1/2 oz. Appleton Estate V/X Rum
1 1/2 oz. Godiva Liqueur
2 ripe bananas
1/2 oz. half & half cream
2 scoops vanilla ice cream
Blend with ice; pour into glass
Float 3/4 oz. St. James Extra Old Rhum
Whipped cream garnish
Sprinkle shaved chocolate

CITY TAVERN COOLER
Bucket glass, ice
Build in glass
1 1/2 oz. Appleton Estate V/X Rum
1 oz. Bourbon Whiskey
3/4 oz. Peach Schnapps
4 oz. fresh apple cider
Apple garnish

COCOMACOQUE
House specialty glass, ice
1 1/2 oz. Bacardi Gold Rum
1 1/2 oz. Red Wine
1 1/2 oz. sweet 'n' sour
1 1/2 oz. pineapple juice
1 1/2 oz. orange juice
Shake and strain
Float 3/4 oz. Cockspur V.S.O.R. Rum
Pineapple garnish

COCOMOTION
House specialty glass, chilled
1 1/2 oz. Mount Gay Eclipse Rum
1 oz. Bacardi Gold Rum
3/4 oz. Tia Maria
1 oz. fresh lime juice
2 oz. coconut syrup
3 oz. pineapple juice
Blend with ice; pour into glass
Float 3/4 oz. Dillon Dark Rhum
Pineapple garnish

COCONUT BREEZE
House specialty glass, ice
1 1/4 oz. Bacardi Light Rum
1 oz. Cruzan Coconut Rum
1/2 oz. simple syrup
1 oz. fresh lime juice
2 oz. mango juice
2 oz. pineapple juice
Shake and strain
Fill with Seven-Up
Lime garnish

COOL CARLOS
House specialty glass, ice
1 1/2 oz. Matusalem Classic Black Rum
1 oz. Orange Curaçao
1 1/2 oz. sweet 'n' sour
2 oz. cranberry juice
2 oz. pineapple juice
Shake and strain
Float 3/4 oz. St. James Extra Old Rhum
Pineapple and orange garnish

CORK STREET COFFEE
Coffee mug, heated
Build in glass
1 1/2 oz. Bacardi Gold Rum
1/2 oz. Cruzan Rum Cream
1/2 oz. Frangelico
Fill with hot coffee
Whipped cream garnish
Drizzle 1/2 oz. chocolate syrup

COVE COOLER
Bucket glass, ice
Build in glass
1 1/4 oz. Pusser's British Navy Rum
1 1/2 oz. sweet 'n' sour
1 1/2 oz. pineapple juice
Splash club soda
Orange garnish

CREOLE
Old fashion glass, ice
1 1/2 oz. Bacardi Light Rum
2 dashes Tabasco Sauce
1 tsp. lemon juice
1 1/2 oz. beef bouillon
Salt and pepper to taste
Shake and strain
Lemon garnish

CRUZAN GLIDE SLIDE
Bucket glass, ice
Build in glass
1 1/2 oz. Cruzan Coconut Rum
3/4 oz. Kahlúa
3/4 oz. Baileys Irish Cream
2 oz. milk
2 oz. pineapple juice
Float 3/4 oz. Matusalem Classic Black Rum

CUBAN COCKTAIL
Cocktail glass, chilled
2 oz. Matusalem Light Dry Rum
2 oz. sweetened lime juice
Shake and strain
Lime garnish

CUBAN PEACH
Cocktail glass, chilled
1 1/2 oz. Matusalem Light Dry Rum
1 oz. Peach Schnapps
1/2 oz. Rose's Lime Juice
Dash simple syrup
Shake and strain
Mint sprig garnish

CUBAN SIDE CAR
Cocktail glass, chilled
1 1/2 oz. Matusalem Light Dry Rum
1 oz. Triple Sec
1 oz. fresh lime juice
Shake and strain
Lime garnish

CUBAN SPECIAL
Cocktail glass, chilled
1 1/2 oz. Matusalem Light Dry Rum
1/2 oz. Triple Sec
1/2 oz. fresh lime juice
3/4 oz. pineapple juice
Shake and strain
Lime garnish

CURAÇAO COOLER
House specialty glass, ice
1 1/2 oz. Mount Gay Eclipse Rum
1 1/4 oz. Blue Curaçao
3/4 oz. Citrónge Orange Liqueur
1 oz. fresh lime juice
1 1/2 oz. orange juice
1 1/2 oz. sweet 'n' sour
Shake and strain
Fill with club soda
Float 3/4 oz. St. James Extra Old Rhum
Lime garnish

DAIQUIRI
House specialty glass, ice
1 1/4 oz. Light Rum
1/2 oz. Rose's Lime Juice
2 oz. sweet 'n' sour
Shake and strain
Lime garnish

DAIQUIRI, BANANA
House specialty glass, chilled
1 1/4 oz. Light Rum
(1 oz. Cruzan Banana Rum optional)
Peeled ripe banana
1/2 oz. Rose's Lime Juice
2 oz. sweet 'n' sour
Blend with ice; pour into glass
Orange and banana slice garnish

DAIQUIRI, BERRY
House specialty glass, chilled
1 1/4 oz. Bacardi Light Rum
1/2 cup raspberries or strawberries
1/2 oz. Rose's Lime Juice
2 oz. sweet 'n' sour
Blend with ice; pour into glass
Float 3/4 oz. Chambord
Pineapple and cherry garnish

DAIQUIRI, CALYPSO
House specialty glass, chilled
1 1/2 oz. Appleton Estate V/X Rum
1 ripe banana
1 tsp. vanilla extract
1/2 oz. half & half cream
2 1/2 oz. sweet 'n' sour
Blend with ice; pour into glass
Float 3/4 oz. Rhum Barbancourt 3-Star Rum
Pineapple and cherry garnish

DAIQUIRI, CHARLES
Cocktail glass, chilled
1 1/2 oz. Bacardi Light Rum
3/4 oz. Angostura Royal Oak
    Extra Old Rum
3/4 oz. Cointreau
1/2 oz. Rose's Lime Juice
1 1/2 oz. sweet 'n' sour
Shake and strain
Lime garnish

DAIQUIRI, COCONUT
Cocktail glass, chilled
1 1/2 oz. Bacardi Light Rum
1 oz. Cruzan Coconut Rum
3/4 oz. coconut cream
1/2 oz. Rose's Lime Juice
1 1/2 oz. sweet 'n' sour
Shake and strain
Lime garnish

D

DAIQUIRI, DEMERARA
House specialty glass, chilled
1 1/4 oz. Cadenhead's
    Green Label Demerara
1/2 oz. Rose's Lime Juice
2 oz. sweet 'n' sour
Shake and strain
Orange garnish

DAIQUIRI de PIÑA (PINEAPPLE)
Cocktail glass, chilled
1 1/2 oz. Bacardi Light Rum
(1 oz. Cruzan Pineapple Rum optional)
2-3 slices cored and peeled pineapple
1/2 oz. Rose's Lime Juice
2 oz. sweet 'n' sour
Blend with ice; pour into glass
Orange, pineapple and cherry garnish

DAIQUIRI, DERBY
Cocktail glass, chilled
1 1/2 oz. Bacardi Select Rum
1/2 oz. Rose's Lime Juice
1 oz. orange juice
1 1/2 oz. sweet 'n' sour
Blend with ice; pour into glass
Float 3/4 oz. Pyrat Pistol Rum
Pineapple and cherry garnish

DAIQUIRI, DON ROLAND
Cocktail glass, chilled
1 1/2 oz. Bacardi Light Rum
1/2 oz. Green Crème de Menthe
1/2 oz. Cointreau
2 fresh mint leaves
1/2 oz. Rose's Lime Juice
1 1/2 oz. sweet 'n' sour
Shake and strain
Garnish with mint sprigs

DAIQUIRI, FLIGHT OF FANCY
House specialty glass, chilled
2 oz. Gosling's Black Seal Rum
1/2 oz. Rose's Lime Juice
1/2 cup raspberries
3 oz. sweet 'n' sour
Blend with ice; pour into glass

DAIQUIRI, FLORIDA
Cocktail glass, chilled
1 1/2 oz. Bacardi Light Rum
1/4 oz. grenadine
1/2 oz. Rose's Lime Juice
1/2 oz. grapefruit juice
1 1/2 oz. sweet 'n' sour
Shake and strain
Lime garnish

DAIQUIRI, FRENCH (1)
Cocktail glass, chilled
1 3/4 oz. St. James Extra Old Rhum
3/4 oz. crème de cassis
1/2 oz. Rose's Lime Juice
2 oz. sweet 'n' sour
Shake and strain
Orange twist garnish

DAIQUIRI, FRENCH (2)
Cocktail glass, chilled
1 3/4 oz. J. Bally Rhum Vieux 7-Year
1/2 oz. Rose's Lime Juice
1 oz. passion fruit juice
2 oz. sweet 'n' sour
Shake and strain
Orange twist garnish

DAIQUIRI, FRUIT (BASIC)
House specialty glass, chilled
1 1/2 oz. Bacardi Light Rum
1/2 cup requested fruit
1/2 oz. Rose's Lime Juice
1 1/2 oz. sweet 'n' sour
Blend with ice; pour into glass
Garnish with appropriate fruit choice

DAIQUIRI, LA FLORIDITA
Cocktail glass, chilled
1 1/2 oz. Bacardi Light Rum
3/4 oz. Cointreau
3/4 oz. fresh lime juice
2 oz. sweet 'n' sour
Shake and strain
Lime garnish

D

DAIQUIRI, LECHTHALER'S
Cocktail glass, chilled
1 oz. Bacardi Light Rum
1 oz. Bacardi Gold Rum
1/2 oz. Rose's Lime Juice
2 oz. sweet 'n' sour
Shake and strain
Lime and orange garnish

DAIQUIRI, MULATA
Cocktail glass, chilled
1 oz. Appleton Estate V/X Rum
1 oz. Mount Gay Eclipse Rum
3/4 oz. Dark Crème de Cacao
3/4 oz. Maraschino Liqueur
1/2 oz. Rose's Lime Juice
2 oz. sweet 'n' sour
Shake and strain
Lime garnish

DAIQUIRI, PAPA HEMINGWAY
Cocktail glass, chilled
1 1/2 oz. Bacardi Light Rum
1/2 oz. Maraschino Liqueur
1 oz. fresh lime juice
1 1/2 oz. grapefruit juice
Shake and strain
Lime garnish

DAIQUIRI, PASSION
Cocktail glass, chilled
1 1/2 oz. Bacardi Light Rum
1/2 oz. Rose's Lime Juice
1 1/2 oz. passion fruit juice
1 1/2 oz. sweet 'n' sour
Shake and strain
Orange twist garnish

DAIQUIRI, PRICKLY PEAR
House specialty glass, chilled
2 oz. Bacardi Limón Rum
1/2 oz. grenadine
1 oz. sweetened lime juice
1 oz. sweet 'n' sour
2 oz. prickly pear syrup (puree)
Shake and strain
Lime garnish

DAIQUIRI, PYRAT
Cocktail glass, chilled
1 3/4 oz. Pyrat XO Reserve Rum
1 oz. orange juice
1 1/4 oz. sweetened lime juice
Shake and strain
Orange twist garnish

DAIQUIRI, RHUM
Cocktail glass, chilled
1 1/2 oz. Rhum Barbancourt 5-Star Rum
3/4 oz. Chambord
3/4 oz. Crème de Banana
2 oz. sweetened lime juice
Shake and strain
Lime and orange garnish

DAIQUIRI, SUMMER SKY
Cocktail glass, chilled
1 3/4 oz. Mount Gay Eclipse Rum
1 1/2 oz. orange juice
1 1/2 oz. sweetened lime juice
Shake and strain
Orange twist garnish

DARK'n STORMY®
House specialty glass, ice
Build in glass
1 3/4 oz. Gosling's Black Seal Rum
Fill with ginger beer
Lime garnish

DEEP SEA DIVER
House specialty glass, ice
1 1/4 oz. Bacardi Gold Rum
3/4 oz. Mount Gay Eclipse Rum
3/4 oz. Citrónge Orange Liqueur
1/2 oz. Rose's Lime Juice
2 oz. sweet 'n' sour
Shake and strain
Float 3/4 oz. Bacardi Select Rum
Orange, lime and lemon garnish

DELICIAS DE LA HABANA
House specialty glass, chilled
1 1/4 oz. Matusalem Light Dry Rum
1 1/4 oz. Matusalem Golden Dry Rum
1 oz. Midori
3/4 oz. Blue Curaçao
1 oz. coconut cream
1 oz. pineapple juice
2 oz. peach nectar
Blend with ice; pour into glass
Pineapple and peach garnish

DHARAMA RUM
House specialty glass, chilled
1 1/2 oz. Appleton Estate V/X Rum
3/4 oz. Dark Crème de Cacao
3/4 oz. Crème de Banana
Peeled, ripe banana
2 scoops vanilla ice cream
Blend with ice; pour into glass
Pineapple and banana garnish

DINGO
House specialty glass, ice
1 1/2 oz. Bacardi Light Rum
3/4 oz. Disaronno Amaretto
1/2 oz. Southern Comfort
3/4 oz. grenadine
2 oz. sweet 'n' sour
2 oz. orange juice
Shake and strain
Float 3/4 oz. Gosling's Black Seal Rum
Orange garnish

DOWN UNDER SNOWBALL
House specialty glass, chilled
1 1/2 oz. Bacardi Light Rum
3/4 oz. Peach Schnapps
1 oz. grenadine
4 oz. orange juice
Blend with ice; pour into glass
Orange garnish

DRUNKEN MONKEY
House specialty glass, ice
3/4 oz. Appleton Estate V/X Rum
3/4 oz. Mount Gay Eclipse Rum
3/4 oz. Cruzan Coconut Rum
3/4 oz. Midori
3/4 oz. Crème de Banana
1 1/2 oz. orange juice
1 1/2 oz. pineapple juice
Shake and strain
Float 3/4 oz. St. James Extra Old Rhum
Orange, lime and lemon garnish

DUKE OF EARL
Coffee mug, heated
Build in glass
1 1/4 oz. XO Café Coffee Liqueur
3/4 oz. Bacardi Select Rum
1/2 oz. Disaronno Amaretto
1/2 fill with hot coffee
1/2 fill with frothed milk
Sprinkle shaved chocolate

ED SULLIVAN
House specialty glass, chilled
1 1/4 oz. Bacardi Light Rum
3/4 oz. Disaronno Amaretto
1/3 cup strawberries
1/2 oz. half & half cream
Blend with ice; pour into glass
Fill with Champagne
Strawberry garnish

EL PRESIDENTÉ COCKTAIL (1)
Cocktail glass, chilled
1 1/2 oz. Light Rum
1/2 oz. Martini & Rossi Extra Dry Vermouth
1/2 oz. Martini & Rossi Rosso Vermouth
1/2 oz. Cointreau
1/4 oz. grenadine
1/4 oz. freshly squeezed lemon juice
Stir and strain
Lime garnish

EL PRESIDENTÉ COCKTAIL (2)
Cocktail glass, chilled
1 1/2 oz. Bacardi Light Rum
1/4 oz. fresh lime juice
1/4 oz. pineapple juice
1/4 oz. grenadine
Shake and strain
Lime garnish

EL PRESIDENTÉ COCKTAIL (3)

Cocktail glass, chilled
1/2 oz. Martini & Rossi
    Extra Dry Vermouth
2 dashes Angostura Bitters
3/4 oz. Mount Gay Eclipse Rum
2 1/4 oz. Bacardi Light Rum
Stir and strain
Lime garnish

FIRECRACKER

Bucket glass, ice
Build in glass
1 1/2 oz. Captain Morgan Spiced Rum
1/2 oz. grenadine
Fill with orange juice
Float 1/2 oz. Bacardi 151° Rum

FLAMINGO (1)

Bucket glass, ice
Build in glass
1 1/2 oz. Captain Morgan Spiced Rum
3/4 oz. grenadine
1/2 fill orange juice
1/2 fill lemonade
  Float 3/4 oz. Gosling's Black Seal Rum
  Lemon garnish

FLAMINGO (2)

House specialty glass, ice
1 1/2 oz. Bacardi Select Rum
1/2 oz. grenadine
2 oz. sweetened lime juice
2 oz. pineapple juice
Shake and strain
Float 3/4 oz. Pusser's British Navy Rum
Lime garnish

FLORIDA T-BACK

Bucket glass, ice
1 oz. Appleton Estate V/X Rum
1 oz. Mount Gay Eclipse Rum
1 oz. Cruzan Coconut Rum
1/2 oz. grenadine
1/2 oz. Rose's Lime Juice
1 1/2 oz. pineapple juice
1 1/2 oz. orange juice
Shake and strain
Pineapple and cherry garnish

FOGCUTTER

House specialty glass, ice
1/2 oz. Brandy
1/2 oz. Light Rum
1/2 oz. Gin
1 1/2 oz. orange juice
1 1/2 oz. sweet 'n' sour
Shake and strain
Float 1/2 oz. Dry Sherry
Lemon garnish

FOGCUTTER, ROYAL NAVY

House specialty glass, ice
1 1/2 oz. Pusser's British Navy Rum
1/2 oz. Brandy
1/2 oz. Gin
1/2 oz. orgeat syrup
1 oz. orange juice
1 oz. sweet 'n' sour
Shake and strain
Float 1/2 oz. Dry Sherry
Lemon garnish

FRAPPÉ, BANANA RUM

Cocktail or champagne saucer, chilled
Fill with crushed ice
Build in glass
1 1/4 oz. Bacardi Light Rum
3/4 oz. Crème de Banana
1/2 oz. orange juice
Short straw

FRAPPÉ, MULATTA

Cocktail or champagne saucer, chilled
Fill with crushed ice
Build in glass
1 1/4 oz. Bacardi Gold Rum
3/4 oz. Dark Crème de Cacao
1/4 oz. Rose's Lime Juice
1/4 oz. fresh lime juice
Lime garnish

FRAPPÉ, TRICONTINENTAL

Cocktail or champagne saucer, chilled
Fill with crushed ice
Build in glass
1 1/2 oz. Bacardi Gold Rum
1/2 oz. grenadine
1/2 oz. Dark Crème de Cacao
Short straw

FRUIT STRIPE
House specialty glass, chilled
Blend first layer with ice
1 oz. Bacardi Light Rum
1/2 cup fresh strawberries
2 oz. sweet 'n' sour
Blend second layer with ice
1 oz. Bacardi Light Rum
2 oz. coconut syrup
3 oz. pineapple juice
Combine both layers
　　in sequence into glass
Float 3/4 oz. Cockspur V.S.O.R. Rum
Whipped cream garnish

FUNKY MONKEY
House specialty glass, ice
1 1/4 oz. Bacardi Light Rum
1 oz. Cruzan Coconut Rum
3/4 oz. Cruzan Banana Rum
3/4 oz. apple grape juice concentrate
2 oz. pineapple juice
Shake and strain
Pineapple garnish

GANGBUSTER
House specialty glass, ice
1 1/2 oz. Bacardi Light Rum
1 oz. Mount Gay Eclipse Rum
1 1/2 oz. guava nectar
1 1/2 oz. pineapple juice
1 1/2 oz. sweet 'n' sour
Shake and strain
Float 1/2 oz. Bacardi Select Rum
Float 1/2 oz. Bacardi 151° Rum
Orange, lime and lemon garnish

GANG GREEN
House specialty glass, ice
1 1/2 oz. Bacardi Light Rum
1 oz. Midori
1/2 oz. Captain Morgan Spiced Rum
3/4 oz. Blue Curaçao
2 oz. orange juice
2 oz. sweet 'n' sour
Shake and strain
Pineapple garnish

GAUGUIN
House specialty glass, chilled
2 oz. Bacardi Limón Rum
1 oz. passion fruit syrup
1 1/2 oz. sweet 'n' sour
1 1/2 oz. sweetened lime juice
Blend with ice; pour into glass
Lemon, orange and lime garnish

GOOM BAY SMASH (1)
House specialty glass, chilled
1 1/4 oz. Bacardi Gold Rum
1 1/4 oz. Malibu Rum
3/4 oz. Crème de Banana
2 oz. pineapple juice
2 oz. orange juice
Blend with ice; pour into glass
Banana garnish

GOOM BAY SMASH (2)
House specialty glass, chilled
1 1/4 oz. Gosling's Black Seal Rum
1 1/4 oz. Cruzan Coconut Rum
3/4 oz. Crème de Banana
2 oz. pineapple juice
2 oz. orange juice
Blend with ice; pour into glass
Banana garnish

GORILLA MILK
House specialty glass, chilled
1 oz. Bacardi Light Rum
3/4 oz. Kahlúa
3/4 oz. Bailey's Irish Cream
3/4 oz. Crème de Banana
1 oz. half & half cream
1 scoop vanilla ice cream
Blend with ice; pour into glass
Pineapple and banana garnish

GREEN REEF
Bucket glass, ice
Build in glass
3/4 oz. Bacardi Light Rum
3/4 oz. Midori
1/2 oz. White Crème de Cacao
Fill with pineapple juice
Float 3/4 oz. Cruzan Pineapple Rum
Pineapple and cherry garnish

GROUND ZERO
Bucket glass, ice
Build in glass
1 1/4 oz. Cruzan Pineapple Rum
3/4 oz. Midori
Fill with pineapple juice
Pineapple garnish

GUAVA MARTINIQUE
House specialty glass, ice
1 1/2 oz. Rhum Barbancourt 3-Star Rum
1/2 oz. Chambord
1/2 oz. Godiva Chocolate Liqueur
1 1/2 oz. guava nectar
1 1/2 oz. pineapple juice
1 1/2 oz. sweet 'n' sour
Shake and strain
Float 3/4 oz. St. James Extra Old Rhum
Orange and cherry garnish

GULF STREAM SCREAM
House specialty glass, ice
1 oz. Bacardi Light Rum
1 oz. Midori
1/2 oz. Peach Schnapps
2 oz. pineapple juice
2 oz. fresh orange juice
Shake and strain
Float 3/4 oz. Mount Gay Eclipse Rum
Orange and cherry garnish

HABANA LIBRE
House specialty glass, ice
Build in glass
1 1/2 oz. Matusalem Light Dry Rum
1/2 oz. fresh lime juice
1/4 oz. grenadine
2 splashes grenadine
Fill with cola
Float 3/4 oz. Bacardi 151° Rum
Lime and mint sprig garnish

HABANOS HAVANA
Cocktail glass, chilled
1 3/4 oz. Matusalem Golden Dry Rum
3/4 oz. Cointreau
1 1/2 oz. sweetened lime juice
Shake and strain
Lime garnish

HALEKULANI SUNSET
House specialty glass, ice
1 1/2 oz. Bacardi Light Rum
3/4 oz. Blue Curaçao
1/2 oz. grenadine
3 oz. guava nectar
1 1/2 oz. sweet 'n' sour
Shake and strain
Float 3/4 oz. Gosling's Black Seal Rum
Pineapple garnish

HAVANA
Cocktail glass, chilled
1/2 oz. Dry Sherry
1 3/4 oz. Amber or Gold Rum
Dash Angostura Bitters
1 1/2 oz. sweet 'n' sour
Shake and strain
Orange twist garnish

HAVANA CLUB
Cocktail glass, chilled
1/2 oz. Martini & Rossi Rosso Vermouth
1 3/4 oz. Amber or Gold Rum
Dash Angostura Bitters
Stir and strain
Cherry garnish

HAVANA COCKTAIL
Cocktail glass, chilled
1 3/4 oz. Matusalem Golden Dry Rum
1/2 oz. lemon juice
1 1/2 oz. pineapple juice
Shake and strain
Cherry garnish

HAVANA ICED TEA
House specialty glass, ice
1/2 oz. Brandy
1/2 oz. Matusalem Golden Dry Rum
1/2 oz. Matusalem Light Dry Rum
1/2 oz. Triple Sec
1 1/2 oz. orange juice
1 1/2 oz. sweet 'n' sour
1 1/2 oz. cola
Shake and strain
Lemon garnish

HAVANA SIDECAR (1)

Cocktail glass, chilled
(Sugar rim optional)
1 1/2 oz. Matusalem Golden Dry Rum
3/4 oz. Cointreau
1 1/2 oz. sweet 'n' sour
Shake and strain
Lime garnish

HAVANA SIDECAR (2)

Cocktail glass, chilled
(Sugar rim optional)
1 1/2 oz. Bacardi 8 Rum
3/4 oz. Cointreau
3/4 oz. sweet 'n' sour
Shake and strain
Lemon garnish

HEAT WAVE

Bucket glass, ice
Build in glass
1 oz. Mount Gay Eclipse Rum
1/2 oz. Peach Schnapps
Fill with pineapple juice
Float 3/4 oz. Appleton Estate V/X Rum
Lime garnish

HEAVYWEIGHT SAILOR

Cocktail glass, chilled
1 1/4 oz. Pyrat Pistol Rum
1/2 oz. Tia Maria
1/2 oz. Rose's Lime Juice
1 3/4 oz. sweet 'n' sour
Shake and strain
Lime garnish

HONEY RUM TODDY

Coffee mug, heated
Build in glass
2 oz. Bacardi Gold Rum
2 tbsp. honey
1 tbsp. fresh lime juice
A thin slice of lime
Fill with 1/2 cup boiling water
Cinnamon stick and lemon garnish

HOT BUTTERED RUM

Coffee mug, heated
Build in glass
1 1/2 oz. Appleton Estate V/X Rum
1/2 oz. simple syrup
2 pinches nutmeg
Cinnamon stick
Fill with hot water
Float pat of butter
Cinnamon stick garnish

HOT RUM COW

Coffee mug, heated
Build in glass
1 3/4 oz. Bacardi Gold Rum
1 teaspoon powdered sugar
1 dash Angostura Bitters
2 dashes vanilla extract
2 pinches freshly grated nutmeg
Fill with hot milk

HOT TROPICO MAMA

Cocktail glass, chilled
3/4 oz. Tropico
3/4 oz. Crème de Banana
3/4 oz. Triple Sec
1 1/4 oz. orange juice
1 1/4 oz. half & half cream
Shake and strain
Shaved chocolate garnish

HUMMER

House specialty glass, chilled
3/4 oz. Bacardi Gold Rum
3/4 oz. Kahlúa
3/4 oz. Dark Crème de Cacao
2 scoops vanilla ice cream
Blend with ice; pour into glass
Float 3/4 oz. Mount Gay Eclipse Rum
Oreo cookie garnish

HURRICANE (1)

House specialty glass, ice
1 1/2 oz. Light Rum
1 1/2 oz. Dark Rum
1/2 oz. Rose's Lime Juice
1/2 oz. simple syrup
1/2 oz. grenadine
2 oz. orange juice
2 oz. pineapple juice
Shake and strain
Orange, lime and lemon garnish

H-I

HURRICANE (2)
House specialty glass, ice
1 1/2 oz. Light Rum
1 1/2 oz. Dark Rum
1/2 oz. simple syrup
1 1/2 oz. passion fruit juice or nectar
1 1/2 oz. fresh lime juice
1 1/2 oz. pineapple juice
Shake and strain
Float 3/4 oz. Overproof Rum
Orange, lime and lemon garnish

INDEPENDENCE SWIZZLE
House specialty glass, crushed ice
Build in glass
1 1/2 oz. Appleton Estate V/X Rum
3 dashes Angostura Bitters
1/4 oz. honey
1/2 oz. simple syrup
1 oz. fresh lime juice
Swizzle thoroughly with spoon
    until glass frosts
Lime garnish

INFUSION, BARRIER REEF
Large jar
2-3 lbs. pineapples
1-2 lbs. cantaloupe
1-2 lbs. honey dew melon
3 cups maraschino cherries
4-5 liters Light Rum
Slice and core pineapples, slice and
    seed cantaloupe and honey
    dew, and steep in jar
Add light rum
Taste test after 2-3 days

INFUSION, BRAZILIAN DAIQUIRI
Large jar
4 lbs. fresh pineapple
3 vanilla beans
1 cup brown sugar
1 liter Bacardi Light Rum
1 liter Bacardi Gold Rum
1 liter Bacardi Select Rum
Cut and core pineapple and place
    in bottom of jar
Steep vanilla beans and brown sugar
Add rums
Taste test after 4-5 days

INFUSION, CHERRY BOMB
Large jar
1 gallon maraschino cherries
2-3 vanilla beans
4-5 liters Light Rum
Steep cherries, vanilla beans and rum
Taste test after 3-4 days

ISLA DE PIÑOS
House specialty glass, ice
1 1/2 oz. Matusalem Light Dry Rum
1 1/2 oz. grapefruit juice
1/2 oz. simple syrup
1/2 oz. grenadine
Shake and strain
Grapefruit slice garnish

ISLAND FLOWER
Cocktail glass, chilled
2 1/2 oz. Cruzan Single Barrel Rum
1/2 oz. Blue Curaçao
2 dashes Rose's Lime Juice
1/2 oz. fresh lime juice
Stir and strain
Lime wheel garnish

ISLEÑA
House specialty glass, ice
Build in glass
1 1/2 oz. Bacardi Light Rum
1 1/2 oz. pineapple juice
Fill with Perrier Sparkling Water
Float 1/2 oz. grenadine
Fresh raspberries garnish

ITHMUS BUFFALO MILK
House specialty glass, chilled
1 1/2 oz. Bacardi Select Rum
1 1/2 oz. Cruzan Estate Light Rum
3/4 oz. Kahlúa
3/4 oz. Cruzan Banana Rum
1 peeled, ripe banana
1 1/2 oz. milk
3/4 oz. chocolate syrup
Blend with ice; pour into glass
Whipped cream garnish
Sprinkle nutmeg

JACKALOPE
House specialty glass, ice
1 3/4 oz. Mount Gay Eclipse Rum
3/4 oz. Kahlúa
3/4 oz. Disaronno Amaretto
3/4 oz. Dark Crème de Cacao
3 oz. pineapple juice
Shake and strain
Float 3/4 oz. Appleton Estate V/X Rum
Orange garnish

JACQUELINE
Cocktail glass, chilled
2 oz. Bacardi 8 Rum
3/4 oz. Grand Marnier
1/2 oz. Rose's Lime Juice
1 oz. fresh lime juice
Stir and strain
Lime garnish

JADE
Cocktail glass, chilled
1 1/2 oz. Bacardi Light Rum
1/2 oz. Triple Sec
1/2 oz. Green Crème de Menthe
1/2 oz. Rose's Lime Juice
Stir and strain
Lime garnish

JAMAICA JUICE
House specialty glass, chilled
1 1/2 oz. Appleton Special Rum
1 oz. pineapple juice
1 oz. orange juice
1 oz. cranberry juice
2 oz. coconut cream syrup
Blend with ice; pour into glass
Float 3/4 oz. Appleton Estate V/X Rum
Pineapple garnish

JAMAICA ME CRAZY (1)
Bucket glass, ice
Build in glass
1 1/2 oz. Appleton Estate V/X Rum
3/4 oz. Tia Maria
Fill with pineapple juice
Orange garnish

JAMAICA ME CRAZY (2)
House specialty glass, chilled
1 1/2 oz. Appleton Estate V/X Rum
3/4 oz. Blue Curaçao
2 oz. coconut cream
2 oz. pineapple juice
2 oz. orange juice
Blend with ice; pour into glass
Pineapple garnish

JAMAICAN BARBADOS BOMBER
Presentation shot glass, chilled
1 3/4 oz. Appleton Estate V/X Rum
1 3/4 oz. Mount Gay Eclipse Rum
3/4 oz. Triple Sec
1/2 oz. Rose's Lime Juice
Stir and strain
Lime garnish

JAMAICAN COFFEE
Coffee mug, heated
Build in glass
1 1/4 oz. Appleton Estate V/X Rum
3/4 oz. Tia Maria
Fill with hot coffee
Whipped cream garnish
Sprinkle shaved chocolate

JAMAICAN CRAWLER
Bucket glass, ice
1 1/2 oz. Appleton Special Rum
1 1/2 oz. Midori
1/2 oz. grenadine
3 oz. pineapple juice
Shake and strain

JAMAICAN DUST
Presentation shot glass, chilled
Build in glass
1/3 fill Myers's Jamaican Rum
1/3 fill Tia Maria
1/3 fill pineapple juice

J

JAMAICAN FEVER
House specialty glass, ice
1 1/2 oz. Appleton Special Rum
3/4 oz. Brandy
3/4 oz. mango syrup
1 1/2 oz. guava nectar
1 1/2 oz. pineapple juice
Shake and strain
Float 3/4 oz. Appleton Estate V/X Rum
Pineapple garnish

JAMAICAN PLANTER'S PUNCH
House specialty glass, chilled
1 1/2 oz. Appleton Special Rum
1 oz. simple syrup
2 oz. fresh lime juice
2 oz. pineapple juice
3 large, peeled and cored
    pineapple slices
Blend with ice; pour into glass
Float 3/4 oz. Appleton Estate V/X Rum
Pineapple and cherry garnish

JAMAICAN RUM COW
House specialty glass, chilled
1 1/2 oz. Appleton Special Rum
3/4 oz. Kahlúa
1/2 oz. chocolate syrup
2 dashes Angostura Bitters
2 oz. milk
2 scoops chocolate ice cream
Blend with ice; pour into glass
Float 3/4 oz. Appleton Estate V/X Rum
Pineapple and cherry garnish

JAMAICAN SHAKE
House specialty glass, chilled
1 1/4 oz. Appleton Special Rum
3/4 oz. Tia Maria
3/4 oz. Disaronno Amaretto
1 tsp. vanilla extract
2 scoops vanilla ice cream
Blend with ice; pour into glass
Whipped cream garnish
Sprinkle shaved chocolate

JAMAICAN SPICE
Bucket glass, ice
Build in glass
1 oz. Appleton Special Rum
1 oz. Captain Morgan Spiced Rum
1/2 oz. Cinnamon Schnapps
Fill with ginger ale
Float 1/2 oz. Crème de Banana

JAMAICAN TENNIS BEADS
Bucket glass, ice
1 oz. Appleton Special Rum
3/4 oz. Bacardi Light Rum
3/4 oz. Midori
3/4 oz. Crème de Banana
1/2 oz. half & half cream
1 oz. pineapple juice
Shake and strain
Float 3/4 oz. Gosling's Black Seal Rum

JAMBA JUICE
Bucket glass, ice
3/4 oz. Captain Morgan Spiced Rum
3/4 oz. Mount Gay Eclipse Rum
1 oz. cranberry juice
1 oz. orange juice
1 oz. pineapple juice
Shake and strain
Float 3/4 oz. Appleton Estate V/X Rum
Orange and cherry garnish

JET FUEL
Bucket glass, ice
Build in glass
1/2 oz. Bacardi 151° Rum
1/2 oz. Malibu Rum
1/2 oz. Gosling's Black Seal Rum
1/2 oz. Angostura Royal Oak
    Extra Old Rum
Fill with pineapple juice
Float 1/2 oz. grenadine
Orange garnish

JULIA
House specialty glass, chilled
1 oz. Bacardi Light Rum
1 oz. Disaronno Amaretto
1 oz. Angostura Caribbean Rum Cream
1/2 cup strawberries
1 1/2 oz. sweet 'n' sour
Blend with ice; pour into glass
Float 3/4 oz. Gosling's Black Seal Rum
Strawberry garnish

JUMP ME
Bucket glass, ice
Build in glass
1 1/2 oz. Bacardi Select Rum
1 oz. Mount Gay Eclipse Rum
2-3 dashes Angostura Bitters
1 oz. fresh lime juice
Fill with pineapple juice
Float 3/4 oz. Gosling's Black Seal Rum

KAMIKAZE, RADIOACTIVE
Cocktail glass, chilled
1/2 oz. Bacardi Light Rum
1/2 oz. Cruzan Coconut Rum
1/2 oz. Bacardi 151° Rum
1/2 oz. Blue Curaçao
1 oz. Rose's Lime Juice
1/2 oz. grenadine
Stir and strain
Lime garnish

KAPALUA BUTTERFLY
House specialty glass, chilled
1 1/4 oz. Mount Gay Eclipse Rum
1 1/4 oz. Bacardi Gold Rum
1/2 oz. grenadine
1 1/2 oz. sweet 'n' sour
1 1/2 oz. pineapple juice
1 1/2 oz. coconut syrup
2 oz. orange juice
Blend with ice; pour into glass
Pineapple and orange garnish

KEY ISLA MORADA
House specialty glass, chilled
1 oz. Conch Republic Light Rum
3/4 oz. Cruzan Coconut Rum
3/4 oz. Cruzan Pineapple Rum
Peeled, ripe banana
1 tsp. vanilla extract
3/4 oz. half & half cream
2 oz. sweet 'n' sour
Blend with ice; pour into glass
Float 3/4 oz. Conch Republic Dark Rum
Orange and lime garnish

KEY LARGO
House specialty glass, ice
1 1/2 oz. Conch Republic Light Rum
3/4 oz. Cruzan Coconut Rum
3/4 oz. DiSaronno Amaretto
Shake and strain
Fill with club soda
Float 3/4 oz. Conch Republic Dark Rum
Orange and lime garnish

KEY WEST
House specialty glass, ice
1 1/2 oz. Conch Republic Light Rum
1 1/2 oz. Conch Republic
    Durdy White Rum
1/2 oz. Crème de Banana
1/2 oz. Chambord
2 oz. sweet 'n' sour
2 oz. orange juice
Shake and strain
Fill with Seven-Up
Float 3/4 oz. Conch Republic Dark Rum
Orange and cherry garnish

KILLER WHALE
House specialty glass, ice
1 1/4 oz. Bacardi Gold Rum
1 1/4 oz. Mount Gay Eclipse
1/2 oz. Chambord
1/2 fill cranberry juice
1/2 fill orange juice
Shake and strain
Fill with Seven-Up
Float 3/4 oz. Grand Marnier
Orange garnish

KISS OF THE ISLANDS
House specialty glass, ice
1 1/2 oz. Gosling's Black Seal Rum
1 1/2 oz. Mount Gay Eclipse Rum
1 oz. Crème de Banana
3/4 oz. Blue Curaçao
1 oz. coconut syrup
1 1/2 oz. pineapple juice
1 1/2 oz. orange juice
Shake and strain
Float 3/4 oz. Appleton Estate V/X Rum
Orange and cherry garnish

KNICKERBOCKER
Bucket glass, ice
1 1/2 oz. Bacardi Limón Rum
1 oz. Mount Gay Eclipse Rum
1/2 oz. grenadine
3/4 oz. pineapple juice
1 oz. orange juice
1 oz. sweet 'n' sour
Shake and strain
Float 3/4 oz. Gosling's Black Seal Rum
Orange and cherry garnish

KNICKERBOCKER SPECIAL COCKTAIL
Cocktail glass, chilled
1 1/2 oz. Bacardi Limón Rum
1/2 oz. Cointreau
1/2 oz. Chambord
3/4 oz. orange juice
1 oz. sweet 'n' sour
Shake and strain
Orange garnish

LARCHMONT (1)
Cocktail glass, chilled
1 1/2 oz. Bacardi 8 Rum
3/4 oz. Grand Marnier
1/2 oz. Rose's Lime Juice
Stir and strain
Orange peel garnish

LARCHMONT (2)
Cocktail glass, chilled
1 1/2 oz. Pyrat Cask 23 Rum
3/4 oz. Grand Marnier
1/2 oz. Rose's Lime Juice
Stir and strain
Orange peel garnish

LARCHMONT (3)
Cocktail glass, chilled
1 1/2 oz. Cruzan Single Barrel Rum
3/4 oz. Grand Marnier
1/2 oz. Rose's Lime Juice
Stir and strain
Orange peel garnish

LASTING PASSION
House specialty glass, chilled
1 1/2 oz. Angostura Royal Oak
    Extra Old Rum
3/4 oz. Forres Park Overproof Rum
3/4 oz. Rose's Lime Juice
2 oz. coconut syrup
2 oz. pineapple juice
2 1/2 oz. passion fruit juice
Blend with ice; pour into glass
Float 3/4 oz. Rhum Barbancourt 3-Star Rum
Pineapple and orange garnish

LATIN LOVE
House specialty glass, chilled
Rim glass with grenadine
    and shaved coconut
1 oz. Cruzan Coconut Rum
1 oz. Cruzan Banana Rum
1 oz. raspberry juice
1 oz. coconut syrup
3 oz. pineapple juice
Blend with ice; pour into glass
Pineapple and cherry garnish

LATIN LOVER (1)
House specialty glass, ice
1 1/2 oz. Pyrat Pistol Rum
1/2 oz. Crème de Banana
1/2 oz. grenadine
2 oz. orange juice
2 oz. pineapple juice
Shake and strain
Float 3/4 oz. Pyrat XO Reserve Rum
Lemon twist garnish

LATIN LOVER (2)
House specialty glass, chilled
1 oz. Cruzan Estate Dark Rum
1 oz. Cruzan Banana Rum
3/4 oz. Chambord
1 oz. raspberry syrup
1 1/2 oz. coconut syrup
3 oz. pineapple juice
Blend with ice; pour into glass
Pineapple and cherry garnish

LAUGHING BACARDI COW
House specialty glass, chilled
1 1/2 oz. Bacardi Limón Rum
1/2 oz. Cointreau
1/2 oz. fresh lime juice
1/2 oz. cranberry juice juice
2 scoops vanilla ice cream
Blend with ice; pour into glass
Orange twist garnish

LETHAL INJECTION
Bucket glass, ice
1 1/4 oz. Bacardi Light Rum
3/4 oz. Mount Gay Eclipse Rum
3/4 oz. Cruzan Coconut Rum
1/2 oz. Crème de Noyaux
1 1/2 oz. orange juice
1 1/2 oz. pineapple juice
Shake and strain
Float 3/4 oz. Gosling's Black Seal Rum
Pineapple garnish

LIFESAVER
House specialty glass, ice
1 oz. Mount Gay Eclipse Rum
1 oz. Bacardi Select Rum
2 oz. orange juice
2 oz. sweet 'n' sour
Shake and strain
Float 3/4 oz. Grand Marnier
Orange and cherry garnish

LIMÓN COSMOPOLITAN
Cocktail glass, chilled
1 1/2 oz. Bacardi Limón Rum
1/2 oz. Cointreau
1/2 oz. fresh lime juice
1/2 oz. cranberry juice juice
Stir and strain
Orange twist garnish

LIMÓN RUNNER
House specialty glass, ice
1 1/2 oz. Bacardi Limón Rum
1/2 oz. Crème de Banana
1/2 oz. grenadine
2 oz. orange juice
2 oz. pineapple juice
Shake and strain
Lemon twist garnish

LOST LOVERS
House specialty glass, chilled
3/4 oz. Bacardi Light Rum
3/4 oz. Captain Morgan Spiced Rum
3/4 oz. Mount Gay Eclipse Rum
3/4 oz. Crème de Banana
1 oz. coconut syrup
2 oz. orange juice
2 oz. pineapple juice
Blend with ice; pour into glass
Float 3/4 oz. Chambord
Orange and cherry garnish

LOUNGE LIZARD
House specialty glass, ice
Build in glass
1 oz. Bacardi Gold Rum
1 oz. Captain Morgan Spiced Rum
1/2 oz. Disaronno Amaretto
Fill with cola
Lime garnish

LOVE POTION #9
House specialty glass, chilled
1 oz. Bacardi Gold Rum
1 oz. Mount Gay Eclipse Rum
2 oz. strawberry puree
1 1/2 oz. coconut syrup
3 oz. pineapple juice
Blend with ice; pour into glass
Float 1/2 oz. Bacardi Select
Float 1/2 oz. St. James Extra Old Rhum
Whipped cream garnish optional

MAI TAI (1)
House specialty glass, ice
1 3/4 oz. Light Rum
1/2 oz. orgeat syrup or Crème de Noyaux
1/2 oz. Triple Sec
2 oz. sweet 'n' sour
Shake and strain
Orange and cherry garnish

M

MAI TAI (2)
House specialty glass, ice
2 1/2 oz. Light Rum
1 oz. Gold Rum
1 oz. Triple Sec
3/4 oz. grenadine
3/4 oz. orgeat syrup
1 oz. fresh lime juice
1 3/4 oz. sweet 'n' sour
Shake and strain
Float 3/4 oz. Overproof Rum
Pineapple and cherry garnish

MAI TAI (3)
House specialty glass, ice
1 oz. Overproof Rum
1 oz. Gold Rum
1 oz. Light Rum
3/4 oz. Orange Curaçao
1/2 oz. grenadine
1 1/2 oz. orange juice
1 3/4 oz. fresh lime juice
Shake and strain
Mint sprig, lime and orange garnish

MAI TAI, MOBAY
House specialty glass, ice
1 oz. Appleton Estate V/X Rum
1 oz. Mount Gay Eclipse Rum
1 oz. Triple Sec
1 oz. orgeat syrup
3/4 oz. grenadine
1 3/4 oz. sweet 'n' sour
1 3/4 oz. sweetened lime juice
Shake and strain
Garnish with sprig of mint

MALIBU SUNSET
Bucket glass, ice
Build in glass
1 1/2 oz. Malibu Rum
1/2 oz. Peach Schnapps
Fill with orange juice
Float 1/2 oz. grenadine

MANHATTAN BEACH
House specialty glass, ice
1 1/4 oz. Matusalem Light Dry Rum
1 1/4 oz. Matusalem Golden Dry Rum
3/4 oz. Disaronno Amaretto
1/2 oz. grenadine
3 oz. pineapple juice
Shake and strain
Float 3/4 oz. Matusalem Classic Black Rum
Orange, lime and lemon garnish

MANHATTAN, CUBAN
Cocktail glass, chilled
3/4 oz. Martini & Rossi Rosso Vermouth
2-3 dashes Angostura Bitters
1 3/4 oz. Matusalem Light Dry Rum
Stir and strain
Cherry garnish

MANHATTAN, CUBAN MEDIUM
Cocktail glass, chilled
1/2 oz. Martini & Rossi Rosso Vermouth
1/2 oz. Martini & Rossi Extra Dry Vermouth
2-3 dashes Angostura Bitters
1 3/4 oz. Matusalem Light Dry Rum
Stir and strain
Cherry garnish

MANHATTAN, LATIN
Cocktail glass, chilled
1/4 oz. Martini & Rossi Rosso Vermouth
1/4 oz. Martini & Rossi
    Extra Dry Vermouth
2 dashes Angostura Bitters optional
1 3/4 oz. Matusalem Light Dry Rum
Stir and strain
Lemon twist garnish

MARASCHINO RUM MIST
House specialty glass, ice
Build in glass
1 1/2 oz. Bacardi Gold Rum
1 1/2 oz. maraschino cherry juice
1 oz. Rose's Lime Juice
Fill with club soda
Orange and cherry garnish

MARGARITA, CONGA
Cocktail glass, chilled
1 oz. Cruzan Banana Rum
1 oz. Cruzan Pineapple Rum
3/4 oz. Citrónge Orange Liqueur
1/2 oz. Rose's Lime Juice
1 1/2 oz. sweet 'n' sour
Shake and strain
Lime garnish

MARGARITA, JAMAICAN
Cocktail glass, chilled
1 1/4 oz. Appleton Estate V/X Rum
3/4 oz. Cointreau
1/2 oz. Rose's Lime Juice
1/2 oz. orange juice
1 1/2 oz. sweet 'n' sour
Shake and strain
Lime garnish

MARGARITA, MONTEGO
Cocktail glass, chilled
1 1/2 oz. Appleton Estate V/X Rum
3/4 oz. Citrónge Orange Liqueur
1/2 oz. Rose's Lime Juice
1/2 oz. orange juice
1 1/2 oz. sweet 'n' sour
Shake and strain
Lime and lemon garnish

MARTINI, BLACK DEVIL
Cocktail glass, chilled
1/4 oz. Martini & Rossi
     Extra Dry Vermouth
2 oz. Cruzan Estate Light Rum
Stir and strain
Black olives garnish

MARTINI, BLACK TIE
Cocktail glass, chilled
1/4 oz. Martini & Rossi
     Extra Dry Vermouth
2 oz. Appleton Estate Extra Rum
Stir and strain
Black olives garnish

MARTINI, EL PRESIDENTÉ
Cocktail glass, chilled
1/2 oz. Martini & Rossi Extra Dry Vermouth
1/2 oz. Martini & Rossi Rosso Vermouth
1/2 oz. Cointreau
2 dashes grenadine
1 1/2 oz. Bacardi Light Rum
Stir and strain
Lemon twist garnish

MARTINI, EMERALD
Cocktail glass, chilled
1/2 oz. Midori
1 1/2 oz. Bacardi Limón Rum
Stir and strain
Lemon twist garnish

MARTINI, HAVANA
Cocktail glass, chilled
1/2 oz. Vintage Tawny Port
1 1/2 oz. Bacardi 8 Rum
Stir and strain
Cherry garnish

MARTINI, MARTINIQUE
Cocktail glass, chilled
Powdered sugar rim
1/2 oz. fresh lime juice
3/4 oz. sugar cane syrup
1 1/2 oz. St. James Extra Old Rhum
Stir and strain
Lime garnish

MARTINI, PYRAT
Cocktail glass, chilled
1/2 oz. Godiva Chocolate Liqueur
1 3/4 oz. Pyrat Cask 23 Rum
Stir and strain
Lemon twist garnish

MARTINI, SMOKED
Cocktail glass, chilled
3/4 oz. Rhum Barbancourt 3-Star Rum
1 1/2 oz. Gin
Stir and strain
Lemon twist garnish

M

MARTINIQUE GIMLET (1)
Cocktail glass, chilled
1 3/4 oz. St. James Extra Old Rhum
3/4 oz. Cointreau
1/2 oz. fresh lime juice
1/2 oz. sweet 'n' sour
Shake and strain
Lime garnish

MARTINIQUE GIMLET (2)
Cocktail glass, chilled
1 oz. J. Bally Rhum Vieux 12-Year
1 oz. Dillon Dark Rhum
3/4 oz. Citrónge Orange Liqueur
1/2 oz. fresh lime juice
1/2 oz. sweet 'n' sour
Shake and strain
Lime garnish

MAUI WOWIE
Cocktail glass, chilled
3/4 oz. Matusalem Light Dry Rum
3/4 oz. Cruzan Coconut Rum
3/4 oz. Midori
1 oz. pineapple juice
1 oz. orange juice
Shake and strain
Float 3/4 oz. Gosling's Black Seal Rum
Orange garnish

MELON MOOSE
Bucket glass, ice
Build in glass
3/4 oz. Bacardi Light Rum
3/4 oz. Midori
Fill with pineapple juice
Float 1 oz. Appleton Estate V/X Rum

MELON SCOOP
House specialty glass, chilled
1 3/4 oz. Mount Gay Eclipse Rum
1 1/2 oz. Midori
3/4 oz. Kahlúa
1/2 oz. grenadine
1 oz. sweet 'n' sour
2 scoops vanilla ice cream
Blend with ice; pour into glass
Float 3/4 oz. Matusalem
  Classic Black Rum
Orange and cherry garnish

MEL'S CHOCOLATE BUTTERSCOTCH SHAKE
House specialty glass, chilled
1 1/2 oz. Kahlúa
3/4 oz. Appleton Special Rum
2 oz. butterscotch topping
1 oz. chocolate syrup
2 scoops vanilla ice cream
4 oz. whole milk
Blend with ice; pour into glass
Whipped cream garnish

MEL'S CHOC/PB/NANA SHAKE
House specialty glass, chilled
1 1/2 oz. Kahlúa
3/4 oz. Appleton Special Rum
1 peeled, ripe banana
1 oz. chocolate syrup
2 tbsp. creamy peanut butter
2 scoops vanilla ice cream
4 oz. whole milk
Blend with ice; pour into glass
Whipped cream garnish

MIDNIGHT EXPRESS (1)
Cocktail glass, chilled
1 3/4 oz. Bacardi 8 Rum
3/4 oz. Cointreau
1/2 oz. fresh lime juice
1/2 oz. sweet 'n' sour
Shake and strain
Lime garnish

MIDNIGHT EXPRESS (2)
Cocktail glass, chilled
1 3/4 oz. Angostura 1824
  Limited Reserve Rum
3/4 oz. Cointreau
1/2 oz. fresh lime juice
1/2 oz. sweet 'n' sour
Shake and strain
Lime garnish

MIDNIGHT EXPRESS (3)
Cocktail glass, chilled
1 3/4 oz. Rhum Barbancourt 5-Star Rum
3/4 oz. Cointreau
1/2 oz. fresh lime juice
1/2 oz. sweet 'n' sour
Shake and strain
Lime garnish

MIDWAY MANHATTAN
House specialty glass, ice
1 1/4 oz. Bacardi Gold Rum
1 1/4 oz. Mount Gay Eclipse Rum
3/4 oz. Disaronno Amaretto
3/4 oz. Tia Maria
2 oz. orange juice
2 oz. sweet 'n' sour
Shake and strain
Orange and cherry garnish

MINCEMEAT MOCHA
Coffee mug, heated
Build in glass
1 1/2 oz. Bacardi Gold Rum
3/4 oz. Tuaca
1 oz. Hershey's chocolate syrup
Fill with hot coffee
Whipped cream garnish
Drizzle 1/2 oz. Apple Schnapps

MOBAY RUNNER
Bucket glass, ice
Build in glass
1 oz. Appleton Estate V/X Rum
1 oz. Mount Gay Eclipse Rum
1 oz. Cruzan Coconut Rum
Fill with papaya juice
Orange garnish

MOCHA JAMOCHA
Coffee mug, heated
Build in glass
3/4 oz. Appleton Estate V/X Rum
1/2 oz. Cruzan Rum Cream
1/2 oz. Tia Maria
1/2 oz. Dark Crème de Cacao
Fill with hot coffee
Whipped cream garnish

MOJITO (1)
Bucket glass
Build in glass
3/4 oz. fresh lime juice
1/2 oz. simple syrup
3-4 sprigs fresh mint
2 lime wedges
Muddle contents and add ice
2 oz. Light Rum
2-3 splashes club soda
Lime and mint sprig garnish

MOJITO (2)
Bucket glass
Build in glass
1 oz. fresh lime juice
2 lime wedges
2 to 3 dashes Angostura Bitters
4 mint leaves (fresh)
1 1/2 tbsp. superfine sugar
Muddle contents and add ice
2 oz. Light Rum
2-3 splashes club soda
Lime and mint sprig garnish

MONKEY JUICE
Rocks glass, ice
Build in glass
1 3/4 oz. Angostura Royal Oak
Extra Old Rum
3/4 oz. Angostura Caribbean
Rum Cream
3/4 oz. Crème de Banana

MONTEGO BAY
Coffee mug, heated
Build in glass
3/4 oz. Tia Maria
3/4 oz. Appleton Special Rum
3/4 oz. Cruzan Banana Rum
Fill with hot coffee
Whipped cream garnish
Sprinkle shaved chocolate

MOP IN A BUCKET
Bucket glass, ice
Build in glass
1 oz. Myers's Jamaican Rum
1/2 fill orange juice
1/2 fill pineapple juice

MOUNT GAY CAFÉ
Cocktail glass, chilled
(Sugar rim optional)
1 1/4 oz. Mount Gay Eclipse Rum
1 oz. Tia Maria
3/4 oz. Grand Marnier
1 oz. cold, freshly brewed coffee
Shake and strain
Layer on frothed milk
Dust with powdered cocoa

N

NÁCIONAL
Cocktail glass, chilled
1 1/2 oz. Bacardi Gold Rum
3/4 oz. Apricot Liqueur
3/4 oz. fresh lime juice
3/4 oz. pineapple juice
Shake and strain
Lime garnish

NAVAL COMMISSION
House specialty glass, ice
1 1/2 oz. Pusser's British Navy Rum
3/4 oz. Matusalem Light Dry Rum
3/4 oz. Matusalem
   Red Flame Rum
1/2 oz. Rose's Lime Juice
1/2 oz. grenadine
1 1/2 oz. orange juice
1 1/2 oz. pineapple juice
Shake and strain
Orange, lemon and lime garnish

NAVY GROG, MODERN
House specialty glass, chilled
2 oz. Pusser's British Navy Rum
1/2 oz. fresh lime juice
1/4 oz. Falernum (sugar cane liqueur)
1 oz. orange juice
1 oz. pineapple juice
1 oz. guava nectar
Blend with ice; pour into glass
Orange garnish

NAVY GROG, NOR'EASTER
Coffee mug, heated
Build in glass
1 oz. Gosling's Black Seal Rum
1 oz. Pusser's British Navy Rum
1/2 oz. Cointreau
1/2 oz. Tia Maria
1/2 oz. Disaronno Amaretto
1 tsp. brown sugar
Pinch powered cinnamon
Fill with hot black coffee
Float 3/4 oz. Bailey's Irish Cream
Whipped cream garnish
Sprinkle shaved chocolate

NAVY GROG, ORIGINAL
Coffee mug, heated
Build in glass
2 oz. Dark Rum
1 oz. Brandy
1 oz. lemon juice
1 sugar cube
1 cinnamon stick
6 cloves
1 slice lemon
Fill with hot water
Lemon garnish

NELSON'S BLOOD (1)
Rocks glass, ice
Build in glass
2 oz. Pusser's British Navy Rum
1/2 oz. fresh lime juice
2 oz. ginger beer
Lime garnish

NELSON'S BLOOD (2)
Bucket glass, ice
Build in glass
2 oz. Pusser's British Navy Rum
1/2 fill with cranberry juice
1/2 fill with pineapple juice
Lime garnish

NEVADA PETE COCKTAIL
Cocktail glass, chilled
1 3/4 oz. Angostura Royal Oak
   Extra Old Rum
3/4 oz. Citrónge Orange Liqueur
1/2 oz. Rose's Lime Juice
1 oz. grapefruit juice
1 oz. sweet 'n' sour
Shake and strain
Lime garnish

NEW ENGLAND SUMMER SPRITZER
House specialty glass, ice
Build in glass
1 3/4 oz. Bacardi Limón Rum
3 oz. white zinfandel
3 oz. cranberry juice
Lemon garnish

NEW ORLEANS BUCK
House specialty glass, ice
1 3/4 oz. Bacardi Limón Rum
1 oz. orange juice
1 oz. sweet 'n' sour
Shake and strain
Fill with ginger ale
Lemon garnish

NEW ORLEANS JAZZ TIME
Champagne glass, chilled
1 1/2 oz. Bacardi Light Rum
1/2 oz. Peach Schnapps
1/2 oz. orange juice
1/2 oz. Rose's Lime Juice
Shake and strain
Fill with Champagne
Orange twist garnish

N'ORLEANS CHILLER
House specialty glass, ice
1 1/2 oz. Bacardi Limón Rum
1 1/2 oz. Cruzan Orange Rum
1 oz. orange juice
1 oz. sweet 'n' sour
2 oz. iced herbal tea
Shake and strain
Orange garnish

NYMPHOMANIAC
Bucket glass, chilled
Build in glass
1 1/4 oz. Bacardi Limón Rum
3/4 oz. Midori
1 oz. sweet 'n' sour
1 oz. Seven-Up

OFFENBURG FLIP
House specialty glass, chilled
3/4 oz. St. James Extra Old Rhum
3/4 oz. Cruzan Coconut Rum
3/4 oz. Cruzan Banana Rum
1/2 oz. Rose's Lime Juice
1/2 oz. fresh lemon juice
1 peeled, ripe banana
1 egg yolk
2 oz. orange juice
Blend with ice; pour into glass
Float 3/4 oz. St. James Extra Old Rhum
Banana and cherry garnish

OTTER WATER
House specialty glass, ice
Build in glass
3/4 oz. Bacardi Light Rum
3/4 oz. Bacardi Gold Rum
3/4 oz. Mount Gay Eclipse Rum
1/2 oz. Chambord
1 oz. orange juice
1 oz. pineapple juice
1 oz. Seven-Up
Float 3/4 oz. Cockspur V.S.O.R. Rum
Orange garnish

OUTRIGGER
Cocktail Glass, chilled
1 oz. Cruzan Junkanu Citrus Rum
1/2 oz. Disaronno Amaretto
1 1/2 oz. cranberry juice
1 1/2 oz. pineapple juice
Shake and strain
Float 3/4 oz. Cruzan Estate
Diamond Rum
Orange and cherry garnish

PAIN IN THE BUTT
House specialty glass, chilled
Two blender canisters required
Step one/canister one
3/4 oz. Crème de Banana
3/4 oz. Blackberry Brandy
3/4 oz. Bacardi Select Rum
1/2 oz. Bacardi 151° Rum
1/2 oz. grenadine
3/4 oz. Rose's Lime Juice
Blend with ice; pour into glass
Step two/canister two
1 1/4 oz. Mount Gay Eclipse Rum
3/4 oz. Chambord
1/2 cup strawberries
1/2 oz. Rose's Lime Juice
2 1/2 oz. sweet 'n' sour
Blend with ice; pour into glass
Pour on top of first drink
Pineapple garnish

P

PAINKILLER
House specialty glass, ice
Build in glass
2 oz. Pusser's British Navy Rum
1 oz. orange juice
1 oz. coconut syrup
4 oz. pineapple juice
Stir ingredients
Orange and cherry garnish
Sprinkle with grated fresh nutmeg

PANAMA
See RUM ALEXANDER

PAPA DOBLES
House specialty glass, chilled
1 3/4 oz. Bacardi Light Rum
3/4 oz. maraschino cherry juice
1 1/4 oz. lime juice
1 1/4 oz. grapefruit juice
Blend with ice; pour into glass
Float 1 oz. Mount Gay Eclipse Rum
Lime and cherry garnish

PARANOIA
Bucket glass, ice
Build in glass
1 oz. Cruzan Coconut Rum
1 oz. Disaronno Amaretto
1/2 fill orange juice
1/2 fill pineapple juice
Float 3/4 oz. Gosling's Black Seal Rum
Orange garnish

PARPLE THUNDER
Bucket glass, ice
1 oz. Bacardi Select Rum
1 oz. Bacardi Light Rum
1/2 oz. Triple Sec
1 1/2 oz. grape juice
1 1/2 oz. cranberry juice
Shake and strain
Splash club soda

PASSIONATE POINT
House specialty glass, ice
1 3/4 oz. Mount Gay Eclipse Rum
3/4 oz. Grand Marnier
3/4 oz. Peach Schnapps
2 oz. orange juice
2 oz. cranberry juice
Shake and strain
Float 3/4 oz. Mount Gay Extra Old

PASSIONATE SCREW
Bucket glass, ice
1 1/4 oz. Bacardi Limón Rum
1 oz. Cruzan Pineapple Rum
1 oz. Chambord
1/2 oz. grenadine
2 oz. orange juice
2 oz. sweet 'n' sour
Shake and strain
Orange and cherry garnish

PAZZO GRAND SPANISH COFFEE
Coffee mug, heated
Build in glass
1 oz. XO Café Coffee Liqueur
1 oz. Courvoisier VS Cognac
3/4 oz. Grand Marnier
1/2 oz. Bacardi 151° Rum
1/2 oz. Citrónge Orange Liqueur
2 pinches ground cinnamon
5 oz. hot black coffee
1 1/2 oz. espresso
Garnish with whipped cream
Dust with powdered cocoa

PEDRO COLLINS
Collins glass, ice
1 1/2 oz. Light Rum
2 oz. sweet 'n' sour
Shake and strain
Fill with club soda
Orange and cherry garnish

PERIODISTA (1)
Cocktail glass, chilled
1 1/4 oz. Light Rum
3/4 oz. Cointreau
1/2 oz. Apricot Brandy
1/2 oz. simple syrup
1 oz. fresh lime juice
Shake and strain
Lime garnish

P

PERIODISTA (2)
Cocktail glass chilled
1 1/4 oz. Gosling's Black Seal Rum
3/4 oz. Cointreau
1/2 oz. Apricot Brandy
1/2 oz. simple syrup
1 oz. fresh lime juice
Shake and strain
Lime garnish

PETER PRESCRIPTION
Coffee mug, heated
Build in glass
1 1/4 oz. Appleton Estate V/X Rum
1/2 oz. Tia Maria
1/2 oz. Grand Marnier
1/2 oz. Chambord
Fill with hot coffee
Whipped cream garnish
Sprinkle shaved chocolate

PILGRIM'S PRIDE
House specialty glass, chilled
1 1/2 oz. Bacardi Light Rum
1 oz. Cruzan Orange Rum
1/2 oz. grenadine
3 oz. cranberry juice
2 scoops orange sherbet
Blend with ice; pour into glass
Float 3/4 oz. Bacardi Select Rum
Orange garnish

PIÑA COLADA
House specialty glass, chilled
1 oz. Light Rum
(1/2 oz. half & half cream optional)
2 oz. coconut syrup
3 oz. pineapple juice
Blend with ice; pour into glass
Pineapple garnish

PIÑA COLADA, AMARETTO
a.k.a. ITALIAN COLADA
House specialty glass, chilled
1 oz. Disaronno Amaretto
1 oz. Bacardi Light Rum
(1/2 oz. half & half cream optional)
2 oz. coconut syrup
3 oz. pineapple juice
Blend with ice; pour into glass
Pineapple garnish

PIÑA COLADA, AUSSIE
a.k.a. FLYING KANGAROO
House specialty glass, chilled
1 oz. Bacardi Light Rum
1/2 oz. Galliano Liquore
1/2 oz. Vodka
1/2 oz. orange juice
2 oz. coconut syrup
3 oz. pineapple juice
(1/2 oz. half & half cream optional)
Blend with ice; pour into glass
Pineapple garnish

PIÑA COLADA, BELLEVUE
House specialty glass, chilled
1 1/2 oz. Matusalem Golden Dry Rum
3/4 oz. Citrónge Orange Liqueur
1/2 oz. Rose's Lime Juice
2 oz. coconut syrup
3 oz. pineapple juice
Blend with ice; pour into glass
Float 3/4 oz. Matusalem Classic Black Rum
Pineapple garnish

PIÑA COLADA, BERMUDA
House specialty glass, chilled
2 3/4 oz. Gosling's Black Seal Rum
2 oz. coconut syrup
3 oz. pineapple juice
Blend with ice; pour into glass
Pineapple garnish

PIÑA COLADA, BLACK PEARL
House specialty glass, chilled
1 1/4 oz. Mount Gay Eclipse Rum
1 oz. Bacardi Gold Rum
3/4 oz. Tia Maria
2 oz. coconut syrup
3 oz. pineapple juice
Blend with ice; pour into glass
Float 3/4 oz. Gosling's Black Seal Rum
Pineapple garnish

PIÑA COLADA, BRAZILIAN
House specialty glass, chilled
1 oz. Bacardi Light Rum
1 oz. Ypióca Cachaça
1/2 cup cored, peeled pineapple
2 oz. coconut syrup
3 oz. pineapple juice
Blend with ice; pour into glass
Pineapple garnish

P

PIÑA COLADA, CANNE BAY
House specialty glass, chilled
1 1/2 oz. Cruzan Coconut Rum
1 1/2 oz. Cruzan Pineapple Rum
1/2 oz. Roses's Lime Juice
1/2 oz. lemon juice
2 oz. coconut syrup
3 oz. pineapple juice
Blend with ice; pour into glass
Pineapple garnish

PIÑA COLADA, CHOCO
House specialty glass, chilled
3/4 oz. Captain Morgan Spiced Rum
3/4 oz. Bacardi Gold Rum
3/4 oz. Mount Gay Eclipse Rum
3/4 oz. Kahlúa
3/4 oz. chocolate syrup
1 3/4 oz. coconut syrup
2 oz. pineapple juice
2 scoops vanilla ice cream
Blend with ice; pour into glass
Float 3/4 oz. Matusalem
    Classic Black Rum
Pineapple garnish

PIÑA COLADA, CHOCOLATE
House specialty glass, chilled
1 1/2 oz. Bacardi Gold Rum
1 oz. chocolate syrup
2 oz. coconut syrup
3 oz. pineapple juice
2 scoops chocolate ice cream
Blend with ice; pour into glass
Float 3/4 oz. Bacardi Select Rum
Pineapple garnish

PIÑA COLADA, EMERALD ISLE
House specialty glass, chilled
1 3/4 oz. Mount Gay Eclipse
1 oz. Cruzan Coconut Rum
1 oz. Blue Curaçao
1 scoop vanilla ice cream
2 oz. coconut syrup
4 oz. pineapple juice
Blend with ice; pour into glass
Float 3/4 oz. Gosling's Black Seal Rum
Pineapple garnish

PIÑA COLADA, FRENCH
House specialty glass, chilled
1 3/4 oz. St. James Extra Old Rhum
3/4 oz. Cognac
3/4 oz. Crème de Cassis
1/2 oz. half & half cream
1 oz. coconut syrup
1 1/2 oz. orange juice
2 oz. pineapple juice
Blend with ice; pour into glass
Pineapple garnish

PIÑA COLADA, FRUIT (BASIC)
House specialty glass, chilled
1 1/2 oz. Light Rum
1/2 cup requested fruit
2 oz. coconut syrup
3 oz. pineapple juice
Blend with ice; pour into glass
Fresh fruit garnish

PIÑA COLADA, GOLDEN BACARDI
House specialty glass, chilled
1 1/2 oz. Bacardi Gold Rum
3/4 oz. Bacardi Light Rum
1/2 oz. half & half cream
1 1/2 oz. orange juice
2 oz. coconut syrup
2 oz. pineapple juice
Blend with ice; pour into glass
Float 3/4 oz. Galliano Liquore
Pineapple garnish

PIÑA COLADA, HAWAIIAN LION
House specialty glass, chilled
1 1/2 oz. Mount Gay Eclipse Rum
1 oz. Chambord
1/2 cup raspberries
2 oz. coconut syrup
3 oz. pineapple juice
Blend with ice; pour into glass
Float 3/4 oz. Kahlúa
Pineapple garnish

PIÑA COLADA, HOLIDAY ISLE
House specialty glass, chilled
1 1/4 oz. Bacardi 151° Rum
3/4 oz. Grand Marnier
2 scoops French vanilla ice cream
Blend with ice; pour into glass
Float 3/4 oz. Mount Gay Extra Old Rum
Pineapple garnish

PIÑA COLADA, ITALIAN
House specialty glass, chilled
1 1/2 oz. Bacardi Gold Rum
3/4 oz. Mount Gay Eclipse Rum
1/2 oz. half & half cream
2 oz. coconut syrup
3 oz. pineapple juice
Blend with ice; pour into glass
Float 3/4 oz. Disaronno Amaretto
Pineapple garnish

PIÑA COLADA, KAHLÚA
House specialty glass, chilled
1 1/2 oz. Bacardi Light Rum
3/4 oz. Kahlúa
1/2 oz. half & half cream
1 scoop vanilla ice cream
2 oz. coconut syrup
3 oz. pineapple juice
Blend with ice; pour into glass
Float 1 oz. Kahlúa
Pineapple garnish

PIÑA COLADA, KINGSTON
House specialty glass, chilled
1 3/4 oz. Appleton Estate V/X Rum
3/4 oz. Cointreau
1 1/2 oz. orange juice
1 1/2 oz. pineapple juice
2 oz. coconut syrup
Blend with ice; pour into glass
Float 3/4 oz. Tia Maria
Pineapple and orange garnish

PIÑA COLADA, KOKOMO JOE
House specialty glass, chilled
3/4 oz. Bacardi Light Rum
3/4 oz. Bacardi Gold Rum
3/4 oz. Mount Gay Eclipse Rum
3/4 oz. Crème de Banana
1 oz. orange juice
2 oz. coconut syrup
3 oz. pineapple juice
Blend with ice; pour into glass
Pineapple and banana garnish

PIÑA COLADA, LEMONADA
House specialty glass, chilled
1 1/2 oz. Bacardi Limón Rum
1 1/4 oz. Lemoncello Lemon Liqueur
1 oz. Mount Gay Eclipse Rum
2 oz. cranberry juice
2 oz. coconut syrup
2 oz. pineapple juice
Blend with ice; pour into glass
Pineapple garnish

PIÑA COLADA, MIDORI
a.k.a. GREEN EYES
House specialty glass, chilled
1 1/2 oz. Midori
1 1/2 oz. Bacardi Limón Rum
1/2 oz. half & half cream
2 oz. coconut syrup
3 oz. pineapple juice
Blend with ice; pour into glass
Pineapple garnish

PIÑA COLADA, MONKALADA
House specialty glass, chilled
1 oz. Appleton Estate V/X Rum
1 oz. Mount Gay Eclipse Rum
1 oz. Cruzan Banana Run
2 scoops vanilla ice cream
2 oz. coconut syrup
2 oz. pineapple juice
Blend with ice; pour into glass
Float 1/2 oz. Appleton Estate V/X Rum
Float 1/2 oz. Tia Maria
Pineapple garnish

PIÑA COLADA, PORT ROYAL
House specialty glass, chilled
1 3/4 oz. Appleton Special Rum
1 oz. Chambord
1 1/2 oz. strawberry juice
1 1/2 oz. orange juice
1 1/2 oz. pineapple juice
2 oz. coconut syrup
Blend with ice; pour into glass
Float 1 oz. Tia Maria
Pineapple, orange and strawberry garnish

P

PIÑA COLADA, PUSSER'S ISLAND
House specialty glass, chilled
1 3/4 oz. Pusser's British Navy Rum
3/4 oz. Sloe Gin
2 oz. coconut syrup
3 1/2 oz. pineapple juice
Blend with ice; pour into glass
Pineapple garnish

PIÑA COLADA, STRAMARETTO
House specialty glass, chilled
1 oz. Bacardi Gold Rum
1 oz. Disaronno Amaretto
1/2 cup strawberries
1/2 oz. half & half cream
2 oz. coconut syrup
3 oz. pineapple juice
Blend with ice; pour into glass
Float 3/4 oz. Bacardi Select Rum
Pineapple and strawberry garnish

PIÑA COLADA, STRAWBERRY BANANA
House specialty glass, chilled
1 3/4 oz. Gosling's Black Seal Rum
1 oz. Cruzan Banana Rum
3/4 oz. Kahlúa
1 peeled, ripe banana
1 1/2 oz. coconut syrup
2 oz. pureed strawberries
2 oz. pineapple juice
Blend with ice; pour into glass
Pineapple garnish
Whipped cream garnish optional

PIÑA COLADA, TOASTED ALMOND
House specialty glass, chilled
1 1/4 oz. Bacardi Gold Rum
3/4 oz. Kahlúa
3/4 oz. Disaronno Amaretto
1/2 oz. half & half cream
2 oz. coconut syrup
3 oz. pineapple juice
Blend with ice; pour into glass
Float 1/2 oz. Kahlúa
Float 1/2 oz. Disaronno Amaretto
Pineapple garnish

PIÑA COLADA, TROPICAL MOON
House specialty glass, chilled
1 1/2 oz. Bacardi Light Rum
3/4 oz. Disaronno Amaretto
3/4 oz. Blue Curaçao
2 oz. coconut syrup
3 oz. pineapple juice
2 scoops chocolate ice cream
Blend with ice
Float 3/4 oz. Appleton Estate V/X Rum
Pineapple garnish

PIÑA COLADA, TROPICAL SPLASHES
House specialty glass, chilled
1 oz. Mount Gay Eclipse Rum
1 scoop vanilla ice cream
2 oz. coconut syrup
3 oz. pineapple juice
Blend with ice; pour into glass
Float 1 oz. Appleton Estate V/X Rum
Pineapple garnish

PINEAPPLE FIZZ
Cocktail glass, chilled
1 3/4 oz. Bacardi Select Rum
3/4 oz. lemon juice
1 3/4 oz. pineapple juice
Shake and strain
Orange garnish

PINK COCONUT
Bucket glass, ice
Build in glass
1 3/4 oz. Cruzan Coconut Rum
1 oz. Chambord
1 1/2 oz. pineapple juice
1 1/2 oz. orange juice
Lime garnish

PINK CREOLE
Cocktail glass, chilled
1 1/4 oz. Bacardi Select Rum
3/4 oz. Chambord
1 oz. orange juice
1 oz. pineapple juice
1 oz. sweet 'n' sour
Shake and strain
Orange garnish

P

PINK LEMONADE
House specialty glass, ice
1 1/4 oz. Bacardi Limón Rum
1 1/4 oz. Stolichnaya Limonnaya
1/2 oz. grenadine
3 oz. lemonade
2 oz. cranberry juice
Shake and strain
Splash Seven-Up
Orange and cherry garnish

PINK PARADISE
House specialty glass, ice
1 oz. Appleton Estate V/X Rum
1 oz. Mount Gay Eclipse Rum
1 oz. Disaronno Amaretto
1 1/2 oz. pineapple juice
3 oz. cranberry juice
Shake and strain
Pineapple and cherry garnish

PINK SLIPPER
House specialty glass, chilled
1 1/2 oz. Bacardi Light Rum
3/4 oz. Matusalem Golden Dry Rum
1 1/2 oz. coconut syrup
3 oz. pink lemonade concentrate
Blend with ice; pour into glass
Float 1/2 oz. Chambord
Whipped cream garnish

PIRANHA CLUB INITIATION
Bucket glass, ice
1 1/2 oz. Bacardi 151° Rum
3/4 oz. Blue Curaçao
1/2 oz. Peach Schnapps
1 1/2 oz. sweet 'n' sour
Fill with orange juice
Float 1/2 oz. Bacardi Select

PIRANHA PUNCH
Punch Bowl, ice
Build in bowl
26 oz. Matusalem Classic Black Rum
12 oz. Matusalem Red Flame Rum
12 oz. lime juice
12 oz. strawberry syrup
32 oz. orange juice
32 oz. pineapple juice
32 oz. mango or peach nectar
Thoroughly stir ingredients
Orange, lime and lemon garnish

PIRATE LOVE
House specialty glass, chilled
1 1/2 oz. Pyrat Pistol Rum
3/4 oz. Tia Maria
3/4 oz. Disaronno Amaretto
1 tsp. vanilla extract
2 scoops vanilla ice cream
Blend with ice; pour into glass
Whipped cream garnish
Sprinkle shaved chocolate

PLANTER'S PUNCH (1)
House specialty glass, ice
1 1/2 oz. Dark Jamaican Rum
1/2 oz. grenadine
2 dashes Angostura Bitters
1 1/2 oz. sweet 'n' sour
1 1/2 oz. orange juice
Shake and strain
Orange and cherry garnish

PLANTER'S PUNCH (2)
House specialty glass, ice
1 1/2 oz. Appleton Estate V/X Rum
1 oz. Bacardi Light Rum
3/4 oz. Triple Sec
2-3 dashes Angostura Bitters
1/2 oz. grenadine
1/2 oz. Rose's Lime Juice
2 oz. orange juice
2 oz. pineapple juice
Shake and strain
Orange, lime and lemon garnish

PLANTER'S PUNCH (3)
House specialty glass, ice
1 1/2 oz. Appleton Estate V/X Rum
1 1/4 oz. Bacardi Select Rum
3/4 oz. Curaçao or Triple Sec
2 or 3 dashes Angostura Bitters
3/4 oz. fresh lime juice
1/2 oz. grenadine
1 1/2 oz. orange juice
1 1/2 oz. pineapple juice
Shake and strain
Float 3/4 oz. Matusalem
Classic Black Rum
Orange, lime and lemon garnish

P

PLANTER'S RUM PUNCH
House specialty glass, ice
2 oz. Pyrat XO Reserve Rum
1 oz. simple syrup
3 dashes Angostura Bitters
3/4 oz. fresh lime juice
2 oz. fresh water
Shake and strain
Sprinkle nutmeg
Lemon garnish

PLYMOUTH ROCKS
Bucket glass, ice
Build in glass
1 1/2 oz. Bacardi Light Rum
1/2 fill grape juice
1/2 fill club soda
Lime garnish

PRESIDENTÉ
Cocktail glass, chilled
1 1/2 oz. Light Rum
1/2 oz. Martini & Rossi
        Extra Dry Vermouth
1/2 oz. Martini & Rossi
        Rosso Vermouth
1/2 oz. Cointreau
2 dashes grenadine
Stir and strain
Lemon twist garnish

PRIMAL SHOOTER
Presentation shot glass, chilled
Layer ingredients
1/2 fill with XO Café Coffee Liqueur
1/2 fill with Bacardi Light Rum

PRIMO BACIO
Champagne glass, chilled
1 oz. Vodka
1 oz. Tropico
1/2 oz. Chambord
1 oz. fresh orange juice
Shake and strain
Fill with Champagne
Orange twist garnish

PURPLE FLIRT
Rocks glass, chilled
1 oz. Gosling's Black Seal Rum
1/4 oz. Blue Curaçao
1/2 oz. sweet 'n' sour
1/4 oz. grenadine
1 oz. pineapple juice
Shake and strain
Orange and cherry garnish

PURPLE PIRANHA
House specialty glass, ice
3/4 oz. Bacardi Light Rum
3/4 oz. Bacardi Gold Rum
3/4 oz. Mount Gay Eclipse Rum
1 oz. Blue Curaçao
1 oz. cranberry juice
1 3/4 oz. sweet 'n' sour
Shake and strain
3/4 oz. Bacardi 151° Rum
Orange and cherry garnish

PUSSER'S DAILY RATION
House specialty glass, ice
2 oz. Pusser's British Navy Rum
1/2 oz. fresh lime juice
2 oz. sweet 'n' sour
Shake and strain
Fill with lemon/lime soda
Lime garnish

PUSSER'S STALEMATE
Coffee mug, heated
Build in glass
1 1/2 oz. Pusser's British Navy Rum
1/2 oz. XO Café Coffee Liqueur
1/2 oz. Dark Crème de Cacao
Fill with hot chocolate
Whipped cream garnish
Sprinkle shaved chocolate

PYRAT GIMLET
Cocktail glass, chilled
1 1/2 oz. Pyrat XO Reserve Rum
1/2 oz. Rose's Lime Juice
1/4 oz. Fresh lime juice
1/4 oz. Citrónge Orange Liqueur
Stir and strain
Lime garnish

QUARTER DECK
a.k.a. QUARTERMASTER
Bucket glass, ice
Build in glass
1 oz. Appleton Estate V/X Rum
1 oz. Mount Gay Eclipse Rum
3/4 oz. Sherry
Dash Rose's Lime Juice
Lime garnish

RAIN MAN
House specialty glass, ice
1 1/4 oz. Bacardi Select Rum
3/4 oz. Midori
4 oz. orange juice
Shake and strain
Orange garnish

RANCHO VALENCIA RUM PUNCH
Wine goblet, ice
1 oz. Bacardi Light Rum
1 oz. Mount Gay Eclipse Rum
1-2 dashes Angostura Bitters
1 1/2 oz. pineapple juice
1 1/2 oz. orange juice
Shake and strain
Float 3/4 oz. Appleton Estate V/X Rum
Orange, lemon and lime garnish

RASPBERRY CREAM
House specialty glass, chilled
1 oz. Bacardi Light Rum
3/4 oz. White Crème de Cacao
1/2 oz. Chambord
1 1/2 oz. raspberry yogurt
1 1/2 oz. half & half cream
2 scoops raspberry ice cream
Blend with ice; pour into glass
Whipped cream garnish
Float 3/4 oz. Chambord

RAZORBACK HOGCALLER
Rocks glass, ice
Build in glass
1 1/2 oz. Bacardi 151° Rum
1/2 oz. Green Chartreuse

RENDEZVOUS PUNCH
Coffee mug, heated
Build in glass
3/4 oz. Angostura Royal Oak Extra Old Rum
3/4 oz. Chambord
Fill with hot spiced apple cider
Garnish with cinnamon stick

RESERVA COCKTAIL
Cocktail glass, chilled
Rim glass with sugar
2 oz. Bacardi 8 Rum
3/4 oz. Cointreau
1/2 oz. fresh lime juice
1 oz. sweet 'n' sour
Shake and strain
Lime garnish

RHODODENDRON
House specialty glass, chilled
1 1/2 oz. Bacardi Light Rum
3/4 oz. Crème de Noyaux
1/2 oz. fresh lemon juice
1/2 oz. fresh lime juice
1/2 oz. simple syrup
2 oz. pineapple juice
Blend with ice; pour into glass
Float 3/4 oz. Gosling's Black Seal Rum
Lime garnish

RHUMBA ESCAPADES
House specialty glass, chilled
1 1/4 oz. Bacardi Light Rum
3/4 oz. Mount Gay Eclipse Rum
3/4 oz. Crème de Banana
1/2 oz. grenadine
1 1/2 oz. pineapple juice
1 peeled, ripe banana
1 scoop vanilla ice cream
Blend with ice; pour into glass
Whipped cream garnish

RHUM BARBANCOURT FREEZE
House specialty glass, chilled
1 3/4 oz. Rhum Barbancourt 3-Star Rum
1 oz. Blue Curaçao
1 oz. grapefruit juice
1 oz. sweet 'n' sour
2 oz. orange juice
Blend with ice; pour into glass
Float 3/4 oz. Rhum Barbancourt 5-Star Rum
Orange, lime and lemon garnish

R

RIVIERA DAYS
Rocks glass, ice
Build in glass
3/4 oz. Bacardi Light Rum
3/4 oz. Cointreau
3/4 oz. Chambord
Lemon garnish

RIVIERA NIGHTS
Rocks glass, ice
Build in glass
3/4 oz. Bacardi Gold Rum
3/4 oz. Bacardi Select Rum
3/4 oz. Citrónge Orange Liqueur
3/4 oz. Chambord
Lemon garnish

RUM ALEXANDER
a.k.a. PANAMA
House specialty glass, chilled
1 1/4 oz. Bacardi Light Rum
1 oz. White Crème de Cacao
1 oz. half & half cream
2 scoops vanilla ice cream
Blend with ice; pour into glass
Whipped cream garnish
Sprinkle nutmeg garnish

RUM AND BLACK
Rocks glass, chilled
1 3/4 oz. Dillon Dark Rhum
3/4 oz. black currant juice or syrup

RUMBALL
Brandy snifter, heated
1 3/4 oz. Pyrat Pistol Rum
3/4 oz. Godiva Chocolate Liqueur

RUM FIX
Bucket glass, ice
Build in glass
2 1/2 oz. Light Rum
2 1/2 oz. sweet 'n' sour
Fill with water
Lemon garnish

RUM MILK PUNCH
Bucket glass, ice
Build in glass
1 tsp. powdered sugar
2 oz. Light Rum
4 oz. milk
Shake and strain
Sprinkle nutmeg garnish

RUM MINT JULEP
House specialty glass, crushed ice
4 sprigs of mint
1/2 oz. simple syrup
2 oz. water
Muddle contents
2 1/2 oz. Light Rum
Mint sprigs garnish

RUM OLD-FASHIONED
Bucket glass
Build in glass
1/2 oz. simple syrup
2-3 dashes Angostura Bitters
1-2 splashes club soda
Orange slice and cherry
Muddle contents
Fill with ice
2 oz. Light Rum
1/2 oz. 151-proof Rum
Lime garnish

RUM PUNCH
Bucket glass, ice
1 1/2 oz. Overproof Rum (strong)
1/2 oz. lemon juice (sour)
2-3 dashes Angostura Bitters (bitters)
1 oz. grenadine (sweet)
2 oz. fresh fruit juice (weak)
Shake and strain
Sprinkle nutmeg
Pineapple and cherry garnish
Note: An island favorite. The traditional
way to remember this recipe: 1 of sour, 2
of sweet, 3 of strong, and 4 of weak, 5
drops of bitters and nutmeg spice, serve
well chilled and lots of ice.

RUM RUNNER (1)
House specialty glass, ice
3/4 oz. Bacardi Light Rum
3/4 oz. Appleton Estate V/X Rum
3/4 oz. Crème de Banana
3/4 oz. Blackberry Brandy
2 oz. orange juice
2 oz. sweet 'n' sour
Shake and strain
Float 3/4 oz. Matusalem
    Classic Black Rum
Orange garnish

RUM RUNNER (2)
House specialty glass, ice
1 1/4 oz. Bacardi Select Rum
1 1/4 oz. Mount Gay Eclipse Rum
3/4 oz. Blackberry Brandy
3/4 oz. Crème de Banana
1 1/2 oz. orange juice
1 1/2 oz. sweet 'n' sour
Shake and strain
Orange garnish

RUMSCAPES
House specialty glass, ice
Build in glass
1 1/4 oz. Bacardi Gold Rum
1 1/4 oz. Mount Gay Eclipse Rum
3/4 oz. Chambord
3/4 oz. Crème de Banana
Fill with ginger ale
Lime garnish

RUM SWIZZLE
House specialty glass, crushed ice
Build in glass
2 1/2 oz. Gosling's Black Seal Rum
3/4 oz. lime juice
1/2 oz. simple syrup
2-3 dashes Angostura Bitters
2 oz. club soda
Orange and cherry garnish

RUM TODDY
Coffee mug, heated
Build in glass
2 oz. Dark Rum
1/2 oz. simple syrup
Fill with hot water
Lemon garnish

SAN ANDREAS FAULT
Coffee mug, heated
Build in glass
1 oz. Bacardi Select Rum
3/4 oz. Cruzan Banana Rum
3/4 oz. Godiva Chocolate Liqueur
Fill with hot coffee
Whipped cream garnish

SANTIAGO (1)
House specialty glass, ice
1 1/4 oz. Bacardi Select Rum
1 1/4 oz. Mount Gay Eclipse Rum
3/4 oz. Cointreau
1/2 oz. Rose's Lime Juice
2 oz. sweet 'n' sour
2 dashes Angostura Bitters
Shake and strain
Fill with Champagne
Lime garnish

SANTIAGO (2)
House specialty glass, ice
1 1/2 oz. Bacardi Light Rum
3/4 oz. Cockspur V.S.O.R. Rum
3/4 oz. Triple Sec
2-3 dashes Angostura Bitters
1/2 oz. Rose's Lime Juice
1 1/2 oz. sweet 'n' sour
Shake and strain
Orange garnish

SAOCO
Highball glass, ice
Build in glass
1 3/4 oz. Light Rum
Fill with coconut milk

SASSAFRAS SUNSET
House specialty glass, ice
1 1/4 oz. Bacardi Gold Rum
1 oz. St. James Extra Old Rhum
3/4 oz. Triple Sec
1 oz. orange juice
1 1/2 oz. cranberry juice
1 1/2 oz. sweet 'n' sour
Shake and strain
Fill with club soda
Orange and cherry garnish

S

SCORPION
House Specialty glass, ice
1 1/4 oz. Light Rum
1 1/4 oz. Gold Rum
1 oz. White Wine
3/4 oz. Gin
3/4 oz. Brandy
3/4 oz. orgeat or Crème de Noyaux
1/2 oz. Rose's Lime Juice
1 1/2 oz. orange juice
1 1/2 oz. sweet 'n' sour
Shake and strain
Pineapple and cherry garnish

SCREAMING GOOD TIMES
House specialty glass, ice
1 1/2 oz. Bacardi Gold Rum
3/4 oz. Bacardi Limón
3/4 oz. Midori
2 scoops vanilla ice cream
Blend with ice; pour into glass
Whipped cream garnish

SCREAMING WEEBIES
House specialty glass, ice
1 oz. Matusalem Light Dry Rum
1/2 oz. Cruzan Coconut Rum
1/2 oz. Midori
1/2 oz. grenadine
2 oz. pineapple juice
2 oz. Seven-Up
Shake and strain
Orange and cherry garnish

SEA SIDE LIBERTY
House specialty glass, chilled
1 oz. Mount Gay Eclipse Rum
1 oz. Cruzan Coconut Rum
3/4 oz. XO Café Coffee Liqueur
1/2 oz. half & half cream
1 oz. coconut cream
3 oz. pineapple juice
Blend with ice; pour into glass
Pineapple garnish

SHARK ATTACK
Bucket glass, ice
Build in glass
1 1/4 oz. Bacardi Light Rum
Fill with lemonade
Float 3/4 oz. Blue Curaçao
Orange garnish

SHARK BITE
Bucket glass, ice
Build in glass
1 oz. Appleton Estate V/X Rum
Fill with orange juice
Float 3/4 oz. grenadine
Orange slice garnish
Note: Immerse orange slice
    to resemble shark's fin

SHARK'S TOOTH
House specialty glass, chilled
1 1/2 oz. Bacardi Light Rum
1 oz. Blue Curaçao
3/4 oz. White Crème de Cacao
2 scoops vanilla ice cream
Blend with ice; pour into glass
Whipped cream garnish
Float 1/2 oz. grenadine

SHORE BOAT
Coffee mug, heated
Build in glass
1 oz. Pusser's British Navy Rum
3/4 oz. Appleton Estate V/X Rum
3/4 oz. Angostura Caribbean Rum Cream
1/2 oz. Kahlúa
Fill with hot coffee
Whipped cream garnish

SHORE BREEZE
Bucket glass, ice
Build in glass
1 1/2 oz. Bacardi Light Rum
2-3 dashes Angostura Bitters
2 oz. cranberry juice
2 oz. pineapple juice
Float 1/2 oz. Mount Gay Eclipse Rum

SHOT THRU THE HEART
Rocks glass, chilled
Build in glass
3/4 oz. Bacardi Select
3/4 oz. Kahlúa
3/4 oz. Bailey's Irish Cream
3/4 oz. Grand Marnier

SLIPPED DISK
House specialty glass, chilled
1 1/4 oz. Bacardi Gold Rum
1 oz. Captain Morgan Spiced Rum
3/4 oz. Disaronno Amaretto
3/4 oz. Grand Marnier
1/2 oz. cranberry juice
1/2 oz. orange juice
1/2 oz. grenadine
1/2 oz. sweet 'n' sour
1 oz. coconut syrup
1 oz. pineapple juice
Blend with ice; pour into glass
Pineapple garnish

SLOPPY JOE'S COCKTAIL
Cocktail glass, chilled
1 1/2 oz. Bacardi Light Rum
1/2 oz. Martini & Rossi Extra Dry Vermouth
1/4 oz. Triple Sec
1/4 oz. grenadine
1/2 oz. fresh lime juice
Shake and strain
Lime garnish

SLOW TROPICO CRUISE
Bucket glass, ice
Build in glass
1 1/4 oz. Tropico
3/4 oz. Sloe Gin
1 1/2 oz. pineapple juice
1 1/2 oz. orange juice
Orange garnish

SMOOTH SCREW
House specialty glass, chilled
3/4 oz. Appleton Estate V/X Rum
3/4 oz. Mount Gay Eclipse Rum
3/4 oz. Tia Maria
1 1/2 oz. pineapple juice
1 1/2 oz. orange juice
Blend with ice; pour into glass
Float 3/4 oz. Cockspur V.S.O.R. Rum

SNEAK & PEAK COCKTAIL
Cocktail glass, chilled
1 1/4 oz. Bacardi Limón Rum
1 oz. Stolichnaya Razberri Vodka
1/2 oz. Chambord
1 oz. Sprite
1 oz. sweet 'n' sour
Shake and strain
Lemon twist and raspberry garnish

SOUTH OF FRANCE
House specialty glass, chilled
1 1/2 oz. Bacardi Light Rum
1 oz. B&B
1 1/2 oz. coconut syrup
2 1/2 oz. pineapple juice
Blend with ice; pour into glass
Pineapple and cherry garnish

SPATS COLUMBO
House specialty glass, ice
Build in glass
1 1/2 oz. Bacardi Light Rum
1 oz. Midori
2 oz. orange juice
2 oz. pineapple juice
Float 1/2 oz. Sloe Gin
Pineapple and cherry garnish

STARBOARD TACK
House specialty glass, ice
Build in glass
1 1/2 oz. Mount Gay Eclipse Rum
1 oz. Mount Gay Special Reserve Rum
1/2 fill cranberry juice
1/2 fill orange juice
Float 3/4 oz. Mount Gay Extra Old Rum
Orange and cherry garnish

STARBURST
House specialty glass, chilled
1 1/2 oz. Bacardi Select Rum
1 1/2 oz. Bacardi Limón Rum
1 oz. Rose's lime juice
2 oz. pureed strawberries
3 oz. orange juice
Blend with ice; pour into glass
Strawberry garnish

STEALTH BOMBER
House specialty glass, ice
1 1/4 oz. Matusalem Light Dry Rum
1 1/4 oz. Matusalem Golden Dry Rum
3/4 oz. Blue Curaçao
1 1/2 oz. grapefruit juice
1 1/2 oz. cranberry juice
Shake and strain
Float 1 oz. Matusalem Classic Black Rum

STORM-A-LONG BAY
House specialty glass, chilled
1 1/2 oz. Matusalem Classic Black Rum
3/4 oz. Chambord
1 oz. cranberry juice
2 oz. pineapple juice
2 scoops vanilla ice cream
Blend with ice; pour into glass
Whipped cream garnish

STRAWBERRY BANANA SPLIT
House specialty glass, chilled
1 1/4 oz. Angostura Royal Oak
    Extra Old Rum
3/4 oz. Crème de Banana
1/2 cup strawberries
1 oz. half & half cream
1/2 tsp. vanilla
2 scoops vanilla ice cream
Blend with ice; pour into glass
Whipped cream and banana garnish

STRAWBERRY SMASH
House specialty glass, chilled
1 oz. Bacardi Gold Rum
1 oz. Chambord
1/2 oz. Bacardi 151° Rum
1/2 cup strawberries
1 ripe banana
1 oz. orange juice
2 oz. sweet 'n' sour
Blend with ice; pour into glass
Strawberry garnish

STRAW HOUSE HUMMER
House specialty glass, chilled
1 1/4 oz. Bacardi Light Rum
3/4 oz. Crème de Banana
3/4 oz. Disaronno Amaretto
1 peeled, ripe banana
1 oz. orange juice
1 oz. sweet 'n' sour
Blend with ice; pour into glass
Float 3/4 oz. Dillon Dark Rhum
Whipped cream and banana garnish

SUFFERING BASTARD
House specialty glass, ice
1 1/2 oz. St. James Extra Old Rhum
3/4 oz. Bacardi Light Rum
3/4 oz. Crème de Noyaux
3/4 oz. Cointreau
1/2 oz. simple syrup
1 1/2 oz. fresh lime juice
Shake and strain
Cucumber peel garnish

SUNRISE
Bucket glass, ice
Build in glass
1 1/2 oz. Bacardi Select Rum
1/2 oz. Triple Sec
1/2 oz. orange juice
Fill with grapefruit juice
Float 1/2 oz. grenadine

SUN SEEKER
House specialty glass, ice
1 1/4 oz. Bacardi Select Rum
1 oz. Mount Gay Eclipse Rum
1 oz. Crème de Banana
2 oz. pineapple juice
2 oz. orange juice
Splash Seven-Up
Orange and cherry garnish

SURF SIDER
Cocktail glass, chilled
1 1/4 oz. Gosling's Black Seal Rum
3/4 oz. Blue Curaçao
3/4 oz. Grand Marnier
1/2 oz. Rose's Lime Juice
1 1/4 oz. pineapple juice
Shake and strain
Lime garnish

THAI SMILE
House specialty glass, ice
1 1/2 oz. Bacardi Light Rum
1 oz. Mount Gay Eclipse Rum
3/4 oz. Blue Curaçao
1 1/4 oz. apple juice
3 oz. pineapple juice
Shake and strain
Float 3/4 oz. Matusalem Classic Black Rum
Pineapple garnish

TIDAL WAVE
Bucket glass, ice
3/4 oz. Bacardi Gold Rum
3/4 oz. Captain Morgan Spiced Rum
3/4 oz. Crème de Banana
2 oz. orange juice
Shake and strain
Float 3/4 oz. Galliano Liquore

TIGHTER CIDER
Coffee mug, heated
Build in glass
1 oz. Appleton Special Rum
3/4 oz. Calvados
3/4 oz. Apple Schnapps
1 tsp. apple butter
2 pinches cinnamon
Fill with hot apple cider
Apple garnish

TOUR de CARIBBEAN
House specialty glass, ice
3/4 oz. Bacardi Select Rum
3/4 oz. Mount Gay Eclipse Rum
3/4 oz. Crème de Banana
2 oz. cranberry juice
2 oz. orange juice
Shake and strain
Float 1/2 oz. Tia Maria
Float 1/2 oz. Appleton Estate V/X Rum
Orange and cherry garnish

TRADE WINDS
House specialty glass, chilled
3/4 oz. Cruzan Estate Light Rum
3/4 oz. Brandy
3/4 oz. Chambord
1 oz. orange juice
2 oz. sweet 'n' sour
Shake and strain
Lemon twist garnish

TRIP TO THE BEACH
House specialty glass, ice
1 oz. Bacardi Gold Rum
1 oz. Bacardi Limón Rum
1/2 oz. Peach Schnapps
3 oz. fresh orange juice
Shake and strain
Orange and cherry garnish

TROPICAL DEPRESSION
Coffee mug, heated
Build in glass
1 1/4 oz. Dillon Dark Rhum
1/2 oz. Disaronno Amaretto
1/2 oz. Godiva Chocolate Liqueur
Fill with hot coffee
Float 3/4 oz. Tia Maria
Whipped cream garnish

TROPICAL ITCH
House specialty glass, ice
1 oz. Bacardi Gold Rum
1 oz. Mount Gay Eclipse Rum
1/2 oz. grenadine
1 oz. orange juice
1 oz. grapefruit juice
1 oz. pineapple juice
Shake and strain
Float 1/2 oz. Cruzan Banana Rum
Float 1/2 oz. Cruzan Pineapple Rum
Orange and cherry garnish

TROPICO TANGO
House specialty glass, ice
2 oz. Tropico
1 oz. Bacardi Limón Rum
2 oz. cranberry juice
2 oz. orange juice
Shake and strain
Orange and cherry garnish

VOODOO JUICE
House specialty glass, ice
1 oz. Cruzan Orange Rum
1 oz. Cruzan Banana Rum
1 oz. Cruzan Coconut Rum
1 oz. Cruzan Pineapple Rum
1 1/2 oz. cranberry juice
1 1/2 oz. orange juice
1 1/2 oz. pineapple juice
Shake and strain
Float 3/4 oz. Cruzan Estate Diamond Rum
Orange and cherry garnish

VOODOO SHOOTER
Presentation shot glass, chilled
Layer ingredients
1/3 fill Tia Maria
1/3 fill Cruzan Rum Cream
1/3 fill Bacardi Select Rum

VULCAN MIND PROBE
Presentation shot glass, chilled
Layer ingredients
1/2 fill with Sambuca
1/2 fill with Bacardi 151° Rum

WYNBREEZER
House specialty glass, ice
1 oz. Rhum Barbancourt 3-Star Rum
1 oz. Cockspur V.S.O.R. Rum
3/4 oz. Citrónge Orange Liqueur
3/4 oz. Rose's Lime Juice
2 oz. orange juice
Shake and strain
Fill with Seven-Up
Float 3/4 oz. Angostura Royal Oak
        Extra Old Rum
Orange slice garnish

YELLOW BIRD (1)
Bucket glass, ice
Build in glass
3/4 oz. Light Rum
3/4 oz. Galliano Liquore
1/2 fill pineapple juice
1/2 fill orange juice

YELLOW BIRD (2)
House specialty glass, chilled
1 oz. Light Rum
3/4 oz. Galliano Liquore
1/2 oz. Crème de Banana
1/4 oz. simple syrup
2 oz. orange juice
2 oz. pineapple juice
Blend with ice; pour into glass
Pineapple garnish

YELLOW DEVIL
Bucket glass, ice
Build in glass
1 oz. Mount Gay Eclipse Rum
1 oz. Galliano Liquore
Fill with orange juice
Orange garnish

ZOMBIE (1)
House specialty glass, ice
2 oz. Appleton Estate V/X Rum
3/4 oz. Crème de Noyaux
3/4 oz. Triple Sec
1 1/2 oz. sweet 'n' sour
1 1/2 oz. orange juice
Shake and strain
Float 3/4 oz. Bacardi 151° Rum
Orange and cherry garnish

ZOMBIE (2)
House specialty glass, ice
1 1/2 oz. Mount Gay Eclipse Rum
1 oz. Bacardi Light Rum
3/4 oz. Triple Sec
3/4 oz. grenadine
1 1/2 oz. pineapple juice
1 1/2 oz. orange juice
1 1/2 oz. grapefruit juice
Shake and strain
Splash club soda
Float 3/4 oz. Bacardi Select Rum
Orange and cherry garnish

ZOMBIE, PINK
House specialty glass, ice
1 1/2 oz. Appleton Special Rum
3/4 oz. Bacardi Limón Rum
1 oz. Crème de Banana
1/2 oz. grenadine
1 oz. fresh lime juice
2 oz. passion fruit syrup
2 oz. pineapple juice
2 oz. pink grapefruit juice
Shake and strain
Float 3/4 oz. Bacardi 151° Rum
Pineapple and cherry garnish

Z STREET SLAMMER
Rocks glass, chilled
1 1/4 oz. Appleton Estate V/X Rum
3/4 oz. Crème de Banana
1 3/4 oz. pineapple juice
1/2 oz. grenadine
Shake and strain

The Glossary of Caribbean Rum

Rums in bold print have been reviewed in the book.

- A. H. RIISE CUSTOM RUMS — A producer of Virgin Island rum located on St. Thomas. The company markets two blends of gold rum, one aged between 3-6 years, the other aged 6-12 years.

- **ANGOSTURA CARIBBEAN RUM CREAM**® — A liqueur made from a blend of fresh cream, proprietary flavorings, and aged, continuous-distilled rum.

- **ANGOSTURA 1824 LIMITED RESERVE**® — A Trinidadian rum made from a blend of continuous-distilled, molasses-based rums that are aged for a minimum of 12 years in charred, American oak barrels. The rums are hand-blended in small batches and then recasked. It is marketed at 40% abv (80 proof).

- **ANGOSTURA OLD OAK GOLD**® — A Trinidadian rum made from a blend of molasses-based, continuous-distilled rums that are aged in charred, American oak barrels between 3 and 5 years. It is marketed at 40% and 43% abv.

- **ANGOSTURA OLD OAK WHITE**® — A Trinidadian rum made from a blend of molasses-based, continuous-distilled rums that are aged in charred, American oak barrels between 3 and 5 years. After aging, the rum is charcoal filtered to remove its color. It is marketed at 40% and 43% abv.

- **ANGOSTURA ROYAL OAK EXTRA OLD TRINIDAD**® — A Trinidadian rum made from a blend of molasses-based, continuous-distilled rums that are aged up to 8 years in charred, American oak barrels It is marketed 40% and 43% abv.

- **APPLETON ESTATE EXTRA JAMAICA**® — A Jamaican rum made from a blend of molasses-based, pot-distilled and continuous-distilled spirits and aged in American white oak barrels up to 18 years. After blending, the rum is rested in large oak vats to allow the blend to marry. 43% abv (86 proof)

- **APPLETON ESTATE 21-YEAR OLD JAMAICA**® — A Jamaican rum made from a blend of molasses-based, pot-distilled and continuous-distilled spirits and aged in American white oak barrels a minimum of 21-years. The blend is aged an additional 2 years to allow the constituent rums to marry. 43% abv (86 proof)

- **APPLETON ESTATE 250**TH **ANNIVERSARY EDITION**® — A Jamaican rum made from a rare blend of molasses-based, pot-distilled spirits, some having aged in American white oak barrels in excess of 50-years. 43% abv (86 proof)

- **APPLETON ESTATE V/X JAMAICA**® — A Jamaican rum made from a blend of molasses-based, pot-distilled and continuous-distilled spirits and aged in American oak barrels for 5 to 10 years. After blending, the rum is rested in large oak vats to allow the blend to marry. It is marketed at 40% and 43% abv.

- **APPLETON SPECIAL JAMAICA**® — A Jamaican rum made from a blend of molasses-based, pot-distilled and continuous-distilled spirits that are aged in American oak barrels. 43% abv (86 proof)

- **BACARDI 8**® — A Puerto Rican rum made from a blend of molasses-based, continuous-distilled and pot-distilled rums that are charcoal filtered and aged a minimum of 8 years in charred, American white oak barrels. The rum is crafted using the original recipe and aging process created by Don Facundo Bacardi in 1862. 40% abv (80 proof)

- **BACARDI® LIMÓN**™ — A Puerto Rican rum made from a blend of molasses-based, continuous-distilled and pot-distilled rums that are aged 1 year in charred, oak barrels. An all-natural blend of lemon, lime and grapefruit extracts is added to the rum during blending. 35% abv (70 proof)

- **BACARDI 151°**® — A Puerto Rican overproof rum made from a blend of molasses-based, continuous-distilled rums, charcoal filtered and aged in charred, oak barrels for up to 2 years. 75.5% abv (151 proof)

- **BACARDI SELECT**® — A Puerto Rican rum made from a blend of molasses-based, continuous-distilled and pot-distilled rums. The constituent rums are aged between 1 and 4 years in charred, American white oak barrels. 40% abv (80 proof)

- **BACARDI SUPERIOR CARTA BLANCA (LIGHT-DRY)**® — A Puerto Rican rum made from a blend of molasses-based, continuous-distilled and pot-distilled rums. It is aged a minimum of 1 year in American white oak barrels. The rum is charcoal filtered to remove its color. Bacardi Carta Blanca is the world's best selling spirit. 40% abv (80 proof)

- **BACARDI SUPERIOR CARTA DE ORO (GOLD)**® — A Puerto Rican rum made from a blend of molasses-based, continuous-distilled and pot-distilled rums. It is charcoal filtered and aged a minimum of 2 years in American white oak barrels. 40% abv (80 proof)

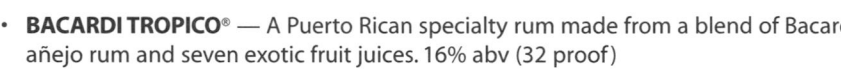

- **BACARDI TROPICO**® — A Puerto Rican specialty rum made from a blend of Bacardi añejo rum and seven exotic fruit juices. 16% abv (32 proof)

- BRITISH ROYAL NAVY IMPERIAL RUM — A naval rum made from a blend of alembic spirits distilled in the West Indies and aged in American oak barrels. The rum is marketed in an authentic, 4.54-liter demijohn flagon with a stainless steel label affixed to the woven wickerwork. 54% abv (108 proof)

- C. J. WRAY — A Jamaican rum produced by J. Wray & Nephew made from a blend of dry, molasses-based, aged white rums. 40% abv (80 proof)

- **CADENHEAD'S ORIGINAL CASK STRENGTH**® **COLLECTION** — A collection of special bottlings by the Scottish firm, Cadenhead's. The cask strength collection is comprised of pot-distilled rums that are bottled unfiltered, undiluted and unaltered in anyway. The cask strength rums range in strength from 70.4% abv (140.8 proof) to 74.1% abv (148.2% proof). The Cadenhead's Collection concentrates on the rums of smaller producers from Jamaica, Barbados and Guyana.

- **CADENHEAD'S ORIGINAL GREEN LABEL® COLLECTION** — A collection of special bottlings by the Scottish firm, Cadenhead's. These rums are similar to the cask strength releases, in as much as they are pot-distilled unfiltered, unaltered and bottled from a single cask. The one point of difference being that the Green Label rums are diluted with pure water to reduce it from cask strength to 46% abv (92 proof). The Cadenhead's Collection concentrates on the rums of smaller producers from Jamaica, Barbados and Guyana.

- CAPTAIN MORGAN BLACK LABEL — A Puerto Rican rum distilled by Serrallès made from a blend of molasses-based, continuous-distilled and pot-distilled rums aged up to 7 years. It is marketed at 37.5% abv and 40% abv.

- CAPTAIN MORGAN ORIGINAL SPICED — A Puerto Rican rum distilled by Serrallès made from a blend of molasses-based, continuous-distilled and pot-distilled rums and a proprietary blend of Caribbean spices. 35% abv (70 proof)

- CAPTAIN MORGAN PARROT BAY — A Puerto Rican rum distilled by Serrallès made from a blend of molasses-based, continuous-distilled rums with tropical flavors and natural coconut added. 25% abv (50 proof)

- CAPTAIN MORGAN PRIVATE STOCK — A Puerto Rican rum distilled by Serrallès made from a blend of molasses-based, barrel-aged continuous-distilled and pot-distilled rums and a proprietary blend of Caribbean spices. 40% abv (80 proof)

- CARONI FÉLICITÉ GOLD — A Trinidadian rum made from a blend of molasses-based rums on the Félicité Estate. Introduced in 1820, it is possibly the oldest label of rum on Trinidad. 40% and 43% abv

- CARONI SPECIAL OLD CASK — A Trinidadian rum made from a blend of molasses-based, continuous-distilled rums and aged for up to 10 years. 40% and 43% abv

- CARONI STALLION PUNCHEON — A Trinidadian rum made from a blend of molasses-based, continuous-distilled rums. At 78% abv (156 proof), it is the strongest rum on Trinidad.

- **COCKSPUR FIVE STAR FINE®** — A Barbadian rum made from a blend of molasses-based, continuous-distilled and pot-distilled rums that are aged a minimum of 2 years in charred, American oak barrels. It is produced in both a gold and white style and marketed at 37.5%, 40% and 43% abv.

- **COCKSPUR OLD GOLD RESERVE®** — A Barbadian rum made from a blend of molasses-based, continuous-distilled and pot-distilled rums that are aged a minimum of 5 years. 43% abv (86 proof)

- **COCKSPUR V.S.O.R. (VERY SUPERIOR OLD RESERVE)®** — A Barbadian rum made from a blend of molasses-based, continuous-distilled and pot-distilled rums that are aged a minimum of 10 years. 43% abv (86 proof)

- **CONCH REPUBLIC ATOCHA GOLD SPICED®** — An American spiced rum made from a blend of molasses-based, continuous-distilled and pot-distilled rums that are aged 2 to 3 years in charred, American oak bourbon barrels. The rum contains 24-karat gold flakes. 40% abv (80 proof)

- **CONCH REPUBLIC DURDY WHITE®** — An American rum made from a blend of molasses based, continuous-distilled and pot-distilled rums, aged 4 to 8 years in charred, American oak bourbon barrels and charcoal filtered to remove its color. 40% abv (80 proof)

- **CONCH REPUBLIC ISLAMORADA LIGHT**® — An American rum made from a blend of molasses-based, continuous-distilled and pot-distilled rums, aged 2 to 3 years in charred, American oak bourbon barrels and charcoal filtered to remove its color. 40% abv (80 proof)

- **CONCH REPUBLIC MATECUMBE DARK**® — An American rum made from a blend of molasses-based, continuous-distilled and pot-distilled rums that are aged 2 to 3 years in charred, American oak bourbon barrels. 40% abv (80 proof)

- CORUBA DELUXE DARK — A Jamaican rum produced by J. Wray & Nephew made from a blend of molasses-based, barrel-aged, continuous-distilled and pot-distilled rums. It is marketed at 37.2% and 40% abv.

- **CRUZAN ESTATE DARK**® — A Virgin Island rum made from a blend of molasses-based, continuous-distilled rums that are lightly filtered and aged in charred, American oak barrels between 2 and 4 years. 40% abv (80 proof)

- **CRUZAN ESTATE DIAMOND**® — A Virgin Island rum made from a blend of molasses-based, continuous-distilled rums that are lightly filtered and aged in charred, American oak barrels between 5 and 10 years. 40% abv (80 proof)

- **CRUZAN ESTATE LIGHT**® — A Virgin Island rum made from a blend of molasses-based, continuous-distilled rums that are aged in charred oak barrels from 2 to 3 years. The rum is charcoal-filtered to its remove color. 40% abv (80 proof)

- **CRUZAN FRUIT-FLAVORED**® — A line of Virgin Island rums made from a blend of molasses-based, continuous-distilled rums that are aged in charred, oak barrels from 2 to 3 years. They are charcoal-filtered and natural orange, banana, pineapple or coconut flavorings are added to create each individual rum. 27.5% abv (55 proof)

- **CRUZAN JUNKANU CITRUS**® — A Virgin Island rum made from a blend of molasses-based, continuous-distilled rums aged in charred, American oak barrels between 2 and 3 years. It is charcoal-filtered to remove color and natural orange and lemon flavors are added. 35% abv (70 proof)

- **CRUZAN RUM CREAM**® — A liqueur produced in Ireland made with Irish cream, caramel, vanilla and Cruzan light rum. 17% abv (34 proof)

- **CRUZAN SINGLE BARREL ESTATE**® — A Virgin Island rum made in limited quantities from a blend of molasses-based, continuous-distilled rums aged in charred, oak barrels between 5 and 12 years. After blending, the rum is placed in a newly charred, white oak cask for secondary aging. 40% abv (80 proof)

- **DILLON DARK**® — A Martinique agricole rhum made in a continuous still and aged a minimum of 6-years in American white oak barrels. It is also marketed as **DILLON RHUM VIEUX CARTE NOIRE**® on Martinique. 40% abv (80 proof)

- **DILLON GRAND RHUM BLANC**® — A Martinique agricole rhum made in a continuous still and aged for a minimum of 3-months, then charcoal filtered to remove its coloring. It is marketed at 50%, 55% and 62% abv.

- **DILLON RHUM PAILLE**® — A Martinique agricole rhum made in a continuous still and aged for a minimum of 1-year in American oak barrels. 50% abv (100 proof)

- **DILLON TRÈSVIEUX**® — A Martinique agricole rhum made in a continuous still and 15-years in American oak barrels. 45% abv (90 proof)

- DOORLY'S FINE OLD BARBADOS — A Barbadian rum produced by R. L. Seale & Company made from a blend of molasses-based, amber spirits that are barrel-aged for 5 years. It is marketed at 40% and 43% abv.

- DOORLY'S HARBOUR POLICEMAN — A Barbadian rum produced by R. L. Seale & Company made from a blend of molasses-based, barrel-aged spirits. It is marketed in a figural bottle at 40% abv (80 proof).

- DOORLY'S MACAW — A Barbadian rum produced by R. L. Seale & Company made from a blend of unaged, molasses-based spirits. It is marketed at 40%, 43% and 75.5% abv.

- DOORLY'S XO — A Barbadian rum produced by R. L. Seale & Company made from a blend of molasses-based, barrel-aged spirits, and finished with a second maturation in sherry oak casks. 40% abv (80 proof)

- **FERNANDES FORRES PARK PUNCHEON**® — An overproof Trinidadian rum made from a blend of continuous-distilled, molasses-based rums. 75% abv (150 proof)

- **FERNANDES "19"**® — A Trinidadian rum made from a blend of continuous-distilled, molasses-based rums that are aged 3 to 5 years in charred, oak bourbon barrels. It is marketed in a white and gold version at 37.5%, 40% and 43% abv.

- **GOSLING'S BLACK SEAL**® — A Bermudian rum made from a premium blend of 3-year old, molasses-based rums according to the original family recipe from 1860. 40% abv (80 proof)

- HAVANA CLUB — A line of Cuban rums made from molasses-based, continuous-distilled rums aged a minimum of 18-months in American white oak vats. The Havana Club line includes SILVER DRY (37.5% abv), 3-YEAR (40% abv), 5-YEAR (40% abv) and the AÑEJO RESERVE (7-years and 40% abv).

- **J. BALLY RHUM BLANC**® — A Martinique agricole rhum made in a continuous still and bottled unaged. 50% abv (100 proof)

- **J. BALLY RHUM PAILLE**® — A Martinique agricole rhum made in a continuous still and barrel-aged a minimum of 12-months. 50% abv (100 proof)

- **J. BALLY RHUM VIEUX MILLÉSIME**® — A Martinique agricole rhum made in a continuous still that is then barrel-aged and vintage-dated. Current vintages include: 1924; 1929; 1955; 1960; 1970; 1975; 1979; 1982; 1985; 1986; 1989 and 1990. All were bottled at 45% abv (90 proof).

- **J. BALLY RHUM VIEUX 7-ANS D'AGE**® — A Martinique agricole rhum made in a continuous still and barrel-aged a minimum of 7 years. 45% abv (90 proof)

- **J. BALLY RHUM VIEUX 12-ANS D'AGE**® — A Martinique agricole rhum made in a continuous still and barrel-aged a minimum of 12 years. 45% abv (90 proof)

- J. WRAY AND NEPHEW WHITE OVERPROOF — A Jamaican rum made from a blend of molasses-based, continuous-distilled and pot-distilled rums that are barrel-aged a minimum of 2 years. It is charcoal filtered to remove color. 63% abv (126 proof)

- LA FAVORITE CUVÉE SPÉCIALE DE LA FLIBUSTE — A Martinique agricole rhum. Barrel-aged 33-years, it has the distinction of being the oldest Martinique vieux rhum. 40% abv (80 proof)

- LA MAUNY HORS D'AGE — A Martinique agricole rhum made in a continuous still and barrel-aged for a minimum of 10 years. 43% abv (86 proof)

- LAMB'S NAVY RUM — A naval rum produced by Alfred Lamb's of London made from a blend of molasses-based, pot- distilled and column-distilled rums from distilleries in Jamaica, Guyana, Barbados and Trinidad. 40% abv (80 proof)

- **MATUSALEM CLASSIC BLACK®** — A rum of Cuban origin made from a blend of molasses-based, continuous-distilled rums and Solera aged a minimum of 7-years. 40% abv (80 proof)

- **MATUSALEM GOLDEN DRY (CARTA ORO)®** — A rum of Cuban origin made from a blend of molasses-based, continuous-distilled rums and Solera aged a minimum of 5-years. 40% abv (80 proof)

- **MATUSALEM GRAN RESERVA®** — A rum of Cuban origin built around a core "blender rum" that has been Solera aged approximately 15 years and is comprised of rums between 8- and 32-years old. Various other rums barrel-aged from 3 to 4 years are added. 40% abv (80 proof)

- **MATUSALEM LIGHT DRY (CARTA PLATA)®** — A rum of Cuban origin made from a blend of molasses-based, continuous-distilled rums, barrel-aged in oak barrels for a minimum of 2-years and charcoal-filtered to its remove color. 40% abv (80 proof)

- **MATUSALEM RED FLAME®** — An overproof rum of Cuban origin made from a blend of molasses-based, continuous-distilled rums and aged in American oak barrels for a minimum of 2-years. 75.5% abv (151 proof)

- **MOUNT GAY ECLIPSE®** — A Barbadian rum made from a blend of molasses-based, continuous-distilled and pot-distilled rums a minimum of 2 years in maturity. It is marketed 37.5%, 40%, 43% and 77% abv.

- **MOUNT GAY EXTRA OLD®** — A Barbadian rum made from a blend of mature pot still and continuous still rums from 12 to 17 years in maturity. 43% abv (86 proof)

- **MOUNT GAY SPECIAL RESERVE®** — A Barbadian rum made from a blend of molasses-based, continuous-distilled and pot-distilled rums a minimum of 2 years in maturity. The rum is charcoal filtered to remove its color and marketed at 40% and 43% abv.

- **MOUNT GAY SUGAR CANE®** — A Barbadian rum blended with a high proportion of pot-distilled rums that range in maturity up to 7 years. It is marketed at 40% and 43% abv.

- MYERS'S LEGEND — A Jamaican rum produced by Fred L. Myers & Son made from a blend of molasses-based, pot-distilled rums that are aged up to 10 years. 40% abv (80 proof)

- MYERS'S ORIGINAL PLANTER'S PUNCH — A Jamaican rum produced by Fred L. Myers & Son made from a blend of molasses-based, pot-distilled rums aged up to 4 years. 40% abv (80 proof)

- OLD BRIGAND BLACK AND WHITE — A Barbadian rum produced by R. L. Seale & Company made from a blend of molasses-based rums aged less than 5 years. 40% abv (80 proof)

- OLD BRIGAND BLACK LABEL SUPERIOR — A Barbadian rum produced by R. L. Seale & Company made from a blend of molasses-based rums and aged up to 13-years. It is marketed at 37%, 40% and 43% abv.

-  **PUSSER'S BLUE LABEL BRITISH NAVY**® — A naval rum made from a blend of six, molasses-based, pot-distilled rums, produced at several West Indies distilleries in Guyana, Trinidad and the British Virgin Islands. 47.75% abv (95.5 proof)

-  **PUSSER'S RED LABEL BRITISH NAVY**® — A naval rum made from a blend of six, molasses-based, pot-distilled rums, produced at several West Indies distilleries in Guyana, Trinidad and the British Virgin Islands. 40% abv (80 proof)

-  **PYRAT CASK 23**® — An Anguillan rum made from a blend of molasses-based, barrel-aged, alembic rums produced by 7 Caribbean distillers. The blend is Solera aged in 55-gallon, French oak barrels. The rums in the blend range in age from 8-40 years. 40% abv (80 proof)

-  **PYRAT PISTOL**® — An Anguillan rum made from a blend of molasses-based, barrel-aged alembic rums produced by 7 Caribbean distillers. The blend is Solera aged in 55-gallon, French oak barrels. The rums in the blend range in age from 8-40 years. 40% abv (80 proof)

-  **PYRAT XO RESERVE RUM—PLANTER'S GOLD**® — An Anguillan rum made from a blend of molasses-based, barrel-aged alembic rums produced by 7 Caribbean distillers. The blend is Solera aged in 55-gallon, French oak barrels. The rums in the blend range in age from 8-40 years. 40% abv (80 proof)

- R. L. SEALE FOURSQUARE SPICED — A Barbadian rum made from a blend of barrel-aged Barbados rum and ground nutmeg, cinnamon and vanilla. 35% abv (70 proof)

- RED RUM — A liqueur made from a blend of Virgin Island rum and natural fruit flavorings. It is produced and imported by the Three-D Company of San Francisco.

-  **RHUM BARBANCOURT FIVE STAR RÉSERVE SPÉCIALE**® — A Haitian agricole rhum double distilled, first in a column still and then in a copper pot still. The rhum is diluted to 50% abv before being aged a minimum of 8 years in Limousin oak vats. It is marketed at 40% and 43% abv.

-  **RHUM BARBANCOURT RÉSERVE DU DOMAINE**® — A Haitian agricole rhum double distilled, first in a column still and then in a copper pot still. The rhum is diluted to 50% abv before being aged a minimum of 15 years in Limousin oak vats. It is marketed at 40% and 43% abv.

-  **RHUM BARBANCOURT THREE STAR**® — A Haitian agricole rhum double distilled, first in a column still and then in a copper pot still. The rhum is diluted to 50% abv before being aged a minimum of 4 years in Limousin oak vats. It is marketed at 40% and 43% abv.

-  RHUM CLÉMENT — A producer of Martinique agricole rhum. Clément is best known for its line of vieux rhums, aged 6, 10 and 15 years. The company also markets three millésimé vieux rhums—vintages 1952, 1970 and 1990.

- RHUM DEPAZ — A producer of Martinique agricole rhum known for its 4-year old vieux rhum (45% abv). The company also markets three RHUM VIEUX PLANTATION MILLÉSIMÉ—vintages 1929, 1950 and 1979.

- RHUMERIE J. M — A producer of Martinique agricole rhum known for its 10-year old vieux rhum 50% abv (100 proof).

- RON CARIOCA — A producer of Virgin Island rum located on St. Croix. The company makes a line of 3 rums: a blanco, gold and dark añejo. 40% abv (80 proof)

- RON DEL BARRILITO THREE STAR — A Puerto Rican rum made from a blend of molasses-based, continuous-distilled rums that are aged a minimum of 6-years in large, oak wine barrels. 43% abv (86 proof)

- RON DEL BARRILITO TWO STAR — A Puerto Rican rum made from a blend of molasses-based, continuous-distilled rums that are aged a minimum of 3-years in large, oak wine barrels. 43% abv (86 proof)

- RONRICO — A Puerto Rican rum made from a blend of molasses-based, continuous-distilled rums. Available in a white and gold version (40% abv) and a 151° overproof (75.5% abv).

- **SAINT JAMES COEUR DE CHAUFFE®** — A Martinique agricole rhum made in a steam-heated pot still. It is an unaged, white rhum marketed at 60% abv (120 proof).

- **SAINT JAMES EXTRA OLD®** — A Martinique agricole rhum made in a continuous still and aged in Limousin oak barrels for a minimum of 3 years. 42% abv (84 proof)

- **SAINT JAMES HORS D'AGE®** — A Martinique agricole rhum made in a continuous still and aged in Limousin oak barrels for a minimum of 6 years. 43% abv (86 proof)

- **SAINT JAMES IMPERIAL BLANC®** — A Martinique agricole rhum made in a continuous still, diluted with purified water and rested for 6 months prior. It is marketed at 50% or 55% abv.

- **SAINT JAMES RHUM BLANC®** — A Martinique agricole rhum made in a continuous still, diluted with distilled water and rested for 6 months prior. It is marketed at 50% or 55% abv.

- **SAINT JAMES RHUM PAILLE®** — A Martinique agricole rhum made in a continuous still aged 12-months in large, oak vats called *tuns*. It is marketed at 50% or 55% abv.

- **SAINT JAMES ROYAL AMBRE®** — A Martinique agricole rhum made in a continuous still and aged in Limousin oak barrels for a minimum of 18-months. 45% abv (90 proof)

- SERRALLÈS DON Q — A Puerto Rican rum made from a blend of molasses-based, continuous-distilled rums. Available in both a white and gold version. 40% abv (80 proof)

- SERRALLÈS EL DORADO — A Puerto Rican rum made from a blend of molasses-based, continuous-distilled rums aged a minimum of 5 years. 40% abv (80 proof)

- SERRALLÈS GRAN AÑEJO — A Puerto Rican rum made from a blend of molasses-based, continuous-distilled rums aged from 3 to 12 years. 40% abv (80 proof)

- STADE'S WHITE — A Barbadian rum produced by R. L. Seale & Company made from a blend of molasses-based, barrel-aged spirits, then charcoal filtered to remove its color. Stade's is the best selli ng white rum in Barbados. 43% abv (86 proof)

Index of Rum Drink Recipes

Index

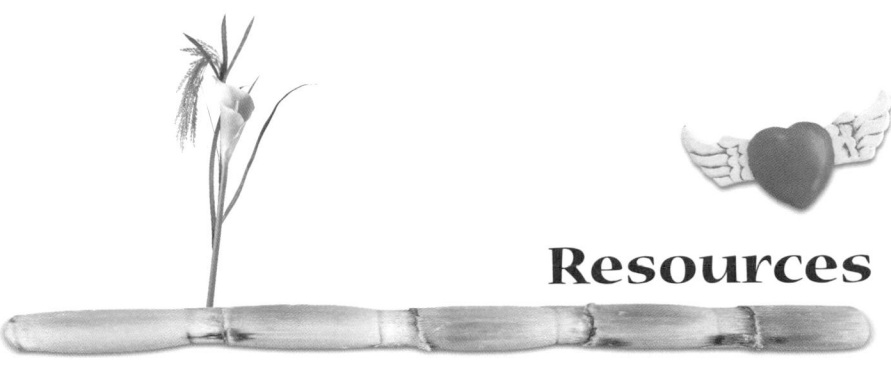

Resources

Following is a list of the companies and products that made Caribe Rum, The Original Guide to Caribbean Rum and Drinks a success. We whole-heartedly recommend that you contact these quality individuals and companies concerning their products and services. If there is a product mentioned in the book that you are having trouble finding and it is not listed, please contact the publisher for further information.

Angostura International Limited
The House of Angostura
Corner Eastern Main Road & Trinity Avenue
(P. O. Box 62, Port of Spain)
Laventille, Trinidad, W. I.
    Phone: 868.623.1841
    Fax: 868.623.1847
  Website: www.angostura.com
Products: Angostura Caribbean Rum
    Cream®, Angostura 1824 Limited
    Reserve® Rum, Angostura Old Oak
    Gold® Rum, Angostura Old Oak
    White® Rum, Angostura Royal Oak
    Extra Old Trinidad® Rum,
    Fernandes Forres Park Puncheon®
    Rum, Fernandes "19"® Rum

Bacardi U.S.A., Inc.
The Baddish Group
552 7th Avenue, Ste. 6C
New York, NY 10018
    Phone: 212.221.7611
    Fax: 212.221.7687
  Website: www.bacardi.com
Products: Bacardi Superior Carta Blanca
    (Light-Dry)® Rum, Bacardi Superior
    Carta de Oro (Gold)® Rum, Bacardi
    Select® Rum, Bacardi 8® Rum,
    Bacardi 151°® Rum, Bacardi
    Limón® Rum, Tropico®

Gosling Brothers, Ltd.
17 Dundonald Street
Hamilton, HM10, Bermuda
    Phone: 441.295.1123
    Fax: 441.292.1775
  Website www.goslings.com
  Product: Gosling's Black Seal® Rum

Heaven Hill Distilleries
1064 Loretto Road
Bardstown, KY 40004
    Phone: 502.348.3921
    Fax: 502.348.0162
  Product: Dillon Dark Rhum®

J. Wray and Nephew, Ltd.
234 Spanish Town Road
Kingston 11
Jamaica, W. I.
    Phone: 876.923.6141
    Fax: 876.937.1160
  Web site: www.appletonrum.com
Products: Appleton Estate Extra Jamaica®
    Rum, Appleton Estate 21-Year Old
    Jamaica® Rum, Appleton Estate
    250th Anniversary Edition® Rum,
    Appleton Estate V/X Jamaica®
    Rum, Appleton Special
    Jamaica® Rum

Mount Gay Distilleries Limited
Exmount Gap Brandon, P. O. Box 298
Bridgetown, St. Michael
Barbados, W.I.
    Phone: 246.425.9066
Products: J. Bally Rhum Vieux Millésime®
    1989, J. Bally Rhum Vieux 12-Ans
    d'Age®, St. James Extra Old Rhum®,
    St. James Hors d'Age Rhum®,
    St. James Imperial Blanc Rhum®,
    St. James Rhum Blanc®, St. James
    Royal Ambre Rhum®

Preiss Imports
323 D Street
Ramona, CA 92065
    Phone: 760.789.6010
    Fax: 760.789.5461
  Website: www.preissimports.com
 Products: Cadenhead's Cask Strength® CRV
    22-Year Rum, Cadenhead's Cask
    Strength® Port Morant 32-Year
    Rum, Cadenhead's Cask Strength®
    WIRR 12-Year Rum, Cadenhead's
    Green Label® Barbados 12-Year
    Rum, Cadenhead's Green Label®
    Demerara 22-Year Rum,
    Cadenhead's Green Label®
    Jamaican 10 -Year Rum

Pusser's Limited
Box 626
Road Town, Tortola
British Virgin Islands, W. I.
    Phone: 809.494.2467
    Fax: 284.494.4267
 Products: Pusser's Blue Label British Navy®
    Rum, Pusser's Red Label British
    Navy® Rum

Remy Amerique, Inc.
1350 Avenue of the Americas
New York, NY 10019
    Phone: 212.424.2205
  Website: www.mountgay.com
 Products: Mount Gay Eclipse® Rum, Mount
    Gay Extra Old® Rum, Mount Gay
    Special Reserve® Rum, Mount Gay
    Sugar Cane® Rum

Ron Matusalem
1205 SW 37th Avenue, Ste. 300
Miami, FL 33135
    Phone: 305.448.8255
    Fax: 305.443.9528
  Website: www.matusalem.com
 Products: Matusalem Classic Black® Rum,
    Matusalem Golden Dry® Rum,
    Matusalem Gran Reserva® Rum,
    Matusalem Light Dry® Rum,
    Matusalem Red Flame® Rum

Sazerac Company
803 Jefferson Highway
New Orleans, LA 70121
    Phone: 504.849.6434
 Products: Cockspur V.S.O.R.® Rum

SMS Ltd.
2955 E. Valley Road
Montecito, CA 93108
    Phone: 805.969.9329
  Website: www.patrontequila.com/pyrat
 Products: Pyrat Cask 23® Rum, Pyrat Pistol®
    Rum, Pyrat XO Reserve Rum—
    Planter's Gold®

Todhunter Imports, Ltd.
222 Lakeview Avenue
West Palm Beach, FL 33401
    Phone: 561.837.6300
    Fax: 561.832.4556
 Websites: www.todhunter.com
    www.conchrepublic.com
    www.cruzan.com
 Products: Conch Republic Atocha Gold
    Spiced® Rum, Conch Republic
    Durdy White® Rum, Conch Republic
    Islamorada Light® Rum, Conch
    Republic Matecumbe Dark® Rum,
    Cruzan Estate Dark® Rum, Cruzan
    Estate Diamond® Rum, Cruzan
    Estate Light® Rum, Cruzan Fruit-
    Flavored® Rums, Cruzan Junkanu
    Citrus® Rum, Cruzan Rum Cream®,
    Cruzan Single Barrel Estate® Rum

Glassware on Cover
Orion Trading
1927 E. 19th St.
Tucson, AZ 85719
    Phone: 520.622.6588

Map
One Treasure Limited
937 Reinli, Ste. #2
Austin, TX 78751
    Phone: 512.320.9161
    Fax: 512.420.9708
  Website: www.onetreasurelimited.com

Photography
Eric Hinote Photography
Contact publisher for information